The Active Defender

The Active Defender

Immersion in the Offensive Security Mindset

Dr. Catherine J. Ullman

WILEY

To my Dad, who has not only been my all-time greatest supporter, but also who I've been lucky to have as a fellow colleague for most of my career. You changed my life without even knowing it, just by switching occupations.

About the Author

Dr. Catherine J. Ullman is a security researcher, speaker, and principal technology architect, security, at the University at Buffalo with over 20 years of highly technical experience. In her current role, Cathy is a digital forensics and incident response (DFIR) specialist, performing incident management, intrusion detection, investigative services, and personnel case resolution in a dynamic academic environment. She additionally builds security awareness among faculty and staff via a department-wide program that educates and informs users about how to prevent and detect social engineering threats and how to compute and digitally communicate safely. Cathy has presented at numerous information security conferences including DEF CON and BlueTeamCon. In her (minimal) spare time, she enjoys visiting her adopted two-toed sloth, Flash, at the Buffalo Zoo, researching death and the dead, and learning more about hacking things to make the world a more secure place.

About the Technical Editor

Jake Williams (aka MalwareJake) is a seasoned security researcher with decades of experience in the technology and security industries. Jake is a former startup founder, former senior SANS instructor and course author, and an intelligence community and military veteran. He loves forensics, incident response, cyber threat intelligence, and offensive methodologies. Today, Jake is an IANS faculty member and an independent security consultant and is performing security-focused research to benefit the broader community. He has twice won the DoD Cyber Crime Center (DC3) annual digital forensics challenge and is the recipient of the NSA Exceptional Civilian Service Award.

Acknowledgments

I have to start by thanking my wonderful husband, Ryan, for his enduring patience and never wavering support during this project. I am so fortunate to have him in my life and would not have had the fortitude to finish the book without his love and encouragement. In addition, I want to express my gratitude for my uncle, Jeffrey Ullman, for his wisdom and assistance during the contractual negotiations. Also, thank you to my mother and stepfather for always encouraging me toward a lifelong love of learning.

Next, I want to acknowledge the many people who helped me build the career that I have today. A very special note of thanks goes to Dave Brady for suggesting that I shift my occupation into IT. Your recommendation was the first step in what has been an amazing career. For your advice, I will always be grateful. Shinil Hong, I am indebted to you for teaching me many of the first IR skills that I learned. To Chuck Dunn and Jeff Murphy who took a chance on me during my early security career: each of you played a critical role in my transition from support to security, and for that I am eternally appreciative.

My first offensive security experiences would not have happened without Justin Elze's recommendation. Thank you for the suggestion to attend a Security BSides conference as well as letting me pick your brain once I began work on the book. Part of what made that first BSides conference so special was the kindness of BSidesROC co-founder Jason Ross. Jason, you were so welcoming and encouraging that very first day that despite being completely out of my element, I had a fantastic time and wanted to return as a volunteer. I am honored to now be able to continue what you started.

Chris Roberts, meeting you on the way to BSides Cleveland was a true gift. Becoming friends has been priceless. I'm still amazed that you were willing to offer suggestions and support for my very first talk, yet I was someone you barely knew. By the way, your cow hacking talk will forever remain one of my favorites.

It might take a village to raise a child, but it took a great deal of help from amazing friends in the hacker community for me to write this book. I'm forever indebted to Jake Williams, Neil Wyler, Sean Metcalf, and Dan Ward for the enthusiasm with which you responded to my original outline. You each provided the encouragement I needed to formally pursue this project. Since those early conversations, I've continued to learn from each of you. Dan, I was so thrilled that you loved the ideas behind the project and appreciate that you have continued to be so encouraging. Neil, I loved exploring our parallel experiences of the "old days" as well as gaining your insights into the world of threat hunting. Sean, thank you for carving out time for me to ask questions and discuss progress on the book each month. Jake, to you I extend my deepest gratitude for your friendship and guidance. I was blown away that you offered to write the Foreword after just reading the outline and so honored that you also agreed to be my technical editor.

A huge thank you goes out to Phil Wylie. When I told you that I had an idea for a book, you were kind enough to introduce me to Associate Publisher Jim Minatel at Wiley. Putting words to the first couple of chapters is always the hardest. Dustin Heywood, you made that process so much easier by letting me brainstorm with you. I am extraordinarily grateful for your help in flushing out those initial ideas and making sure the terminology I was using was consistent with my vision for the book. You really understood the nature of what I was trying to capture.

A note of heartfelt thanks, Nick Chapel, for our lengthy discussions of hacking and philosophy. Your encouragement and suggestions for how to synthesize these topics in the early chapters was invaluable. I am extremely grateful to Tyler Hudak, for being a second set of eyes before I submitted each chapter to the editorial folks. Your willingness to preview the chapters and give me honest feedback was extremely reassuring. In addition, your never wavering encouragement kept me moving forward even when I felt stuck.

Robert M. Lee, I am grateful that you were able to make time to discuss your white paper with me and further clarify the concept of "Active" that I ultimately used as a basis for the "Active Defender." When writing about offensive security business practices, Joe Vest and Daemon Small were particularly instructive. Thank you, Joe, for your insights into the offensive security world and the importance of focusing on the goals rather than engagement names. Daemon, I will always cherish all of our detailed conversations about the book and our mutual love of academia. Your thoughts about threat modeling from the offensive security perspective were particularly useful. I must also thank you, Joe Grey, for your additional insights into the world of OSINT. I'm so excited that I finally had a chance to read through your book! Bryson Bort, I very much appreciate you making time during your very busy schedule to share your insights on attack simulations versus emulations as well as the SCYTHE material on purple teaming.

The topic of cloud computing required some additional expertise and, fortunately, I found some amazing folks to spend hours to help educate me beyond the initial research that I did on my own. Thank you to Cassandra Young and Zack Glick for giving me a fantastic overview of many of the concepts. Bren Briggs, your knowledge of all things AWS and cloud in general was indispensable. In addition, our conversations helped shape the topics that I knew needed to be included. Likewise, Edwin David, your expertise in the Azure world was incredibly helpful and assisted me in better understanding the challenges there. Thank you each for putting up with all the little questions that I had throughout writing that chapter.

Another topic that required some additional expertise was that of effective detections. Jared Atkinson, your work was absolutely pivotal to this chapter, and I am immensely grateful for all the time you spent with me to flush out ideas and clarify concepts. I love that we both have an active interest in philosophy and I thoroughly enjoyed our conversations. You gave me a new way to think about detections that I will always carry with me.

I would be remiss if I didn't also thank David Bianco and Christopher Peacock for the use of their Pyramid of Pain and TTP Pyramid images, respectively. Your ideas are so pivotal to understanding many of the challenges that defenders face, and I'm so glad that I was able to include them with your individual blessings! To all the people that I had great brainstorming sessions with, including Joe Shottman, Fiona Redmond, Brian Martinez, John McCarty, Keren Elzari, and Casey Smith as well as several members of the Packet Hacking Village, I cannot thank you enough for your inspiring words and ideas.

There are not sufficient words to thank Forrest Fuqua for the inspiration that led to the cover art and Doc for making it a reality. Forrest, you are so amazingly creative. I am positive I wouldn't have come up with the idea without you. Thank you! Doc, I am indebted to you for your ability and willingness to make that idea come alive to become my cover art, despite a supremely busy schedule. PHV family is the best!

Jim Minatel, Cathleen Small, Pete Gaughan, Satish Gowrishankar, Saravanan Dakshinamurthy, and the rest of the team at Wiley, thank you for helping me bring my idea to life and walking me through the process. I am deeply grateful for your patience as I made my way through this whole writing a book thing, which I never thought I'd accomplish.

Contents at a Glance

Contents

Foreword

When I was a US government hacker, I regularly contemplated how system administrators could take trivial steps to make my job infinitely harder. Later in my career, as an incident responder helping victimized organizations around the world, I saw the same: system admins not taking basic steps to stop attacks. But this time I was in a different position. I could talk to them and understand why they made the choices they did to defend their networks. What I learned completely changed my world view.

Most system admins I talked to weren't simply ignoring security best practices as I had assumed from my position on the other side of the keyboard. The vast majority were simply devoting their limited time and resources to the wrong things. When I talked them through how attackers viewed the steps they were taking, I was met with near universal shock. Some were even disgusted, feeling that they had been misled about the most important steps to take in securing a system. The security of these systems is their charge after all, and many system admins take it personally when their systems are compromised.

In these discussions, it became clear that the root cause of incorrectly prioritizing security controls was their mindset. System administrators were learning security "best practices" from other, more senior system administrators. This is a fine model for many professions but fails spectacularly in the face of a sentient adversary. When you want to learn how to stop a thief, it's true that talking to a locksmith provides some value. But talking to a thief is the only way to truly understand how an adversary views the security controls emplaced by defenders. We see the same with cybersecurity. If you want to know how to stop hackers from breaching your systems, talk to a hacker.

Of course this trite "talk to a hacker" advice has several pitfalls. For one, where does the average system administrator find a hacker to talk to in the first place?

Even assuming they can find one, how can they vet the hacker? Listening to bad (e.g., negligent or intentionally harmful) advice is probably worse than doing nothing at all. While some large organizations have the resources to find and vet "good hackers," most system admins simply lack this luxury.

But there's another critical problem with the "just ask a hacker" trope. Whether it is the deep technical understanding of their craft, that hacking disproportionately draws neuro-atypical people, or some combination of other factors, getting answers in ordinary terms is often more challenging than locating the hacker in the first place. The fact that many hackers have no experience with enterprise defense makes any recommendations all the more difficult to follow. Junior cybersecurity analysts often experience similar struggles getting their bearings in this community. This book will serve them well too.

What system administrators needed were clear and actionable explanations of where to focus their limited resources, from an attacker perspective, communicated in ways they can understand. This book distills years of experience in thinking like an attacker and communicates it clearly to readers with no background in offensive cyber. To put it bluntly, the information technology and cybersecurity industries have sorely needed this book for years. If my incident response customers mentioned earlier had been reading this book, I'd have had a lot less business.

Cathy is the perfect person to write this book—one the community so dearly needs. As Cathy describes in her Preface, she was a system administrator who has pivoted into a senior information security analyst. That alone would make her qualified to write this book. But there's another factor that makes Cathy uniquely qualified to discuss securing systems from an attacker's mindset.

With more than 20 years of experience working at the same university, Cathy is now securing some of the same systems that she doubtlessly administered more than a decade ago. Very few people have this type of lens to look through. In fact, I'd be surprised if you can point me to another cybersecurity professional with 10 years' system administration experience at an organization who now has another 13 years' experience as an information security professional *at the same organization*. This provides the reader with unparalleled perspective, not only of how defenders should think about offensive cybersecurity but also of the specific challenges they may face in operationalizing her recommendations. This type of experience (akin to a longitudinal study) is sorely missing in cybersecurity, and this book also addresses that gap.

But beyond all that, Cathy is just a great human being and I'm a better person for knowing her. She has firmly embedded herself into the cybersecurity community and is a regular fixture at the DEF CON Packet Hacking Village and BSides Rochester (among others). Her volunteer work, presentations, and mentoring of others would be an amazing body of work in its own right.

I was aware of Cathy's contributions in the cybersecurity community prior to formally meeting her a few years ago. We instantly bonded over our common work as emergency first responders (mine prior, hers current). When Cathy told me about her idea for this book, I was certain it would fill an important void. When Wiley signed on to publish the book and Cathy asked me to be the technical editor, I was even more excited.

I'll close by thanking Cathy for giving me the honor of being technical editor and writing the foreword you're reading now. I'm really excited for the value this book will bring to countless system administrators, junior information security analysts, or anyone else who wants more background in offensive security. I hope you have as much fun reading this book as I had watching it come together. I'm certain you'll come away with more secure systems after reading it.

— Jake Williams (aka MalwareJake)

Preface

In the early days of computing, neither the term *cybersecurity* nor the term *information security* existed. Instead, the original goals of computer security focused around government risk assessment, policy, and controls. By the mid-1980s, the ARPANET was expanding rapidly, the personal computer boom had begun, and companies were starting to use this thing called the Internet for communications, leading to concerns about security and privacy. At about the same time, some people were trying to gain access to what were then relatively primitive computer networks by nibbling mostly around the edges of equally primitive security measures. Sometimes their goal was just to see where they could go and what they could access. Others had more nefarious goals. Still others, however, had legal access via equipment located in their homes by virtue of a parent's employment responsibilities, providing a fairly unusual early exposure to the technology of the time. I was one of these lucky people and this book is an indirect consequence of that exposure.

Like many Gen-Xers, I was fortunate to have access to a personal computer in my home and at school from a very early age. However, unlike most children of that generation, my first foray into computing began not with a personal computer but with a mainframe terminal located in my house. We acquired this terminal as the result of my father taking a job running the college's computing center in a small town in 1977. My earliest tinkering with this terminal involved mostly playing text-based games, such as *Adventure*, *Zork*, and *Wumpus*, but I also was able to use the early equivalent of instant messaging to chat with my father while he was at work. Uniquely, not only was there no telecom charge for the use of this terminal, there was no need to hear the screech of a modem, tie up the local phone line, or pay for the call, because terminal connectivity to the college was facilitated by a dry copper line. What I never realized was that this early exposure to the technology, which I took for granted, planted seeds that led me into an information security career.

My interest in computer security started long before I was officially a member of a computer security team. My earliest involvement in computer security revolved around updating antivirus software and patching the Windows NT 4.0 machines I was responsible for supporting. Installing intrusion detection/ firewall software on servers was still a new concept, but it was a requirement on our systems that I had self-imposed. I was tenacious enough to prevent an outbreak of Nimda in our offices by returning to work after getting a tip to patch immediately. I also had the opportunity to learn the basics of incident response from a friend who had been attending SANS incident response training and was willing to share his knowledge. Over time, I became one of the people called when a machine was behaving strangely. Eventually, I took some formal training in digital forensics and landed my first job as an information security analyst. Always looking for an opportunity to grow my skills, I got involved with a cyber-defense course where I met my first offensive security practitioner. Intrigued by the experiences he shared with the group, I asked how I could learn more about offensive security. He recommended attending something called a Security BSides conference. I chose to attend BSidesROC (BSides Rochester), because it was the closest to my location. Not only did it open a whole new world to me, it also helped me realize what I had been missing as a defender. Today, I am one of the organizers of that conference.

Protecting computers, networks, software programs, and data from attack, damage, or unauthorized access is a difficult job, as evidenced by the fact that successful attacks continue to be on the rise. This book introduces the idea of the Active Defender as an alternative approach to the way cybersecurity defense has typically been practiced. The traditional approach is usually passive or reactive, waiting to respond to alerts or other indications of attack. The Active Defender, by comparison, is someone who seeks to understand a hacker mindset and embraces the knowledge gained from the offensive security community in order to be more effective. Offensive security entails testing the defensive mechanisms put in place to determine whether they can prevent attacks or at least detect them once they have occurred. Unfortunately, many defenders are either unaware of offensive security or choose to avoid it. By being ignorant of, or choosing to avoid, offensive security, defenders are missing half the larger story and thus are at a significant disadvantage. Immersion into the offensive security community helps the defender to have a broader, more comprehensive view of the effectiveness of their detections and defenses as well as providing many additional resources to further their understanding, which will be covered throughout the subsequent chapters.

Cybersecurity suffers when defenders don't know what they're missing. However, in the same way that I was unaware of the unique situation I had and the power it granted me as a child, many defenders are unaware of the additional power they already possess to be better at defensive security. Ultimately, being an Active Defender involves using many of the same sorts of tools, skills, and access that the traditional defender already has, but in a unique way. The Active Defender is, in a sense, a defensive hacker and, because I know the term *hacker* comes with some baggage, we'll be discussing the term further in Chapter 2, "Immersion into the Hacker Mindset."

The inspiration for this book came from my own eye-opening experiences while immersing myself in the offensive security world. These experiences helped me realize that not only was there more to effective defense than I previously understood, but, as I also discovered, many other defenders were equally in the dark. As they say, knowledge is power. Therefore, I wanted to share my discoveries so that full-time defenders like myself as well as those who are responsible for securing their particular environments, such as system administrators and network administrators, might benefit from them as well. Once a defender opens the door to the offensive security world, they too can be Active Defenders and take their defensive skills to the next level.

Who Is This Book For?

This book is for anyone tasked with cybersecurity defense in general, those in the security-specific roles such as information security analysts, SOC analysts, security engineers, security administrators, security architects, security specialists, and security consultants. It is also meant for people whose jobs involve aspects of security such as system administrators, networking administrators, developers, and people interested in transitioning to information security roles. Realistically, all information technology roles including, but not limited to, IT support, engineers, analysts, and database administrators are responsible for some elements of security, regardless of whether it is part of their formal job description. Everyone should be cognizant of the role they play in securing their environment rather than it being only the purview of one group.

Regardless of your security role, this book will help you shift from a traditional passive or reactive defensive mindset to cultivating a hacker mindset and becoming an Active Defender. As a result, you'll gain a more intimate understanding of the threats you're defending against. Ready to get started?

Introduction

Defense from a Different Perspective

A team of security analysts is working diligently around the clock monitoring for alerts and to prevent attackers from entering the network. They detect and contain any intrusions that slip by the preventative measures in place. A criminal threat actor sends a successful phishing email with a link that downloads malicious software, bypassing the company's antivirus detections. The attacker has now gained entry, unbeknown to the security analysts. The attacker goes to work, disabling security software to hide their activities and using built-in operating system tools to blend in with legitimate user activity. As a result, no security alerts fire. The security analysts continue to work, unaware of the malicious activity that's happening right under their noses. Shortly thereafter, the company receives a notification that a number of enterprise passwords and other company secrets have been compromised and made available for sale to other bad actors—all because the defenders were acting like traditional defenders and not thinking like members of the offensive community. Had they done so, they might have had a chance to avoid this catastrophic and all-too-common outcome. Enter the Active Defender.

The Active Defender is an alternative approach to the way cybersecurity defense has typically been practiced. The traditional approach is usually passive or reactive, waiting to respond to alerts or other indications of attack. The Active Defender, by comparison, is someone who seeks to understand an attacker mindset and embraces the knowledge gained from the offensive security community in order to be more effective. While we'll explore what, exactly, an Active Defender is in Chapter 1, let's first define the notions of defensive and offensive security teams used here.

In the broadest sense, defensive security teams consist of security professionals who are responsible for defending an organization's information systems against security threats and risks in the operating environment. They may work toward identifying security flaws, verifying the effectiveness of security measures put in place, and continuing to monitor the effectiveness of any implemented security measures. They may also provide recommendations to increase the overall cybersecurity readiness posture—in other words, how ready an organization is to identify, prevent, and respond to cybersecurity threats. I will be using defensive security teams here to also include folks who are responsible for securing the services they provide, such as system and network administrators, as well as developers, who are also responsible for operational functions, because it is not unusual for smaller organizations to rely solely on these folks for their cybersecurity needs.

Offensive security teams, on the other hand, consist of security professionals who are responsible for testing the defensive mechanisms put in place to protect an organization's information systems to determine whether they prevent attacks or at least detect them once they have occurred. One team of offensive security professionals might be responsible for penetration testing (pen testing). Pen testing only goes as far as mapping the risk surface of an application or organization to evaluate the potential routes of exploitation for an attacker and does testing against those routes to see whether they are in fact exploitable. Other offensive security teams may be responsible for full adversarial emulation, which completely emulates a high-capability, and/or well-resourced, goal-driven adversary that is attempting to compromise the network environment to achieve a set of operational goals. The goal of this activity is to assess threat readiness and response. Historically, these teams have sometimes been referred to as blue and red teams respectively, but the imprecise nature of this terminology is problematic. Therefore, I will be utilizing some form of defensive and offensive security professionals throughout this book.

Where We Are Now

Defensive security teams continue to be up against some pretty significant challenges. According to research provided by the Identity Theft Resource Center (ITRC), the number of data breaches reported as of the end of 2022 was 1,802, the second highest number of publicly reported data compromise events in a single year.[i] The average cost of a data breach in 2022 increased by 2.6 percent compared to the previous year, from $4.24 million to an all-time high of $4.35 million.[ii] Yet, organizations are spending more than ever on cybersecurity. Costs are up another 12.1 percent from the previous year and were expected to surpass $219 billion before the end of 2023.[iii]

Compromised credentials continued to be the most common initial attack vector, costing organizations an average of $4.57 million.[iv] The average time to discover and contain an attacker in an organization's network in 2022 was 277 days, down only slightly from 287 in 2021.[v] Furthermore, both the *2021 Verizon Data Breach Investigations Report (DBIR)* and the *Ransomware Report 2023* found that overall, older vulnerabilities continue to be what attackers are more often exploiting.[vi] Therefore, it should be no surprise that one area in particular with which organizations continue to struggle is vulnerability management.

Vulnerabilities are any method that a threat actor can use to gain unauthorized access or privileged control over an application, service, endpoint, or server, such as hardware or software flaws or misconfigurations. For example, there may be an unpatched weakness in the operating system on a server that would allow a threat actor to log in without needing the proper credentials. Vulnerability management is generally defined as the process of identifying, categorizing, prioritizing, and resolving vulnerabilities in hardware and software before they can cause harm or loss. Important to note that vulnerability management is not the same as a vulnerability assessment. The former is a full process, whereas the latter is a point-in-time view of discovered vulnerabilities.

The good news is that there have been some improvements in certain areas of vulnerability management. For example, the *SANS 2022 Vulnerability Management Survey* reports that the number of organizations stating that they have vulnerability management programs, whether formal or informal, increased from 92 percent to 94 percent over the previous year.[vii] Most notably, as of 2021, all organizations reported either having a program in place or plans to create one.[viii]

The bad news is that several issues continue to plague organizations in this area. For example, many organizations are not budgeting properly for vulnerability management, in terms of either time or resources. In addition, while defensive security teams are typically accountable for the vulnerability management process, they are not actually responsible for the work in many cases. Those who are responsible for addressing vulnerabilities typically have operational roles such as system administrators or network engineers. These operational teams are already overwhelmed with the amount of work they're facing, and they're often not rewarded for the efforts they expend in this area. Furthermore, while the business may expect that vulnerabilities are managed properly, it often does not require anyone to do so and, as a result, does not recognize or reward the work done by operational staff in this area. Perhaps most importantly, because new vulnerabilities can come from anywhere at any time and in any format, vulnerability management is a never-ending battle.

Another area where defensive security professionals are currently struggling is cloud computing, as evidenced by the fact that in 2021, according to the DBIR report, external cloud assets were more prevalent in both incidents and breaches than on-premises assets.[ix] As organizations adopt new technology, they often leave established security practices and monitoring tools behind, either because existing practices and tools will not work with the new environment and they don't realize they need new tools for this purpose or because they do not realize that they need to secure cloud resources. As a result, the maturity level of security in cloud computing for most organizations is often significantly lower than in their on-premises locations. Unfortunately, that leaves organizations blind to attacks in this space and, in some cases, can put on-premises assets at an unrecognized risk. For example, Azure Active Directory and Windows Active Directory are often tied together such that if one becomes compromised it can lead to a much larger problem. Furthermore, assumptions about who is responsible for managing cloud security and/or accidental misconfigurations can lead to data compromise or loss.

Offensive security teams seem to have a much easier time accomplishing their objectives. The *NUIX Black Report*, the only industry report to focus on responses from offensive security teams rather than focusing on data from specific incidents or interviews from cybersecurity leadership, offers some insight into their experiences. For example, while 18 percent of respondents stated they could breach the perimeter of a target within an hour, all of them were able to achieve that goal within 15 hours. Once inside the perimeter, more than half were able to move laterally to find their target within five hours, and in certain industries, such as hospitals and healthcare, hospitality, and retail, they could accomplish the same goal within a single hour.

Not only are offensive security teams able to easily breach and access their targets, rarely were they identified by defensive security teams. How good are they at not being caught? Seventy-seven percent of respondents said they were rarely identified by their target's defensive security teams, less than 15 percent of the time. When asked whether they thought defenders understood what they were looking for when detecting an attack, 74 percent of them said no.

While on the one hand, these results may appear to be ideal from the offensive security community perspective, they often report that repeating the same kinds of tests with the same results all the time is boring. More importantly, because the job of the offensive security practitioner is to test defenses, these results reinforce the fact that defenders and their defenses are not what they need to be in most organizations. In the end, the goal of both teams should be the greater security position of the organization for whom they are working.

How Did We Get Here?

Clearly what numerous defenders are currently doing is ineffective. But how did we get here? To understand and appreciate how we've gotten to this current state of our industry, it's important to understand how cybersecurity evolved over time.

Antivirus Software

The first significant security product to become mainstream for the PC was antivirus software. Although the first PC virus, Brain, was written as a copyright infringement tool and not intended to harm systems, it caused a wide-spread response from the media in January of 1986 after numerous people flooded the developers' phone line with complaints that Brain had wiped files from their computers.[x] The only remediation at that time was to format and reinstall the operating system, which was frustrating and time-consuming.

Brain was also the catalyst for John McAfee to enter the antivirus market after he reverse engineered its code in the hopes that he could help individuals remediate their systems. Intending to profit only from corporate customers, he launched McAfee Associates at the end of 1987 and by 1990 was making $5 million a year.[xi] McAfee wasn't the only successful antivirus vendor in this realm. Symantec and Sophos also made their debuts in the late '80s. Although the prevalence of viruses and other forms of malware continued to slowly increase, by 1989 there were actually more antivirus vendors than viruses.[xii]

The fear of being hit by a virus infection was also beginning to grip the US government. US government computer security experts were quoted in an article titled "Future bugs Computer world dreading electronic 'virus' attack," published in the Toronto *Globe and Mail* on August 5, 1986, using phrases such as "potentially devastating weapon" to describe a virus and further stating that "the 'virus' is a high technology equivalent of germ warfare."[xiii]

To some degree, their anxiety was well founded as only two years later the Morris Worm rapidly spread to and crashed one-tenth of all the computers on the Internet at that time. It was the first worm to gain significant mainstream media attention and ultimately lead to the formation of the first Computer Emergency Response Team (CERT) Coordination Center at Carnegie Mellon University for the purposes of research and responsible disclosure of software vulnerabilities. Moreover, during a subsequent 1989 hearing before Congress about the Morris Worm, John Landry, executive VP of Cullinet Software Inc., stated that "virus attacks can be life threatening. Recently a computer used in real time control of a medical experiment was attacked. If the attack had not been detected, a patient might have been injured, or worse."[xiv]

By 1990, both corporate reliance on the Internet and the acceleration of new viruses being propagated were inexorably tied together. However, the projected cost to the worldwide microcomputing community to remove malicious software was approximately $1.5 billion per year. At this point, the cost of either purchasing protective software at $5 to $10 per month per machine or hiring two additional staff members to triage infected systems at an estimated $120 thousand to $150 thousand now seemed reasonable.[xv] Companies were finally realizing that the need for something to combat the growing problem was absolutely necessary, thus giving rise to beginnings of the Internet security industry.

Firewalls

As more and more systems connected to the Internet, fear of attacks from external networks grew. Enter the network firewall, which first appeared in the late '80s but became commercially available in the early '90s. The goal of a network firewall, which originally provided only basic packet filtering, was to provide a secure gateway to the Internet for private networks and keep out unwanted traffic from external networks. As Frederic M. Avolo, a well-known early security consultant, observed, "Firewalls were the first big security item, the first successful Internet security product, and the most visible security device."[xvi] For some time, firewalls were thought to be "virtually fail-safe protection," but that all changed when Kevin Mitnick attacked the San Diego Supercomputer Center (SDSC) in December 1995. Despite the SDSC having a properly configured firewall in place, Mitnick was able to spoof his address and utilize a sequence prediction attack. As a result, his system was able to appear to the firewall as a trusted host allowing him access past it.[xvii] From that point forward, it was understood that what had been viewed as the ultimate protection from external networks was no longer the reassurance it once had been.

Secure Sockets Layer

About the same time, the Secure Sockets Layer (SSL) protocol was first introduced by Netscape in response to concerns about security and privacy on the Internet. The goal of this protocol was to enable users to access the Web securely and to perform activities such as online purchases. Unfortunately, the first version of SSL released, SSL v2, was not as secure as originally expected and was deprecated in 2011, as was its successor SSLv3 in 2015 for comparable reasons. The replacement for SSL, Transport Layer Security (TLS), which was originally released in 1999, also went through a number of revisions in 2006 and again in 2018 as more serious security flaws were uncovered.[xviii]

Intrusion Detection Systems and Intrusion Prevention Systems

The next significant security product to debut commercially was the intrusion detection system (IDS). Early IDSs were built on technology similar to that used in antivirus software in that they used signatures to continuously scan for known threats. Unfortunately, that meant that they could only detect known threats. Furthermore, updating the signature set was a hassle. IDS versions released in the 1990s moved to anomaly detection instead, which attempted to identify unusual behavior patterns that traversed the network.[xix] Eventually, misuse detection, which detected behavior violations of stated policies, was also an added feature.

By the mid '90s, commercially available products were available. The two most popular software packages at the time were Wheelgroup's Netranger and Internet Security Systems's RealSecure.[xx] After building products that could help detect threats, the next logical step was creating something to prevent them, which became known as an intrusion prevention system (IPS).

While IDSs became best practice by the early 2000s, very few organizations were using IPSs. IPSs were inline solutions that could take automated actions in response to a detected threat. For example, they could block an IP address, limit access, or block an account. Unfortunately, the original implementation of IPS technology was unreliable and cumbersome. It often blocked legitimate traffic, which was a headache for administrators who then had to remove the blocks. Furthermore, it used a single signature for each type of exploit associated with a vulnerability, which could lead to hundreds of signatures slowing down traffic significantly. However, by 2005 the model changed to use a single signature for an entire category of vulnerability rather than for a specific exploit. Once more vendors entered the market, the technology also became more reliable. The combination lead to an increase in IPS adoption. Shortly thereafter, systems offering combination IDS/IPS solutions became the standard.[xxi]

Next Generation Intrusion Prevention Systems

Between 2011 and 2015 came next generation intrusion prevention systems (NGIPSs), which added some additional features to the existing IDS/IPS technologies. User and application control was added in order to address vulnerabilities in specific applications such as Java or Adobe Flash, and sandboxing technology was added to test the behavior of files not already known to be good or bad. While these technologies have come a long way from their origins, human expertise and time are still needed both to tune the solution to prevent an overwhelming number of alerts and to review the alerts that are generated. Furthermore, false positive detections remain problematic.

Data Loss Prevention

One of the more recent security offerings, data loss prevention (DLP), got its start in the early 2000s but did not gain popularity until the late 2010s.[xxii] The goal of a DLP software solution is to prevent an organization's data from either being accidentally exposed by being leaked to some unauthorized entity, such as when someone sends an email they should not, or stolen by a bad actor during an attack.

While the significant increase in the use of cloud, mobile, and remote computing have made this an attractive solution, it is often difficult for organizations to implement properly. In order to prevent data loss, an organization has to understand both what data they have and what kinds of data they wish to prevent falling into the wrong hands. Each of these goals takes a significant amount of resources beyond the purchase of DLP software. Inventorying what data is available and categorizing it to know what is sensitive can often involve considerable overhead. Many organizations either do not have the resources or choose not to assign the resources they do have to this process.

Security Information and Event Management

One of disadvantages of all of the previous security solutions mentioned was the necessity of looking at the logs and alerts of these systems individually. Security information and event management (SIEM) was introduced around 2006 as a product to solve this problem. A SIEM system aggregates log data, security alerts, and events in a centralized repository in order to provide real-time, correlated analysis of this data. The goal of SIEM is both to provide a single place where defenders could look to see alerts from multiple systems and to make connections between the various data sources.

The first SIEM systems introduced around 2006 had significant scaling limitations. In particular, they were able to add resources to only a single system. Furthermore, both data ingestion and output were particularly challenging, causing reports and dashboards to be equally as limited. The next versions of SIEM tools, which came about in roughly 2011, solved the scalability problem almost too well because at least architecturally, they had the potential for unlimited data sources. As a result, defenders were quickly overwhelmed when trying to make sense of what they were seeing. The most recent iteration of SIEM systems, which became available in about 2015, focuses more on analytical data than pre-built alerts in order to provide better visibility into unknown threats.[xxiii]

Ultimately, the expectation is that having more data from more sources with a more powerful means of aggregation will lead to better security management. However, even with these most recent SIEM systems, there remain inherent challenges. For someone to understand what an unknown threat is in an environment requires the creation of a baseline of activity. Creating this baseline helps to determine what is "normal" for the environment in question. This task requires a defender to have specialized knowledge of the SIEM being used as well as advanced knowledge of an organization, its networks, and its data.

Active Defense

Each of the previously discussed products was created to address a particular security problem, and although the technology continues to improve over time, unfortunately no solution can be a silver bullet providing perfect protection. Furthermore, it is impossible for a single product to address the problem of cybersecurity holistically. More importantly from a historical perspective, it's critical to note that the solutions described previously have something in common: they are reactive and passive in nature. Most of them require waiting for some alert to trigger or information to appear in a log before acting, whether directly or indirectly. Even the ones that appear to be active, such as IPS and DLP, do not truly meet the definition of "active" that I will be using, because they do not require some form of constant human interaction but instead are automated and can be ignored. Therefore, it is not too surprising that defenders have gotten into the habit of being passive and reactive as well. To understand what I have in mind by the terms *active* defense and *passive* defense, let's turn to Robert M. Lee's 2015 white paper, *The Sliding Scale of Cybersecurity*.

Lee provides some illuminating explanations of these terms as part of a framework that he developed. Within it, he outlines five interconnected categories of actions, competencies, and investments of resources: architecture, passive defense, active defense, intelligence, and offense. We will focus on two for the purposes of this discussion: passive defense and active defense.

Lee notes that traditionally these two forms of defense have always been acknowledged. Taking a cue from the original intended notion of "passive defense" from the Department of Defense, Lee defines it as "systems added to the architecture to provide consistent protection against or insight into threats without constant human interaction." The key here, he indicates, is the lack of regular human interaction and he cites firewalls, antimalware systems, intrusion prevention systems, antivirus, and intrusion detection systems as examples fitting this category. The intent of "active defense," on the other hand, is not some form of attacking back as has been previously misinterpreted from its military origins but rather the maneuverability and adaptability of a defender to contain and remediate a threat. Thus, Lee explains that active defense for cybersecurity is "the process of analysts monitoring for, responding to, learning from, and applying their knowledge to threats internal to the network."

Crucial to this definition is the focus on the analysts themselves and not specific tools. As he maintains, "Systems themselves cannot provide an active defense; systems can only serve as tools to the active defender. Likewise, simply sitting in front of a tool such as a SIEM does not make an analyst an active defender—it is as much about the actions and process as it is about the placement of the person and their training."[xxiv] Therefore, it is this definition of active defense that will be used in describing the Active Defender in Chapter 1.

What Keeps Us Stuck?

There are two overarching elements that contribute to keeping us stuck in this reactive, passive defensive space: inertia and organizational culture. Let's dive into each in turn in the following sections.

Inertia

Despite this notion of active defense, most organizations continue to suffer from certain pitfalls that perpetuate a passive and reactive security posture. Perhaps the most common pitfall is simply inertia—"That's how we've always done it." Change and growth are hard, and people are often resistant, organizations even more so. For example, many organizations are still focusing predominantly on perimeter security, which is a way of thinking that goes back to the 1990s and those early firewalls. This philosophy involves providing robust security for the exterior of the network and assumes that the people and assets inside this network can be trusted.

Concentrating mainly on the perimeter was particularly useful both when the employees spent their days working the office and when all data was centrally managed in the organization's on-premises data center. Now, with employees often working remotely, the potential for data to be stored in the cloud, and email connecting people around the world, perimeter security, while still necessary, is no longer sufficient. Current best practices dictate a far more thorough and layered approach called defense in depth, in which companies put multiple layers of security controls in place to protect their assets, not just perimeter protection. Yet, defenders continue to return to this mindset because it's what they know and have always done.

Inertia impacts a number of areas such as how defenders use their tools, alert fatigue, and financial constraints. Let's next explore each of these in turn.

Tool Usage

Inertia can impact one of the most basic fundamentals of defense: tool usage. The way traditional defenders have always utilized their tools perpetuates a passive or reactive culture. Most of the tools described earlier fit Lee's definition of passive by providing "consistent protection against or insight into threats without constant human interaction." As a result, defenders often focus on waiting for alerts to come in rather than actively hunting for threats.

The assumption is that antivirus, firewalls, IDS/IPS, and other tools are providing adequate protection for the organization until an alert is generated. In medium to large organizations that have implemented SIEM technology, it can be particularly problematic. SIEM systems often lead people to have tunnel vision with respect to defense. In other words, the people responsible for monitoring them wind up focusing exclusively on the alerts, dashboards, and other data this tool provides rather than the broader picture of security at an organization. As a result, they often wind up trapped in a vicious cycle of investigating false positive alarms, tuning existing rules, or adding new rules, which leaves time for little else.

Alert Fatigue

The hyper focus on SIEM or other tool data can lead to something called alert fatigue. Alert fatigue is what many defenders experience when they are constantly barraged by warnings and alerts from their tools.

There are several reasons for warnings or alerts to be generated that turn out to be false positives. A false positive might be triggered because the information being fed into a tool is problematic. For example, it is not uncommon for the intelligence data being fed into the tools that defenders use for detecting malicious activity to contain IP addresses that host both legitimate and malicious sites. Without having the proper context to make an informed decision, the defender may accidentally block legitimate traffic, generating a number of alerts that each have to be investigated.

In addition, these feeds can provide indicators of compromise that, without the proper context, are misleading. For example, it is not uncommon for legitimate tools to be detected by antivirus as malicious, such as the application netcat. Netcat, while often used by some system administrators for its flexible network capabilities, can also be used by attackers to set up malicious network connections. However, just because there's an indication that it's being used does not mean that it's an indicator of something malicious occurring. We need the proper context to answer that question such as, Where is it being used? By whom? For what purpose? Without that information, a defender has no way to know whether an alert on this application is legitimate.

Another way these tools can generate a false positive is if oversensitive rules have been deployed within the tools. In other words, a rule that detects brute force attacks might fire as the result of a user having forgotten their password after returning from vacation. The threshold may need to be adjusted to take these cases into account. It is also possible for certain applications to generate what appears to be anomalous traffic but is actually legitimate for that particular application. If the systems generating these alerts are not particularly well tuned, they could create thousands of false positives that could very easily overwhelm defenders. Proper tuning of these systems isn't just about preventing false positives but also involves setting the level of severity for each of the alerts. If all alerts are considered to be the same priority level, really serious incidents will get lost in all the noise.

There are also some psychological reasons for alert fatigue, such as bright red blinking lights found in some tool user interfaces. These notifications are meant to indicate some level of malicious activity, but they can be extremely misleading, leading to nothing more than fear, uncertainty, and doubt. Seeing these indicators incessantly, regardless of whether they are legitimate, can cause people to tune them out. In addition, continuously reading articles about zero-day vulnerabilities and large breaches can be emotionally draining and mentally detrimental. Reinforcing negative outcomes of this nature can cause defenders to feel as if they are fighting a losing battle. These things can lead to significant stress, burnout, and high turnover. [xxv]

Financial Constraints

Inertia is further reinforced by financial constraints. If a business has not experienced a reason to make significant change, such as a massive breach, it is not likely to do so in part because cybersecurity is typically seen as a cost center rather than a revenue driver. In other words, unlike a sales department that brings money into the company, the perception is that spending money to have a more secure environment is, instead, a drain on the organization's resources with little or no obvious return on investment. Rather than implementing some form of validation on their existing security controls such as with penetration tests, adversarial emulation, or active threat hunting, which is a topic we will discuss in later chapters, these organizations just become further mired in passivity.

Furthermore, because they are unwilling to commit more money to defend their cybersecurity assets, most organizations are frequently understaffed. These companies view security as a burden and nothing more. In addition, the staff they do have typically are not able to maintain sufficient training for their positions, much less find the time to learn new skills or tools. As a result, they are often missing the level of expertise needed to take defending their organizations from a passive to a more active state.

The unfortunate result of being shorthanded is that those who are working never have any downtime, which means more possibilities for mistakes and the potential for burnout, among other problems. In this particular case, it also means security staff are constantly responding to alerts or other urgent matters. Thus, they have no time to consider, much less implement, any proactive approaches.

It also prevents them from looking into emerging trends both within and external to their environments. Even if they managed to find the time, an environment that views security as a cost center is likely to consider some of these investigations "unproductive" because they turn up nothing of consequence. However, a hypothesis that is researched is still a result regardless of the outcome. As long as this result is documented, communicated, and discussed, it still has value to the organization. Focusing only on productivity severely limits visibility into new potential attacks or other noteworthy risks.

While it may seem counterintuitive, studies have shown that having some flexibility throughout the workday actually increases productivity.[xxvi] A company that views security as something that enables an organization to be more flexible provides substantial funding in order to integrate it more fully into its environment, leading to far better outcomes overall. Assuming all the necessary controls are in place for the right reasons and people are working well together doing the right things and communicating appropriately, companies can take better, well-managed risks.

Another way to see this thought process in action is to consider race car driving. The brakes on a race car make it go faster, not slower. How is that possible, you ask? While driving on a track, you must brake into a corner in order to accelerate out of it. If you don't brake and you go around the corner too fast, you either crash or have a lower corner entry speed. Slow is smooth. Smooth is fast. In other words, it's all about the deliberate choices that we make today helping us to move faster tomorrow.

Organizational Culture

The culture of the organization and its organizational processes can cause defenders to remain passive and reactive as well as perpetuate existing inertia. Cultural elements include how resistant to change an organization is; the presence of siloing, outsourcing, shadow IT, or BYOD (bring your own device); and lack of support from leadership.

Resistance to Change

If the environment tends to be extremely conservative in terms of change, it can be very difficult to institute more preemptive security practices. For example, some companies will only allow a firewall rule change during a prescribed window. If the rule change is meant to block an active attack, this window might be too late. These organizations often exhibit considerable hesitancy or pushback about blocking anything because they are afraid that it might interrupt production.

The same is true for network access. In large organizations, it is common for multiple departments to take part in a single change, which slows down the process further and prevents any possibility of agility, which is often required for proactive security changes. Other organizations, such as in higher education, resist activities like the manual removal of dangerous messages from their email system for fear that their users might view this as too intrusive or a privacy violation. Furthermore, consider the situation where an existing employee becomes an internal threat and their access needs to be terminated immediately. Organizations often resist making immediate changes to an established process such as cutting off access to an account. However, in this case, if this process takes any significant amount of time, the employee could use their access to cause malicious damage or steal company data.

Siloing

If siloing is common within the organization, security-related observations from other departments such as networking, QA, or development may never make it to the security team. In some companies, these silos are created because communication is blatantly forbidden or strongly discouraged between certain groups. Instead, it may be because these groups do not have a connection within the security team and thus no easy way to share information. The possibility also exists that these other groups want to avoid additional work, so they intentionally do not seek out the security team after making a problematic discovery. As a result of this delay, reactionary measures may be the only options once a problem is brought to light. Furthermore, the security team may not have the necessary insight into what the other teams are doing or what requirements must be met before those requirements become a last-minute problem.

Outsourcing

Whether a company outsources its IT services is another organizational factor that can perpetuate a reactive and passive security posture. Outsourcing is the practice of hiring a third party to manage some or all of the IT services that a company utilizes in its day-to-day operations. While a common practice, outsourcing has a number of hidden costs/risks associated with it that are often overlooked.

If taken to extremes, outsourcing can leave your internal team bereft of the ability to effect change in a timely manner, making them little more than vendor managers. In other words, they can cause the in-house staff to get to a point where they cannot make any changes without asking the vendor how to handle the request. If the vendor is not reasonably responsive, it may take an extremely long time for any changes to be made, including security-related requests. Furthermore, service level agreements for outsourced IT services often do not align with an organization's security demands.

Selecting the right vendor can make a difference too. A vendor that hires cheap, unqualified, or unethical employees can contribute to an already poor security posture through mistakes, oversights, and potentially malicious activity. They may not even notify the organization if there has been an intrusion or data theft.

Some vendors are genuinely interested in providing good quality service with the intention to improve an organization's security posture. However, if the majority of IT is outsourced and the vendor is paid based on the number of tickets they resolve rather than on real results, they may be less interested in doing the right thing.

Shadow IT

A passive security attitude may also lead companies to allow shadow IT to fulfill user requests, further preventing their ability to cultivate proactive security practices. Shadow IT is the practice of deploying information technology systems outside of an organization's normal central IT structure. It can include the use of file storage solutions or email accounts with online providers such as Microsoft or Google, productivity solutions like Trello or Zoom, and instant messaging apps such as WhatsApp or Signal.

Users who are frustrated by the inability of central IT or security departments to provide the services they need, or they find services provided are too complicated to use, turn to shadow IT to solve these problems. For example, if they are not allowed to share data the way they feel they should be able to, they might store information in a cloud service beyond the company's control. As a result, the organization will likely have no knowledge that these tools were implemented, or what data is contained within them. Without this information, the organization cannot possibly take proactive steps to configure or secure this environment properly.

Ultimately, shadow IT increases the overall attack surface requiring protection. Vulnerabilities will either remain unpatched or not be patched in a timely fashion. Furthermore, there is a significant likelihood that data will be shared with individuals who should not have access to it, leading to a potential breach. The use of shadow IT may also mean that compliance regulations, standards, and laws are not being followed, leading to fines and other legal consequences. Each of these issues can generate additional incidents, adding more work to what was likely an already overburdened, understaffed security team and, in turn, causing them to have a more passive and reactive stance.

One important point to note is that to a certain degree, shadow IT is inevitable. Typically, it occurs as a product of the business doing what it needs to survive when existing central IT or security processes introduce too much friction into the business. However, instead of just shutting it down, the discovery of shadow IT should be used as an opportunity to learn and streamline processes to remove this friction and better enable the business. Otherwise, another group will spin up more shadow IT and the practice will repeat itself.

BYOD

A topic that can overlap with shadow IT is that of employees being allowed to use personal devices, rather than company-issued ones, to connect to their organization's networks and access work-related systems as well as potentially sensitive or confidential data. This practice is known as BYOD (bring your own device).

Devices can include anything from laptops to mobile devices, such as smartphones or tablets. Depending on organizational policy, BYOD could be shadow IT that is sanctioned by the company. Typically, sanctioned BYOD is done to reduce costs and provide some user flexibility in device choice but still allows for management of the devices in some capacity by the business. For example, some BYOD systems are governed by the organization's mobile device management software, which monitors, secures, and enforces policies such as patching level or software installed. Instead, BYOD could be shadow IT that is only partially approved.

Consider a situation in which a particular outsourced department wants to use BYOD systems that are outside of the standards of the company, perhaps with an alternative operating system. When consulted, the security office refuses to authorize this request, perhaps because no management controls exist for this platform. However, a senior executive outside of their office approves the request anyway. As a result, BYOD winds up on the network as partially approved but not entirely sanctioned.

The third case involves BYOD as completely unsanctioned shadow IT. For example, a user just brings in a personal device and attaches it to the network without telling anyone or without any controls having been added to protect both the device and the resources on the network.

An organization that permits BYOD without requiring at least some form of management of these devices has the potential to suffer from the same kinds of challenges as that of shadow IT. The overall attack surface increases in all cases, although that may be at least partially mitigated if the devices are managed by the organization. However, in all other cases, these devices are likely to add to the operational overhead, creating more work for the security team and ultimately leading to additional reactivity and passivity. Just as with shadow IT, they are likely to be unpatched or not be proactively securely configured, and the users are unlikely to be aware of any compliance regulations required. Furthermore, if the device is regularly shuttled between the office and home, there is a greater risk of theft both of the device and the data that it contains if the device is stolen.

The one situation where BYOD can be much less of a risk is if it is connecting to a virtual desktop interface (VDI) just to stream the desktop down, limiting exposure to the corporate environment to just a mouse and a keyboard. Company data, in this example, remains in the business network and does not directly interact with the local machine. That said, something like keylogging malware on the BOYD device could still capture passwords used to log into the VDI systems, so multi-factor authentication is still critical.

Leadership Support

One of the key cultural factors that can impact security posture is support from leadership. If they do not buy into the idea of moving from being reactive to a more proactive approach to security, it is unlikely that the status quo will change. Ultimately, management drives whether any kind of transformation can be accomplished within an organization and often how quickly (or not) these changes can occur. It's imperative that they give more than lip service to these modifications and actively work to make them happen. Because they're the ones who usually drive security policy changes, if leadership doesn't actively advocate for policies that create the agility necessary for proactive security practices, defenders will remain stuck. For example, it is not uncommon for business units to demand to deploy Internet of Things (IoT) devices without any type of security review. Without leadership taking a stand to prevent this behavior, it will perpetuate.

Furthermore, if members of leadership circumvent changes put in place to implement a more proactive approach for their pet projects, undoubtedly other people will do the same. Executives who strictly emphasize uptime, performance statistics, and the latest security gadgets rather than the actual security posture of their organization continue to promote passivity. These are the leaders who refuse to fight for proper monetary resources and staffing, refuse to provide flex time for research, put off patching vulnerabilities whenever possible, and discourage real-time information sharing. This attitude is often what causes defenders to remain trapped in a passive security posture.

The Missing Piece

Many of the challenges to the traditional defender just discussed are fairly well known and have been at least touched on in other articles, blog posts, and books. However, I believe there is one specific challenge that I have not seen in any other discussions: either defenders are unaware of the existence of offensive security practices and practitioners or they intentionally avoid them for a variety of reasons.

Leadership attitude plays a role here too. Some managers are extremely uncomfortable allowing their employees to study something they view as outside of their job scope and reprimand them for doing so. If the organization is particularly siloed, any defenders outside of the immediate security world, such as system or network admins, who attempt to explore the world of offensive security might be chastised for what is perceived to be stepping on the toes of the security group. Furthermore, some companies fear their employees might expose operational secrets once they start talking externally about the things they are learning.

Another reason why defenders might avoid learning more about offensive security practices is in situations where their environments are frequently audited. To them, offensive security practitioners doing any testing are viewed as just another form of audit. Defenders in this situation may view audits as a negative experience in which the goal is to prove their incompetence. As a result, these defenders do whatever they can to limit the exposure of systems they are responsible for to the tests being run in order to prevent what they perceive as direct criticism of their work. This situation can be further exacerbated if reports generated by the offensive security team are poorly written either because they don't understand the business context or because they have not taken the time to communicate their findings in a clear, effective manner.

Some offensive security practitioners are also known for their egotistical reputations, which can be off-putting. Naturally, some defenders can be equally arrogant. The combination of challenging personalities potentially on either side, with one team auditing another, can create an adversarial dynamic that does not lend itself well to a learning environment.

Unfortunately, this lack of information leads to defenders having only a partial understanding of the security risks their organizations face. Effective defense requires an intimate understanding of offensive techniques and strategy, not just following best defensive practices. A willingness to open the door to the offensive security community provides the first steps to not only learning about what I call "the other half of the security story" but also to becoming a much stronger and more capable defensive practitioner. As your knowledge deepens, you will find that the way you think about defense changes. Ideally, it will encourage you to take a more proactive approach and encourage you to work toward becoming an Active Defender. As a result, you will have a broader, more comprehensive view of the effectiveness of your detections and defenses as well as access to many additional resources to further your understanding.

The aim of this book will be to both introduce what it means to be an Active Defender and explore the steps necessary to become one. As we will see, becoming an Active Defender rather than a traditional one can begin to break the inertia and address many of the concerns discussed earlier. In the right environment, the Active Defender can even become an organizational champion for change.

What Is Covered in This Book?

The *Active Defender: Immersion in the Offensive Security Mindset* contains nine chapters.

> Chapter 1: What Is an Active Defender? In this chapter I will explain what an Active Defender is and describe what qualities one needs to embody to be an Active Defender. The focus here is on the practitioner, not the practice per se, but I will describe some of the common activities in which an Active Defender participates. I will also explain how my concept of active defense differs from traditional defense models or from other existing definitions of active defense. In particular, I'll explore the idea that being an Active Defender does not necessarily involve the use of offensive security tactics but rather cultivating the hacker mindset to better understand an attacker's thought process. Therefore, they are more easily able to grasp the nature of the risks and threats in their environments. We'll also discuss what the hacker mindset is, generally speaking, and how it differs from

the traditional defender mindset, but I'll leave how to begin to develop this new way of thinking until Chapter 2.

Furthermore, I will also explore how being an Active Defender is better than being a passive defender, using specific examples from the current state. One of the examples discussed will include how threat hunting can reduce the time to discovery of a breach, reduce dwell time, and increase speed and accuracy during incident response. The ability to recognize reliable, relevant intel for your organization is another example of when the Active Defender will be far more valuable than someone who is passive. In addition, because Active Defenders have a better understanding of existing threats, and since the majority of attacks do use known exploits, Active Defenders are well poised to help their organizations to defend against these attacks.

Chapter 2: Immersion into the Hacker Mindset. To become an Active Defender requires an intimate understanding of the threats you're defending against, which requires you to immerse yourself in the offensive security community. It is through this immersion that you can begin to build a hacker mindset. Unfortunately, the media has taken to portraying the offensive security community in a negative light. This chapter will begin by examining some of the media-perpetuating negative perceptions of the offensive security community that might be off-putting to a defender, followed by my own initial personal experiences with the offensive security practitioners at hacker conferences.

Next, it will explore the realities of this community as a response to the reservations a person might have as a result of these preconceived notions. The chapter will discuss how Active Defenders regularly engage with people working in offensive security such that they understand both the attack methodologies in a variety of attack types and how to best defend against them in their own environments.

Finally, it will encourage readers to engage with the community and offer specific strategies that someone can take to get involved. I'll discuss finding local and remote offensive community groups, gatherings, and events, including some examples of where you can find them and generally what to expect if attending.

Chapter 3: Offensive Security Engagements, Trainings, and Gathering Intel. One way to better understand what offensive security practitioners know is to understand what their engagements look like and the goals of each step. In addition, it can be particularly useful to attend some training classes in their methodologies. Thus, the first portion of this chapter will discuss what a typical offensive security engagement entails to provide a foundation for further discussion. The second part will explore some places where one can find a variety of training opportunities, including both inexpensive and pricey options such as BSides and SANS, respectively.

The last portion of this chapter will discuss places where offensive security practitioners often obtain their intel information, such as social media sites. The discussion will include what the site is as well as both why and how the information can be used for attacks.

Chapter 4: Understanding the Offensive Toolset. This chapter will contain a discussion about tools often used by those in offensive security roles. The discussion will explore how, why, and in what circumstances they use these tools as well as how to mitigate them as defenders. However, this discussion is not a walk-through of how to use them, but it will include places to get additional information.

Note that several of these tools are regularly used by defenders, just in different ways. The chapter will categorize these tools using the ATT&CK matrix to illustrate where in the process of an attack they can be used. Using this same context, the chapter will also consider why certain defensive practices are recommended as best practices, such as having an inventory of data, software, hardware, and services.

Chapter 5: Implementing Defense While Thinking Like a Hacker. This chapter will explore applying the hacker mindset in unique ways to some traditional defensive activities as an Active Defender would do. For example, they can recognize vulnerabilities in their organizations that may not have been previously obvious, such as how seemingly innocuous public information about their organizations, known as open-source intelligence (OSINT), can be used against them. Another example involves understanding how binary files built into the operating system, known as LOLBins, can be easily used as attack vectors. In addition, the chapter will cover some proactive methods the Active Defender can use to defend their environments, such as threat modeling, threat hunting, and attack simulations.

Chapter 6: Becoming an Advanced Active Defender. This chapter will discuss how to take being an Active Defender to the next level. The Advanced Active Defender not only engages with the offensive security community, but they are capable of more advanced testing practices, such as automated attack emulations, in part because of this mindset they've been regularly cultivating. They also know how to work with a variety of deceptive technologies and often engage directly with offensive security teams in various ways to improve their own organization's security posture, including something known as purple teaming.

Chapter 7: Building Effective Detections. While this chapter is not intended to teach you to be a detection engineer, it will provide some insights to the challenges they face. Relying on work done by Jared Atkinson, this chapter will first explore the purpose of detection, the two main phases of building detections, and the four overall challenges to creating effective detections. With that information in mind, we will return to the Pyramid of Pain and the TTP Pyramid and discuss why defenders have difficulty detecting attacks. Knowing how detections can be problematic, we will consider at what level we should be testing to know whether or not a detection is effective. Furthermore, we will discuss how proper validation of these tests includes a consideration of both telemetry and detection coverage. Finally, we will consider some options for testing existing detections.

Chapter 8: Actively Defending Cloud Computing Environments. This chapter will examine some of the challenges to defending a cloud computing environment in terms of how it differs from its strictly on-premises counterpart even as a hybrid entity. In particular, it will highlight how the relationships between the two major segments of all cloud computing environments, the data plane and the control plane, can be used against each other from an offensive security perspective. Ultimately, suggestions for how the Active Defender should view defense of this space through the eyes of an offensive security professional will be provided.

Chapter 9: Future Challenges. This chapter will examine some newer challenges that are starting to be thrown at defenders, continuing to push them toward the passive stance. The chapter will consider problems such as the increasing use of supply chain attacks, the growing number of Bring Your Own Vulnerable Drive (BYOVD) attacks, the ease with which threat actors can attack entities thanks to many of the existing frameworks in place, and the topic of API security.

Notes

i. Identity Theft Resource Center Annual Data Breach Report 2022, `www.idtheftcenter.org/publication/2022-data-breach-report`.

ii. IBM Security. *Cost of a Data Breach 2022*, `www.ibm.com/reports/data-breach`.

iii. `www.idc.com/getdoc.jsp?containerId=prUS50498423#:~:text=NEEDHAM%2C%20Mass.%2C%20March%2016,International%20Data%20Corporation%20(IDC)`

iv. IBM Security. *Cost of a Data Breach 2022*, `www.ibm.com/reports/data-breach`.

v. Ibid.

vi. 2021 Data Breach.

Investigations Report, `www.verizon.com/business/resources/reports/dbir`. Ransomware Report 2023, `https://cybersecurityworks.com/howdymanage/uploads/file/Ransomware%20Report%202023_compressed.pdf`.

vii.   www.sans.org/white-papers/sans-vulnerability-management-survey-2022

viii. www.sans.org/white-papers/sans-vulnerability-management-survey-2022

ix.   2022 Data Breach.

Investigations Report, www.verizon.com/business/resources/reports/dbir.

x.   T. Radeska (2016). "Brain -The first computer virus was created by two brothers from Pakistan. They just wanted to prevent their customers of making illegal software copies." Retrieved Oct 19, 2018, from www.thevintagenews.com/2016/09/08/priority-brain-first-computer-virus-created-two-brothers-pakistan-just-wanted-prevent-customers-making-illegal-software-copies.

xi.   J. Davis (2012). "John McAfee Fled to Belize but He Couldn't Escape Himself." Retrieved Sept 25, 2018, from www.wired.com/2012/12/ff-john-mcafees-last-stand.

xii.   L. DiDio (1989). "To Keep your System virus-free, use proper computer hygiene." Network World: 90.

xiii.   (1986). "Future bugs Computer world dreading electronic 'virus' attack." *Globe and Mail*.

xiv.   Government, U. (1989). Computer Viruses: Hearing Before the SubCommittee on Telecommunications and Finance of the Commuttee on Energy and Commerce House of Representatives. C. o. E. a. C. H. o. Representatives. Washington, DC, US Government Printing Office,: 14., ibid.

xv.   M. Alexander (1990). "Health insurance for computers." *ComputerWorld*. Framingham, MA, IDG News Service. *XXIV*: 1.

xvi.   F. Avliolo (1999). "Firewalls and Internet Security, the Second Hundred (Internet) Years." *The Internet Protocol Journal* 2(2).

xvii.   A. Radding (1995). "Crash course in 'net security." *ComputerWorld*. Framingham, MA, IDG News Service. *XXIX*: 10.

xviii. www.acunetix.com/blog/articles/history-of-tls-ssl-part-2

xix.   www.verizon.com/business/small-business-essentials/resources/great-applied-technology-typically-needs-enabling

xx.   G. Bruneau (2021) *The History and Evolution of Intrusion Detection*, SANS white paper. www.sans.org/white-papers/344.

xxi.   www.secureworks.com/blog/the-evolution-of-intrusion-detection-prevention

xxii. www.spirion.com/data-loss-prevention

xxiii. https://cybersecurity-magazine.com/a-brief-history-of-siem

xxiv. R. Lee. *The Sliding Scale of Security*. www.sans.org/white-papers/36240.

xxv. https://ioactive.com/cybersecurity-alert-fatigue

xxvi. https://hbr.org/2012/12/the-upside-of-downtime

What Is an Active Defender?

Chinese general Sun Tzu is perhaps best known for his fifth century BC seminal treatise, *The Art of War*, in which he presents the basic principles of warfare and explains to military leaders how to fight. In particular, the text emphasizes ways to outsmart one's opponent rather than resorting to physical combat, and as a means of ensuring victory if a battle ensues. As Sun Tzu said, "To know your enemy, you must become your enemy." In other words, you must do more than have a superficial understanding of your enemies' behaviors and tactics: you must deeply learn their motivations, thought processes, problem-solving approaches, and patterns as well. Likewise, in the *Republic*, Plato said that "the one who is most able to guard against disease is also most able to produce it unnoticed." Conversely, one who is able to embrace and embody the hacker mindset enough to take appropriate action to contain and excise attackers, as well as better prevent intrusion in the first place, can more easily grasp the nature of the risks and threats in their environments. Acquiring this deep understanding is what transforms a traditional defender into an Active Defender.

The Hacker Mindset

The Active Defender is someone who is aware of and actively engaged with the offensive security community in order to cultivate the hacker mindset.

But what is the hacker mindset? First, let me address the term *hacker* and then we can address the mindset they cultivate.

When I use the word *hacker* I am referring to the original use of the term coined at the Tech Model Railroad Club of MIT in the 1950s: someone who applies ingenuity to create a clever result, called a *hack*.[i] While the media has taken to using hacker in an exclusively pejorative way, tying it to someone who breaks into computer networks to steal or vandalize, nothing about this original definition implies anything illegal or immoral. I will not spend time rehashing the debate over this word, but simply say that this is what I mean when I use it here. In contrast, the word *attacker* is what will refer to someone who breaks into computer networks for the purposes of theft or to cause damage.

With the term *hacker* defined, we can now move to a discussion of the hacker mindset. Generally speaking, this mentality is one of curiosity, creativity, patience, persistence, agility, and nonlinear thinking. Hackers by their nature are curious individuals and believe strongly in freely sharing information. At a young age, they're often the ones who take apart their toys to see how they work. They love to experiment and make something do things it was never intended to do, just because they can. Most people ask why? A hacker is more likely to ask why not? When problem solving, they frequently consider the unintended or overlooked properties of a thing or situation, leading to a new and unique solution only a hacker could produce. As avid security researcher Casey Smith noted in a recent presentation, when paraphrasing a quote by Jon Erickson, "Hackers get their edge from knowing how things really work."[ii]

For example, some of the earliest technological hackers, known as phreakers because they were focused on phone networks, spent hours reading obscure telephone company technical documentation and listening to the patterns of tones used in these networks to figure out how calls were routed. This research led to a full understanding of how telephone networks operated, and as a result, these hackers determined how to make free long-distance calls. After some experimentation, they realized that by producing a 2,600 hertz tone, they could manipulate the phone line into thinking it was idle, thereby allowing a free long-distance call to be placed. This tone could be created by someone with perfect pitch whistling or by a small plastic toy whistle that happened to be a prize found in boxes of Cap'n Crunch cereal at the time. Later, tone-generating devices called blue boxes, which could be readily assembled from some parts at Radio Shack, made this process even easier.

Hackers approach problems in unique and creative ways, often thinking outside the box and challenging assumptions about how things work. When tackling a new problem, they may not focus on a particular goal but rather just start pulling at a thread to see where it goes. Even when there is a goal, the journey, as they say, may be far more interesting to a hacker than the destination. They are not afraid to get lost in tangents and are known to follow the rabbit hole to wherever it leads regardless of any failures they might experience. For every success a hacker has, they likely have a multitude of failures from either continuously trying new techniques or trying new combinations of existing ones. They often have an enhanced way of looking at the world and can make connections others cannot, often by asking one simple question: what if? To view the world in this way requires literally questioning everything you know or think you know in order to defeat confirmation bias. In other words, to prevent interpreting new evidence as just a confirmation of one's existing beliefs or theories requires this level of skeptical analysis.

Perhaps the most important element of the hacker ethos is the fact that hackers investigate and explore simply because of their enthusiasm for learning and the love of the investigative journey. As a result, hackers love to share what they're learning and are willing to spend copious amounts of time doing so. In other security communities, whether in defense or offense, this joy, discovery, and inquisitiveness often becomes subservient to the duties and necessity of the job. Unfortunately, that not only leads these practitioners to burn out and struggle harder to get through each day but also be less inclined to share information or teach others what they know.

Traditional Defender Mindset

One critical problem with traditional defenders is that they don't typically think in this way. As John Lambert, Distinguished Engineer, Microsoft Threat Intelligence Center says, "Defenders think in lists. Attackers think in graphs. As long as this is true, attackers win."[iii]

While hackers and attackers are definitely not the same thing, the hacker mindset is certainly more in line with how attackers think. The difference, however, is one of intent. The hacker, as already described, is curious and wants to understand the possibilities, while the attacker wants to use these possibilities to cause harm.

Regardless, whether they realize it or not, defenders often focus on lists as part of what are considered best practices. For example, the CIS Critical Security Controls, NIST standards, and PCI controls are just some of the lists they often are required to follow, whether for compliance reasons or simply because they've been taught these controls are expected as industry standards.

The problem with thinking in lists is that, broadly speaking, it is linear thinking. Consider an example where a defender is tasked with hardening a web server. The defender can follow all the best practices, such as documenting an inventory of what hardware and software is installed, scanning the machine for vulnerabilities and mitigating anything discovered, running the latest fully patched firmware and operating system, locking the system down to only communicate over port 443, and even restricting what and who has access to the machine both locally and over the network. At the end of the day, the defender believes they have done everything they can do to protect this system and considers it as secure as possible. They move on. The attacker, reflecting on this same system, begins to wonder what they could do with that open port that perhaps it was not meant to do. Someone with the hacker mindset is more likely to recognize the possibilities than the traditional defender.

Even the SANS incident response process, where you have separate, discrete phases of preparation, investigation, containment, eradication, remediation, and lessons learned, is an example of this limited type of thinking. The investigative approach they provide is a linear process in that it's more of a flowchart walk-through rather than having the investigator's actions informed by a deep understanding of the activity observed and its implications as well as an understanding of attacker mindset, goals, and anticipated moves.

In contrast, thinking in graphs is holographic in nature. In other words, it draws connections among disparate data points and uses those connections to inform the attackers actions in wise fashion at a holistic and instinctual level. Each data point informs and enriches all the others such that what you wind up with is essentially a fancy mesh network of information rather than a traditional flat Ethernet network, thus making it more efficient and resilient.

Of course, that's not to say that the process SANS provides is ultimately not useful—it absolutely is. However, I'd argue that it's only meant to be a starting point, providing a sense of the components that need to be considered. An investigation typically begins as the result of some form of initial activity that causes an alert to fire or a defender to become suspicious. With this preliminary evidence as a starting point, you should be looking for context, which in turn will typically result in additional evidence. As a result, there are many paths an investigation could take. However, only someone who cultivates the hacker mindset and has the right experience will be able to efficiently uncover the graph an attacker left behind. Otherwise, they remain stuck, unable to connect the dots.

Another way of explaining this idea is that as a defender trying to piece together the narrative of what an attacker did on a system, you typically have no insight into what the process looked like for the attacker. You look for artifacts that point to activities, and you generally assume those activities were done with intention and were successful unless you see reason to believe otherwise. However, someone who spends enough time within the offensive security space to begin to cultivate the hacker mindset understands that, despite their best efforts, attempts made by attackers often fail in unexpected ways.

Getting from Here to There

As a traditional defender becomes more engaged with the offensive security community, they gain emergent insight into how hackers, and consequently attackers, operate. It opens the door to a world that they didn't know exists, and, if they remain involved, can lead them to becoming Active Defenders. However, unlocking that knowledge requires making a choice.

Long before Neo was asked to choose between the blue and the red pill in the Matrix and saw just how far down the rabbit hole goes, the Greek philosopher Plato had his famous cave. This emblem of a theory of knowledge highlights the blind spots we all possess and parallels the choice we are forced to make. The "Allegory of the Cave" tells the story of a group of prisoners chained together inside a cave facing a blank wall their entire lives. They are unable to turn their heads. Behind the prisoners is a fire. Between the fire and the prisoners is a raised walkway with a low wall. As a result, anyone or anything that moves along the walkway appears as shadows on the wall the prisoners are facing. The prisoners perceive these shadows to be all the things that exist in the world. It is, of course, the only world they know. The story further considers what would happen if one of these prisoners were to escape their bonds, discover the real world that lies beyond those shadows, and then try to return to liberate their former cave-mates. It posits that the rest of the prisoners would reject the knowledge of this "reality," choosing instead to stay in the safety and darkness of the world as they know it.

As defenders, we cannot afford to stay in that darkness if we want to be increasingly effective. We are only as good as what we know—and until we can shine a light on our own blind spots, we cannot begin taking the first steps in breaking the shackles of passivity and transition toward becoming an Active Defender. By continuing to spend time immersed in the offensive security community, we can begin to better recognize the connections into and within our networks that make a variety of attacks possible. Consequently, this understanding facilitates attacker behavior discovery, which is a key part of what makes the Active Defender special. It is key because it is what peels away the blinders and exposes the previously unknown knowledge gaps.

Being an Active Defender requires more than the ability to break through the darkness. They also must understand the difference between the ability to "see" and the ability to "observe" the various pieces of information that they discover, whether in log files, security tools, or incoming intelligence. Simply "seeing" something is a passive function, whereas "observing" something is an active function. This ability is part of the hacker mindset and is crucial to making the connections often overlooked by traditional defenders.

No less illustrious a detective than Sherlock Holmes himself, Arthur Conan Doyle's master of deduction, hints at this difference in "A Scandal in Bohemia." John Watson expresses amazement with how the results of Holmes's investigation seem plain and simple when explained but seem to elude him, despite the fact that they both see through perfectly capable eyes. Holmes gently admonishes him, saying of his friend, "You see, but you do not observe." Both men have trudged up the front steps of 221B Baker Street countless times, and have seen the same steps, but only Holmes knows that the steps are 17 in number, because he has "both seen and observed."

To be clear, though, what Holmes has in mind does not merely equate the idea of observation with memorization of what has been seen. Instead, it involves consciously ingesting the data presented and recognizing the relevant pieces as actual information that can provide context. It is important to understand that data by itself is unstructured with no real meaning. It's not until that data is coupled with context that it becomes information. In other words, what were once simply points of data, with the appropriate context, become organized, analyzed, and interpreted to be useful information. Thus, Active Defenders must not merely uncover the correct artifacts and see them; they must also draw upon their understanding of the artifacts themselves, the context in which the artifacts were found, their knowledge of attacker motivation and behavior, and countless other pieces of information in order to not merely see the data but to observe its significance.

Active Defenders take the joyful and creative exploration of the hacker mindset and apply it to their defensive roles. By their nature, they have a proactive security ethos. In other words, it is in their character to actively seek out ways for their organizations to become more secure, whether by traditional means such as network segmentation or more innovative ways such as taking extra steps to understand how specific attack vectors work.

They view the notion of "security" as a verb, something that they actively work at doing or being rather than a destination or an ultimate goal to achieve. They understand that an organization can never truly be 100 percent secure but that being situationally aware and engaged with the offensive community can help improve their security posture. Furthermore, they recognize that excellence in security is not a matter of achieving a particular and static level of mastery but rather requires regularly practicing this proactive behavior.

What I mean by excellence here comes from the Greek philosopher Aristotle. He believed that excellence consists of being the best possible version of whatever you are, which means you are good at doing whatever it is you are supposed to do. An excellent knife is good at cutting, and an excellent fish fork is good at removing fish meat from small bones. For humans, excellence is more complicated than performing one simple function, but it involves being the best person you can be. This requires both the moral character to see the wisest course of action in any given situation and the technical knowledge to translate that vision into effective action. Similarly, in security, being excellent requires both the wisdom to discern the most appropriate path to take and the technical knowledge to get us there.

Active Defender Activities

First and foremost, as I've said, the Active Defender engages with the offensive security community. They do so in a variety of ways, both in person and online, such as by attending local or national conferences, going to meetups, or participating in forums and on social media. Chapter 2, "Immersion into the Hacker Mindset," will explore some of these options and how to get involved with them. However, they also participate in a number of proactive activities that make them stronger defenders, such as threat modeling, threat hunting, and attack simulations.

Threat Modeling

The Active Defender regularly participates in threat modeling in terms of both the business they are protecting and the technology it employs. Threat modeling, at a very basic level, is a proactive, risk-based evaluation of what attacks are likely or possible for a given person, environment, or situation with an eye toward evaluating particular scenarios. It requires considering what you or your organization has that is of value to a potential attacker. Where these elements are cyber assets most critical to the accomplishment of the organization's mission, they're often referred to as the "crown jewels."[iv]

Threats include anything that has the potential to cause harm (whether reputational or technical), do damage, or in the case of a company, interrupt business. Risk involves the likelihood that a threat could be successful.

Threat modeling also involves considering what vulnerabilities, or weaknesses, a threat can use against you or your organization. Attackers never act without motive, and it is impossible to separate the attack from what it is the attacker is hoping to gain. Therefore, understanding what a threat actor might hope to gain can help you identify where the greatest need for security is in your organization. It can also help determine, to some extent, the path that an attacker might take after landing on a system.

Typically, formal threat modeling occurs at the beginning of a project, whether building new software or deploying a new system to prevent introducing new risks into an organization. Several formal methodologies are available to use for performing an evaluation of this nature. For example, Microsoft offers a model called STRIDE, which is an acronym that stands for Spoofing, Tampering, Repudiation, Information Disclosure, Denial of Service, and Elevation of Privilege. STRIDE specifically focuses on finding potential threats against software.[v]

CVSS, the Common Vulnerability Scoring System, is another well-known model created by NIST (National Institute of Standards and Technology) that provides a numerical score for the severity of vulnerabilities. Furthermore, many books and articles have been written about the topic of threat modeling, mostly intended for an audience of people who create software, such as developers, as well as those responsible for building operational systems, such as analysts or architects. Most recently, a working group of security and privacy professionals came together to develop a methodology-neutral guide called the Threat Modeling Manifesto.[vi] They wanted a way to share their collective threat modeling knowledge to "inform, educate, and inspire other practitioners to adopt threat modeling as well as improve security and privacy during development."[vii]

Although these formal approaches exist, the reality is that each of us threat models regularly, just without referring to it with that name. Anytime we do something involving potential threats, such as traveling or even crossing the street, we consider the threats we might face. For example, when planning a shopping trip for the Friday after Thanksgiving, which is commonly known as Black Friday here in the United States, we must consider several threats such as the possibility of being trampled at large box stores, the potential for vehicle vandalism, potential loss from theft, and the amount of time spent waiting in lines versus opportunities for theft. Contemplating each of these concerns in advance may cause us to take different actions than we would have otherwise. Therefore, I believe the idea of threat modeling can be extended to be useful beyond developers and architects to also include all practitioners of defensive security as we've already defined it, including system administrators, network administrators, and other security professionals. In Chapter 5, "Implementing Defense While Thinking Like a Hacker," we'll examine this topic further and discuss what threat modeling as an Active Defender with the hacker mindset engaged looks like.

Threat Hunting

The Active Defender also may engage in threat hunting regularly. Threat hunting is a human-centric activity by defenders who proactively search through data to find threats that evade traditional security measures.[viii] It forces them to look beyond the alerts generated by SIEMs and other tools, which, as we've already discussed, can lead to tunnel vision. As a result, it is possible to find previously undetected threats, thereby reducing dwell time and limit attacker persistence.

Dwell time is the period between when a system gets compromised and when the compromise is detected. Threat hunting can also help uncover previously overlooked misconfigurations, detect poor user/administrator practices, reduce the overall attack surface, and identify gaps in existing defenses. Ideally, with this information documented, these issues can be resolved. Furthermore, by identifying these threats, the defender may even be able to adjust existing detections or create new ones for their environment. We'll discuss the topic of building effective detections in Chapter 7.

The process used for hunting should be one that is readily repeatable and not random. Furthermore, despite what some may claim, threat hunting does not require the defender to have a significant amount of experience or for the business to have a high level of security maturity. Even a defender who is entry level can threat hunt and do so regardless of the sophistication of the organization's security program. Almost all organizations will have some logs or other places to hunt, even if they're not the ideal central logging repositories of advanced security programs.

Threat hunting does require having at least some knowledge about the environment. However, one of the hidden advantages to engaging in threat hunting is that this activity ultimately helps increase the defender's knowledge of the network and the datasets available. As a result, their responses are typically more accurate and response times are reduced. We'll explore what threat hunting looks like as an Active Defender in Chapter 5. Keep in mind, though, that what gets uncovered during a threat hunt can lead to the need for incident response. The defender should be prepared to take the necessary steps to transition to the appropriate person or team if the need arises.

Attack Simulations

Attack simulations are another area that the Active Defender pursues whenever feasible. As the name implies, attack simulations attempt to create actions and behaviors that mimic what an attacker might be expected to do against the environment being defended. While not a real attack, it allows the defender to get a feel for what a particular type of attack might look like against their environment and whether any detections for it alert as expected.

Utilizing attack simulations allows the defender to continuously test these detections, develop new ones, tune configurations, and compare security products to get a feel for what is more effective in a particular environment against different kinds of attacks. There are a number of different options for employing attack simulations, including both free software such as Atomic Red Team, offered by Red Canary, and paid software such as the SCYTHE adversary emulation platform.

Active Defense

Now that you're starting to get a feeling for what an Active Defender is and what they do, I want to explore the distinction between the type of active defense they practice compared to that proposed by other entities.

"Active Defense" for the Active Defender

The origin of the phrase *active defense*, which is briefly mentioned in the introduction in conjunction with Robert M. Lee's white paper, comes from a paper about the 1973 Arab/Israel war written by US Army General William E. DePuy. It was used to describe the necessity for ground troops to be able to be mobile rather than remain static while defending their position. Specifically, he stated that the purpose of active defense is to "wear down the attacker by confronting him successively and continuously with strong combined arms teams and task forces fighting from mutually supported battle positions in depth throughout the battle area."[ix]

Unfortunately, despite being added to an Army Field Manual in 1976, debate continued about what the term really meant. In 2015 the Department of Defense adopted *active defense* to mean "the employment of limited offensive action and counterattacks to deny a contested area or position to the enemy" in the context of traditional warfare, which further confused matters. As a result, use of the term *counterattacks* in this definition was taken to literally mean "hack-back" with regard to the cybersecurity space.

However, even in the traditional warfare notion of the term "active defense," the word *counterattack* was only meant to occur inside the defended area. For example, the military provides what is known as force protection to safeguard DoD personnel within their defensive zone, including their families, resources, and critical information.[x] These preventative mitigations do not extend beyond the border of protection. In other words, defenders can take proactive steps for protection within their space but not step across this border to go after an attacker.

A similar example from popular culture, for those unfamiliar with military concepts, can be found in the movie *Home Alone*. While the main character sets up a variety of booby traps inside his house to deter a pair of burglars from robbing it, he does not pursue the burglars beyond the entrance to the home itself. Instead, as Rob Lee states, "counterattack in cybersecurity would be more properly reflected in the concept of incident response where personnel 'counterattack' by containing and remediating a threat."[xi]

Thus, rather than "hacking back," Lee's description of active defense for cybersecurity involves the original intent of the term *active defense*, with a focus on the flexibility, intelligence acquired, and application of this intelligence within their networks and, as explained earlier, is what I take to be at the heart of the Active Defender's actions.

Another Take on Active Defense

In contrast, John Strand defines active defense as "the employment of limited offensive action and counterattacks to deny a contested area or position to the enemy."[xii] He describes the actions that make up active defense as being proactive, anticipatory, and reactionary against attackers. In his book *Offensive*

Countermeasures: The Art of Active Defense, Strand outlines three active defense categories: annoyance, attribution, and attack.[xiii]

Annoyance

Annoyance, which is also known as "cyber deception" in certain organizations, involves finding ways to make an attack more time consuming, such as making a website appear like something else, providing nonexistent DNS records, or including a random URL generator on a website. In addition, he recommends the use of honeypots. A honeypot is a decoy that consists of data or a service that looks legitimate to an attacker but is meant to detect and deflect their efforts, thereby increasing the efforts of an attacker by attacking systems that are not real.

Attribution

Attribution entails attempting to figure out who is attacking and, ideally, how to track any intellectual property that has been stolen by an attacker.

Attack

The category of attack he proposes begins similarly to the traditional warfare concept of counterattack that happens within the defender's boundaries. It is done by drawing the attacker into the systems being defended and encouraging them to steal intellectual property and take it back to their own systems. However, this last step is where what Strand has in mind diverges significantly from that meaning of counterattack. What the attacker does not know is that by stealing this data, they've taken more than what they intended. The files contain malware and, as a result, allow defenders to gain access to the attacker's system.

He does caution that while these techniques can be extremely effective, they do require significant caution, preparation, and potential coordination with legal counsel and law enforcement. I agree that there can be some merit to his concept of counterattacks in very specific circumstances. However, the form of active defense practiced by the Active Defender I have in mind would predominantly stick to the strategies he offers within the categories of deception and attribution. The Advanced Active Defender, who will be discussed in a subsequent chapter, might embrace the attack strategies he describes, but only (as Strand himself recommends) with blessings from management and legal and even coordination with law enforcement where appropriate.

Active Defense According to Security Vendors

Several well-known security vendors also offer devices or software that they claim use some form of "active defense," but they often provide limited insight as to what is meant by that term. Fortinet, a cybersecurity company that sells physical firewalls, antivirus software, intrusion prevention systems, and endpoint security components, defines active defense as "the use of offensive tactics to outsmart or slow down a hacker and make cyberattacks more difficult to carry out."[xiv] They claim that it involves using deception technology that misdirects attackers, causing them to waste time and processing power and, although it can sometimes involve striking back at the attacker, they assert that this action should be reserved for law enforcement agencies that have the authority to do so.

Similarly, Illusive offers a product called its Active Defense Suite. This product claims to provide visibility into lateral movement by "creating a hostile environment and accelerating the time to detection for an attacker that has established a beachhead."[xv]

Acalvio Technologies claims to be "a pioneer in Active Defense strategies" and embraces something it calls "deception-based detection" that falls slightly outside of the description.[xvi] Founded in 2015, it describes its product Shadowplex as an alternative to passive defense. Fundamentally, it claims the product detects attacks; impedes attacks through obfuscation and deception; gathers intelligence through an attacker's tactics, techniques, and procedures; and remediates assets.

The problem with all of these technologies is that they are each automated products, not taking the context of the environment they are protecting into account. While it is possible these tools could be helpful in the defense process, at the end of the day true active defense requires human intervention to provide and apply this context.

Active > Passive

Active defense has several significant advantages over passive defense. Being passive, as we saw earlier, implies a distinct lack of involvement or direct interaction on the part of the defender. It can cause tunnel vision from strictly focusing on the information from certain systems like a SIEM and alert fatigue from the constant barrage of alerts and blinking lights as well as burnout from insufficient staffing.

Being active, on the other hand, is an interactive practice that provides insight into the effectiveness of existing defenses, the potential for new defense capabilities, and an ongoing cycle of responding to threats internal to the network, learning from them, and then applying the knowledge gained across the environment, providing better detection and prevention where possible. Being active avoids many of these problems because the emphasis is on proactively seeking out threats and looking at the environment holistically rather than focusing on constant alerts.

Active Defense by the Numbers

One set of statistics that is particularly illustrative in showing how active forms of defense outshine their passive counterparts involves threat hunting. According to the SANS 2021 Threat Hunting Survey, organizations saw a 10–20 percent improvement in their overall security posture as a direct result of their active threat hunting programs.[xvii] Furthermore, 37 percent of these same organizations saw a marked reduction in their overall attack surface. Forty-three percent of them also saw a significant improvement in the creation of more accurate detections and fewer false positives. Nearly 27 percent saw a significant decrease in breakout time, which is the time between initial compromise and lateral movement, as well as a 25 percent improvement in the ability to detect data exfiltration. They also saw a 29 percent decrease in the resources needed for remediation, such as staff hours and expenses.

While these statistics are specific to the survey from 2021, a similar pattern can be seen for many of the previous surveys. With these kinds of statistics, it's easy to see that the benefits of an active approach to security are undeniable.

Active Defense and Staffing

While it cannot directly address insufficient staffing issues, an active defensive environment is one in which people are more likely to want to work for several reasons. An organization that encourages proactive security practices typically has leadership that will fight for the appropriate resources and staffing necessary to do the job properly, not to mention allowing flextime for research and encouraging real-time information sharing. As a result, it is not uncommon for security practices in these spaces to be more efficient, thereby potentially needing fewer people. For example, we've already discussed that threat hunting can reduce the time to discovery of a breach and reduce dwell time as well as increase speed and accuracy during incident response.

Active Defender > Passive Defender

There are a number of different reasons why the Active Defender is better at defending their organizations than their traditional defender counterparts. Let's examine a few of them now.

Relevant Intel Recognition

Because the Active Defender is engaged at this level, they have a much greater ability to recognize reliable, relevant intel when it is discovered directly or provided to them by an outside entity. Defenders regularly receive intelligence from a variety of sources, including but not limited to social media, federal agencies (FBI, Secret Service, CISA), vendors, ISACs (information sharing and analysis centers), and scanning services like Shadowserver. This intel might be in the form of a data feed, an email, or a report.

The problem is that not all threat intelligence is created equally. The glut of information being provided is often out of date, non-actionable, or not relevant to a particular environment. However, in a proactive environment where Active Defenders are regularly engaging with the data being collected by their tools and actively looking for signs of attack, they will typically recognize what portion of that intel is relevant to their environments. Furthermore, they may also be able to articulate to other areas within their organization to explain how and why what they found matters from a business perspective.

Understanding Existing Threats

Generally speaking, because they are engaging with, learning from, and potentially training with offensive security professionals, Active Defenders also have a better understanding of existing threats. The majority of traditional attacks use the same well-known exploits, which can also be used by the offensive security community for testing purposes.[xviii] Therefore, the Active Defender engaging with this community is likely to be familiar with them as well.

Furthermore, by understanding how legitimate services in their networks can be leveraged by attackers for nefarious purposes, Active Defenders are in a stronger position to help their organizations. For example, PowerShell, which is a cross-platform framework that contains a command-line shell, scripting language, and configuration management capabilities, is used regularly by defenders to automate tasks, access certain settings, and configure systems. Unfortunately, the ubiquity of this framework makes it particularly easy for attackers to use it as well, hiding their activities in legitimate traffic. This technique is called a living off the land attack because it specifically abuses legitimate services that are native to the operating system or the user environment. We'll see more examples of how living off the land attacks can be used in Chapter 5.

Attacker Behavior

Most importantly, because of their relationship with the offensive security community, as we've already mentioned, the Active Defender can more easily discover attacker behavior. They have insight into what it means for an attacker to live off the land, what kind of tools they're likely to need and upload for post-exploitation, and what legitimate things on the network can be leveraged in malicious ways.

When alerts do fire that make references to tools well-known to be used by attackers, or they observe certain patterns of malicious behavior, the Active Defender will recognize the potential for real risk rather than mentally lumping these alerts in with all the others they receive. For example, because they are immersed in the offensive security community, Active Defenders are also more likely to recognize any similar tactics, techniques, and procedures (known as TTPs) used in offensive security engagements. In order to understand why this matters, let us explore how TTPs fit into a defender's detection capabilities.

Pyramid of Pain

In 2013, security professional David J. Bianco created the Pyramid of Pain, which ranks the indicators used to detect an attacker's activity by the "pain" it would cause them if they are discovered by the defender.[xix] The higher the indicator, the more pain for the attacker, because these higher indicators are more difficult for the attacker to alter and still continue their nefarious activity. Likewise, the higher the level, the more challenging it is for the defender to uncover and block an attacker. For example, at the bottom of the pyramid are hash values, because it is trivial for an attacker to change the hash value of a file but fairly easy for the defender to detect. At the very top are the TTPs, because these steps are how the adversary actually accomplishes their goals, which requires the defender to understand attacker behaviors, not just the tools they use. Obviously that also means that detecting these TTPs is the most difficult challenge for the defender.

MITRE ATT&CK

The MITRE ATT&CK framework built on this idea in 2015, offering a way to catalog the tactics and techniques used by attackers as well as more specific techniques known as sub-techniques, such that it became possible to strategically track specific groups of attackers.[xx] In particular, understanding an attacker's technique of choice can be useful because it provides the types of data a defender needs for detection purposes.

TTP Pyramid

Taking this idea a step further, in 2022 Christopher Peacock breaks down the top of the original Pyramid of Pain by further separating tactics and techniques from procedures in something he calls the TTP Pyramid.[xxi] He explores each of these levels, explaining how they differ. Tactics are the bottom of this pyramid and include what the attacker is strategically attempting to achieve, such as credential access.

While useful to know, this information provides little actionable detail. At the next level we find techniques, which are at the heart of the ATT&CK framework previously described. They provide an overall insight into the tactical goal of the procedure in question—for example, doing credential dumping via LSASS memory. However, what the techniques by themselves do not provide is exactly how the attacker meets this objective. There are a number of methods to dump LSASS memory, such as by using tools such as Mimikatz or ProcDump among others. The specific way in which the adversary carries out their techniques is known as a procedure and is found at the top of the TTP Pyramid.

To further clarify the idea in nontechnical terms, we can think of the tactics as any desired outcome. Take, for example, climbing a mountain. The technique is the general plan for achieving that outcome. In this case, that might involve putting on the appropriate gear and moving upward in elevation. The procedure is specifically how one goes about implementing this technique. For example, in terms of putting on the gear, the procedure might include putting the right foot into the right boot, tying laces in a counterclockwise bow knot, and then repeating that process with the left.

Toward a Deeper Understanding

If a defender truly hopes to build effective detections, they need to understand not only the technique but the procedures being used during an attack. While traditional defenders are often familiar with the tactics used by attackers, they typically only have limited familiarity with attacker techniques. While possible, it is even less common for them to be acquainted with the various procedures the attackers use.

By virtue of their immersion in the offensive security community, the Active Defender is not only aware of more of these techniques, but understands them and how they work as well as the distinction between techniques and procedures. The Advanced Active Defender may even have a working knowledge of these procedures. This knowledge is a key feature of the Active Defender, making them significantly more valuable than their passive counterparts.

Return to the Beginning

Let's return now to the scenario we saw at the beginning of the introduction in which the attacker sends a phishing message that leads to the download and detonation of malicious software. Once the user unknowingly launches the malware in question, it pops up a cloned system authentication dialog box that asks for their username and password and relays them back to the attacker. At the same time, the malware calls back to the command-and-control (C2) framework that the attacker is using such as Cobalt Strike or Metasploit. Using that connection, the attacker opens a command shell on the victim's computer and attempts to run the password stealing software Mimikatz to gather additional passwords, but the antivirus software stops them in their tracks. Completely undaunted, they instead choose to use `rundll32.exe` with `comsvcs.dll` to dump memory and capture passwords.

The attackers do some basic reconnaissance next to determine what legitimate processes running on the local system can be used to provide camouflage, such as drivers, OneDrive, or `explorer.exe`. The selection might be based on the legitimacy of the process, communication patterns, and/or stability. Once this decision is made, the attacker injects the same malware into this process, which helps their activity blend into the normal traffic and behavior of the local machine.

The attacker focuses next on initial network reconnaissance and finds a terminal server on the network. They are able log into it using the initial credentials stolen from the user. Once logged in, the attacker downloads and executes additional malware, giving them a second C2 via a different domain. Although this new malware triggers a Network Security Monitoring (NSM) alert, it does not prevent the malware from running. As a result, the attacker was able to exfiltrate passwords and other company data stored on the terminal server via the second C2 environment they've established.

The security analysts do a good job of initially responding to the case. Because they had a basic understanding of well-known attack tactics, such as gaining initial access, and techniques, such as phishing, they went about deleting the phishing message and looking for others. They also noticed the malicious traffic coming from the initial C2 domain used by the attacker and took appropriate steps to block it.

Unfortunately, because they are traditional defenders, they made some common mistakes and missed some key evidence. For example, they were unaware that there was a pivot to a second machine because they reimaged the initially infected system to expunge the attacker from it without further investigation.

In addition, although alerts for the attempted Mimikatz install were observed, they assumed because it was blocked, no further investigation was warranted. While an NSM alert did fire against the second machine, indicating that elements of Cobalt Strike were being used, the analysts thought it was a false positive. Furthermore, because the attacker switched C2 domains and used long sleep times, the additional C2 was missed—and so the intrusion on the second computer was never detected.

Being unfamiliar with some of the attacker techniques or procedures, they also did not recognize the connection between the attempt to use Mimikatz and the framework of Cobalt Strike, which might have led them to uncover the second C2 implementation. Furthermore, because there is no visibility into file exfiltration, and since the file was downloaded over the C2 channel, there aren't any artifacts to determine what files might have been taken. By the time the initial user's credentials were rotated, the attacker had already compromised other accounts and systems, working their way toward Domain Admin.

Had there been an Active Defender in the house who understands how attackers operate and could recognize more of the techniques and procedures being used, they would most likely have known that attackers commonly attack one system with the goal to pivot to others. Therefore, they would not only know what techniques to look for that indicated evidence of lateral movement but be able to start actively hunting for it.

In addition, the Active Defender would expect that just because the procedure of running Mimikatz did not work for the technique of credential dumping, the attacker would likely try another procedure. As a result, they should be looking for evidence of other procedures that could achieve the same goal. They would also examine other systems for possible related strange behavior, such as unusual process execution or additional services added. They might also know to seek out potential evidence of additional C2 channels or evidence of data exfiltration.

Summary

The Active Defender, through their immersion in the offensive security community, is someone who cultivates the hacker mindset. They use this mindset to think differently about attacks and attackers, focusing on relationships and connections rather than lists. We've seen how the "active" part of Active Defender involves an agility in monitoring, responding to, and learning from the threats on their networks rather than some form of attacking back as well as why being active is better than being passive. Furthermore, we've discussed how Active Defenders often participate in proactive activities such as threat modeling, threat hunting, and attack simulations. Finally, we discussed what an Active Defender is likely to understand compared to their traditional counterparts and how that could be useful in a particular scenario. Now let's turn to Chapter 2, where we'll begin to discuss how to become an Active Defender.

Notes

i. http://tmrc.mit.edu/hackers-ref.html

ii. Casey Smith. "Hackers Teaching Hackers keynote," Columbus OH. November 4, 2022.

iii. https://medium.com/@johnlatwc/defenders-mindset-319854d10aaa

iv. www.mitre.org/publications/systems-engineering-guide/
enterprise-engineering/systems-engineering-for-mission-assurance/
crown-jewels-analysis

v. https://docs.microsoft.com/en-us/azure/security/develop/
threat-modeling-tool-threats

vi. www.threatmodelingmanifesto.org

vii. Ibid.

viii. Neil Wyler, "Practical Threat Hunting: Straight Facts and Substantial
Impacts" presentation, 11/19/20.

ix. Robert M. Lee, *The Sliding Scale of Cyber Security*, 2015. www.sans.org/
white-papers/36240

x. www.jcs.mil/Portals/36/Documents/Doctrine/pubs/dictionary.pdf

xi. Ibid.

xii. ACM course slides, 2019.

xiii. J. Strand, *Offensive Countermeasures: The Art of Active Defense. 2nd Ed.* 2017.

xiv. www.fortinet.com/resources/cyberglossary/active-defense

xv. https://go.illusivenetworks.com/hubfs/
Platform%20Overview%20-%20Illusive%20Active%20Defense%20Suite.pdf

xvi. www.acalvio.com/us-federal/#:~:text=Active%20Defense%20is%20
%E2%80%9CThe%20employment,and%20hoping%20for%20the%20best

xvii. www.sans.org/white-papers/
sans-2021-survey-threat-hunting-uncertain-times

xviii. www.bleepingcomputer.com/news/security/
90-percent-of-companies-get-attacked-with-three-year-
old-vulnerabilities

xix. http://detect-respond.blogspot.com/2013/03/
the-pyramid-of-pain.html

xx. https://attack.mitre.org

xxi. www.scythe.io/library/
summiting-the-pyramid-of-pain-the-ttp-pyramid

Immersion into the Hacker Mindset

To become an Active Defender requires an intimate understanding of the threats you're defending against. The best way to begin to gain this insight is immersion in offensive security culture, initially by attending community gatherings.

Reluctance

Before you can join the offensive security community, you have to be willing to enter it. Unfortunately, there are a variety of reasons why people may not seek out these opportunities. Let's examine a few of them.

Media Portrayal

First and foremost, many reservations about interacting with those working in offensive security involve the media's perception of hackers. Most offensive security professionals are hackers, and many of the gatherings in which you will find them are known as hacker gatherings, meetups, or conferences. Because the media has taken to portraying the term *hacker* in an exclusively pejorative way, the attendees of these conferences are often equated with attackers rather than people who research and test the defenses of an organization.

Headlines such as "Hackers compromise FBI email system, send thousands of messages"[i] or "Russian-Speaking Hackers Hijack Satellite Links To Hide Cyberspying Operation"[ii] do nothing to encourage those unfamiliar with the actual offensive security communities to join. Furthermore, as the result of the media's portrayal, they're sometimes viewed as "hackers for hire" with the assumption that hackers will do anything for money, regardless of whether or not the activity is ethical.

A second negative outcome from media portrayals involves perpetuating the myth that the only individuals who are capable of being involved with offensive security are some kind of extraordinary savants. For example, in the series *Mr. Robot*, the main character, Elliot Anderson, is portrayed as a brilliant hacker who ultimately is convinced to use his skills as a vigilante. The expectation set by this show and others like it is that only people at this extraordinary level of skill are capable of understanding how to use offensive security effectively.

Fear of Government Retribution

For those who actually do know something about offensive security, the ongoing contentious relationship between hackers and government entities may be off-putting enough to keep them from investigating the community further. Although many organizations now regularly hire offensive security professionals to work for them, there remains a significant fear of prosecution, preventing reporting of bugs by some independent researchers. In a recent well-publicized example, Missouri governor Mark Parson vowed to prosecute the security researcher who discovered a flaw on the Missouri website leaking over 100,000 social security numbers and then alerted the Missouri state Department of Elementary and Secondary Education (DESE) to get the issue fixed.[iii] The reality is that this flaw could have been viewed by anyone using a standard web browser since it can be viewed by reviewing the source code. Despite Parson's claim to the contrary, it seems very unlikely to have been done with malicious intent.

Stories of persecution against well-intentioned researchers are unfortunately plentiful. Therefore, fear of becoming embroiled in these contentious issues may keep people from exploring the world of offensive security, where research is common.

The Rock Star Myth

Another reason defenders might have some reservations about getting involved with offensive security professionals involves the reputation of some of the participants. Certain individuals are viewed as "infosec rock stars" because they are often frequent speakers at conferences, and have a very strong presence on social media and, as a result, are presumed to be extremely knowledgeable. However, there is also an assumption that these folks are typically egotistical prima donnas who believe that they are somehow above the masses, making people uncomfortable to potentially engage.

Imposter Syndrome

Finally, some defenders are concerned about the possibility of feeling like they do not belong when engaging with the offensive security community. Imposter syndrome and other types of emotional challenges can cause people to feel as though they are not competent enough to spend time in this community. As a result, they avoid meetups, conferences, or other opportunities to spend time in this culture.

While I can understand each of these reasons for avoiding the offensive security community, my experience has shown me that not only are they unfounded overall, the value in being part of this community is immeasurable. Certainly, as in any group, there are problematic individuals who may not be worth interacting with, but I've found most people to be open and welcoming to folks willing and interested in learning, regardless of your level of knowledge or background. In general, I've found the community to be welcoming and eager to share what they know.

A Leap of Faith

My first significant experience with a member of the offensive security community happened as part of my involvement with a cybersecurity course offered at the university where I work. The course was the brainchild of a former student together with a faculty member who both saw that there was value in learning hands-on computer security skills in part to compete in the Collegiate Cyber Defense Competition (CCDC) and because these skills are in great demand in real life.

At a meeting of this course, I was lucky enough to meet someone actively working in offensive security. As a traditional defender, I was completely unaware of this particular skill set. Intrigued, I started asking questions about what his job entailed. The more I learned, the more I wanted to know. He suggested that I attend something called a "BSides." What he was referring to was a Security BSides conference. BSides is a framework for a loosely affiliated group of information security conferences all over the world. Security BSides conferences will be discussed in more detail later.

My First Security BSides

Through my research, I discovered that the next BSides offering near me was BSidesROC 2015, held in Rochester, New York. I registered for a ticket and made plans to attend. Despite what was shown on the website in terms of talks and other activities, I had no real idea what to expect.

Bright and early, I made my way to the conference location and walked inside. I was greeted with a warm welcome and checked into the conference. I was given a badge to be worn as proof of my registration and a small bag of free swag (i.e., stuff we all get) and encouraged to explore all the events happening at the conference. Wandering into the main room that contained a number of round tables with chairs, I noticed there were games and puzzles to play with at the center of each table. Overall, the venue itself was big enough to host a variety of activities and yet casual and intimate enough to not feel immediately overwhelming.

I opted to sit in on some of the presentations because I was unfamiliar with the other activities offered. Some of the information from these talks I understood and some I did not. Whether or not I knew specifically what was being discussed, the presentations served to pique my interest and provide new avenues for discovery. What I found particularly comforting was that people were asking questions at all levels. It was obvious to me that not everyone in the room was at the same technical level, and yet these speakers were willing to do their best to answer questions regardless of the ability of those asking. Furthermore, speakers appeared to be open to further discussion once their talk was over.

At lunch time, I purchased a boxed lunch and sat with some people participating in something called Hacker Battleship. Hacker Battleship was a capture-the-flag (CTF) game. CTF games are security competitions in which participants compete in security-themed challenges attempting to obtain the highest score. Flags are typically strings of some kind that competitors must "capture" (by figuring out) to increase their scores. They usually require bringing your own laptop in order to participate. Knowing nothing about Hacker Battleship and even less about capture-the-flag games, I asked many questions. Everyone was incredibly helpful and at no time did I feel judged in any way or stupid for asking.

Overall, I found the experience to be enjoyable. Participation at any level was encouraged regardless of whether you wanted to just watch from the sidelines to take it all in or jump in with both feet and attempt some of the hands-on hacking opportunities available. I never felt that I had to do anything but observe, and yet when I did decide to get more involved, I was always encouraged.

My First DEF CON

Because I had such a great experience with BSidesROC, I started thinking about attending other conferences where I might be able to engage with offensive security practitioners. While investigating my options, I learned that the biggest conference of this nature was something called DEF CON. DEF CON is one of the oldest, continuously running hacker conventions held annually in Las Vegas, Nevada, typically at the end of July or beginning of August. I discovered a few of the other people involved in our cybersecurity course were also planning to attend, so I made plans to go with my husband.

As I began to tell people I knew that I was going to be attending my first DEF CON, I was given numerous warnings and pieces of advice. Some people were horrified that I would want to spend time in a conference full of hackers and expressed worry for both my digital and personal safety. I was told everything from "Do not bring any technology with you except a burner phone" (which is a disposable cell phone with a prepaid service) to "Be very careful what you eat or drink, even if you purchase it yourself." I cannot deny that despite my curiosity, all of this well-meaning advice made me uncomfortable. Still, I spent time scouring the website, reading about all the activities available, the talks I could hear, and making a plan for what I wanted to do when we arrived.

Ultimately, I took what I thought were reasonable precautions. Before I left, I made sure that Wi-Fi and Bluetooth were both off on my cell phone and I made sure that any important data was backed up. I carried a small, cross-body purse rather than a traditional one and kept all my valuables in that or my backpack, which I wore continuously. My husband carried his wallet in a front pocket rather than a rear pocket.

Not only was this my first trip to DEF CON, it was also my first trip to Las Vegas. I can't deny that I was overwhelmed by the sheer magnitude of the infamous Vegas Strip upon arrival. Inside the hotel/casinos was just as chaotic as outside. The conference itself was no better. Everything we wanted to do, whether attending talks, attempting to participate in workshops, and even registration involved extremely long lines. The long process of standing in these lines is affectionately referred to as "LineCon," which involves a variety of spontaneous things happening such as beach balls bouncing around in the air, pizza being shared among line goers, or even a singing animatronic beaver.

As much fun as that sounded, I was lucky in that a friend who was teaching a workshop there had an extra badge for me, so at least I was able to avoid the initial registration line. My husband was not so lucky. It took him nearly three hours to get his badge and a small bag containing a lanyard, conference book, and stickers as well as some other goodies. We both stood in a similarly long line to purchase official DEF CON merchandise, known as "merch," which included T-shirts, mugs, pins, and other souvenirs. Thankfully we were successful in buying what we wanted before they sold out.

Ultimately, my first experience at DEF CON was disappointing and uncomfortable. Even as someone who is an extrovert and very comfortable around people, I was overwhelmed. The long lines meant that I only made it in to see one talk, though I admit what I did see was amazing, and my husband did make it to one workshop, which he enjoyed. As a result of all the warnings I'd been given up front, I felt uneasy during our entire stay, viewing every single person I saw as a potential threat. I was theoretically looking over my shoulder the entire time and was constantly waiting for something bad to happen, though it never actually did.

The one significant bright light in this otherwise disheartening experience was when we happened to stumble into the Packet Hacking Village, where the Wall of Sheep is located. Villages are smaller, dedicated spaces at hacker conferences centered around a particular topic. Packet Hacking Village, for example, focuses on networking. The Wall of Sheep is an educational portal that passively monitors the DEF CON network looking for traffic utilizing insecure protocols. Everyone was amazingly friendly. I was encouraged to wander around and explore the hands-on activities available, but no one pushed me to do anything. Before I left, I asked one of the people working how one might obtain one of the Wall of Sheep T-shirts I'd seen several people holding. "Just for asking so nicely," was the reply as I was handed a T-shirt in the size I'd requested, and I walked away with a smile.

After that first trip, I felt that I had what I considered to be *the* DEF CON experience. Therefore, despite nothing bad actually happening, I had no plans to ever return. Fast-forward to six months later after continuing my exploration of the offensive security community and additional hacker conferences. I started working on building a talk with someone I'd met at BSides Cleveland. We discussed where I might give this talk and the possibility of Packet Hacking Village emerged. Thinking back on my positive experience there, I agreed to submit it. When I got the notification it was accepted I was stunned! Of course, it meant that if I were to accept, I would be heading back to DEF CON.

After lengthy consideration, I accepted the speaker spot and made plans to head back to DEF CON. This time, fortunately, my experience was completely different. Not only was I going as a village speaker, but by then I had attended more offensive security conferences and gotten to know a number of people in that space who were also attending.

I made a point to reach out to the person who'd suggested attending my first Security BSides and asked about reasonable technology precautions to take with my devices. He told me that a burner was unnecessary and that I should take the same precautions at DEF CON that I take anywhere else. Because you never know what threats could be looming no matter where you go, your protections should be consistent regardless of location. He explained that even the folks who could create novel attacks would not waste them on some random person's devices at DEF CON but rather sell them to the highest bidder. His words made sense and really helped me to relax.

I also knew enough to be selective in the talks I wanted to personally attend or to watch them from the comfort of my hotel room. As a result, my return became more of a homecoming of sorts, reconnecting with friends and making new ones. I spent a fair amount of time in Packet Hacking Village (PHV) getting to know more about the activities they offer and the people running those activities. It was hard to believe that this was the same conference I had been prepared to previously completely abandon.

While in my case being a speaker was part of changing my overall experience, the point that I want to draw out here is that getting to know people in the community before I returned made a huge difference in my second trip to DEF CON, both in terms of obtaining more reliable advice about attending and enjoyment of the event in general. The folks at PHV were fantastic ambassadors for the hacking community in general and provided a comfortable, smaller niche in a very large conference.

Finding the Community

Now that I've described a couple of the places where I found offensive security professionals and my own experiences with this amazing community, let's explore where you might find them, such as conferences, local meetups, and online spaces.

Security BSides

As previously described, one place you can interact with offensive security practitioners is at a Security BSides event. The first Security BSides took place in Las Vegas, Nevada, in July of 2009. According to their website,

> BSides was born out of number of rejections to the CFP for Black Hat USA 2009. A number of quality speakers were rejected, not due to lack of content but lack of space and time. Any constrained system must operate within the bounds to which it has defined itself. Conferences constrain themselves to the eight hours a day for however many days they run. Our goal is to provide people with options by removing those barriers and providing more alternatives for speakers, topics, and events.[iv]

As of 2022, there have been more than 725 BSides events around the world, hosted in 198 cities spanning 56 countries.[v] Security BSides can be in a Structured format, an Unconference format, or some combination of both. Regardless of format, the underlying goal was to create something that focused on conversations and personal interaction with other members of the security community.

Structured Format

Structured events are more like a traditional conference in that organizers call for presentations and send out acceptances in advance. These events may coincide with other conferences, such as how BSidesLV typically overlaps with Black Hat

USA, or they may stand on their own. If an overlap does exist, members from both conferences may intermingle and attend one or both events. A Structured event offers a more traditional schedule but somewhat limited opportunities for direct participation beyond question and answer sessions.

Unconference Format

The Unconference format is attendee-driven, where people show up; suggest ideas for talks, discussions, or questions; and then collectively decide on the day's schedule guided by expert facilitators. There may or may not be a theme to guide what is being discussed for the day. Attendees are encouraged to lead what interests them and contribute as much or as little as they desire. Generally, there is more opportunity for active contribution, including discussion leadership, in an Unconference format than in a Structured format.

Hybrid Format

The Hybrid format brings pieces of each of these formats together. In a Hybrid event, the event begins much the same as the Unconference, opening up suggestions for talks, discussions, or questions to the attendees and setting up the schedule based on desires of the attendees. Yet, it also allows speakers to submit talks in advance. A track of each type is then made available to attendees, and they can choose to participate as much or as little as they desire.

Additional Events

Beyond the talks, there may be additional activities, including contests, such as capture-the-flag (CTF) competitions, or dedicated spaces called "villages" where the focus is on a specific security topic. For example, Lockpick Village can be commonly found at many Security BSides conferences. In this village, people learn about the vulnerabilities of various locking devices and the ways these vulnerabilities can be exploited and are able to practice on a variety of locks of different difficulties. By understanding how and where these weaknesses are present, participants become better consumers in the marketplace. Thus, they are able to make decisions based upon sound fact and research rather than the mystery that usually surrounds these devices.

Security BSides events are typically either free or inexpensive and are manageable in size for many people. Although there are some large Security BSides events, such as BSides Las Vegas (BSidesLV) which hosts around 3,000 people, and some tiny ones with only a few dozen people, the average conference is around 300 attendees. Security BSides events may also offer training the day before the conference or as an option during the conference itself.

Other Security Conferences

Offensive security professionals can not only be found at Security BSides, but at other security conferences all over the world, typically those that encourage elements of hacker culture. Many of them tend to be small conferences, with reasonable price tags compared to many corporate, larger conferences. While in the following sections I will mention a few that I've found to be particularly enjoyable, there are many more than could possibly be listed here. While ticket prices are subject to change, I'll give you an idea of what to expect in a general sense. I'll use ($) to indicate that the cost of a ticket is about $50 to $100, ($$) to indicate a cost of about $101 to $299, and ($$$) to indicate a cost of about $300 to $500.

CircleCityCon

CircleCityCon is an annual three-day security conference held in downtown Indianapolis, Indiana, typically in June. The cost of a ticket to this conference depends in part on when you purchase it. Early bird tickets can be pretty cheap ($) and discounts are available for students. Free training is offered as part of the basic ticket, regardless of purchase date. More information can be found here: https://circlecitycon.org.

GrrCON

GrrCON is a two-day security conference held in the fall in Grand Rapids, Michigan. This conference offers multiple levels of tickets: early bird ($), regular admission ($$), student ($), and VIP ($$$). All tickets get you into the conference and a free T-shirt. The VIP ticket also includes a special space with free snacks and drinks throughout the day as well as priority seating. Training workshops are available for a nominal fee. More information can be found at https://grrcon.com.

Thotcon

Thotcon is an annual two-day conference held in Chicago, Illinois, typically in the spring. The exact location of the conference is kept a secret to everyone except attendees and speakers, who obtain the information a week before the event. Three levels of tickets are available: VIP ($$$), General Admission ($$), and Student General Admission ($). General Admission tickets include a badge, t-shirt, swag, and admission to the after party. VIP tickets include lunch, snacks and drinks all day. All tickets include the opportunity to attend free training workshops during the con. Thotcon tickets do sell out quickly, so it's important to make note of whatever day they go on sale. More information can be found here: www.THOTCON.org.

ShmooCon

ShmooCon, is a two-day security conference held annually in Washington, DC, typically in January. Tickets are not particularly pricey ($$), but getting a ticket to ShmooCon can be particularly difficult. In 2021, they sold out in three rounds, each within seconds, a total 1,425 tickets. However, if you really want to attend, there are usually extra tickets floating around right before the conference, and even the night before, that people are willing to sell. Some people will post that they have extras on Twitter and others might mention it in passing in the lobby of the hotel where the conference is held. More information on ShmooCon can be found here: www.shmoocon.org.

Wild West Hackin' Fest

Wild West Hackin' Fest is a three-day security conference held in Deadwood, South Dakota, typically in the fall. Tickets to this conference are a little more expensive ($$$), but it does include a lunch buffet for all attendees each day and a sit-down dinner on the last night. Pre-conference training classes are offered for a fee. More information can be found here: https://wildwesthackinfest.com.

DEF CON

Of course, I would be remiss if I didn't also mention DEF CON, despite discussing it earlier. However, be aware that attending DEF CON means subjecting yourself to an attendee count of around 30,000 people. DEF CON offers free workshops as part of an attendee ticket, but they are on a first-come, first-served basis, which means they fill up quickly. The current cost of a DEF CON ticket is a bit higher than some of the others ($$$), but it definitely gives you access to a ton of people and resources that other conferences do not. More information can be found here: https://defcon.org.

Local Security Meetups

Other places where you can find offensive security professionals are at a variety of local security meetups. Each of these meetups is different, typically influenced by the culture of the local community. I'll highlight a few with which I am familiar in the following sections, but an Internet search or asking around will no doubt lead to many more—hopefully in your area!

Infosec 716

For example, in the Buffalo, New York, area there is a meetup called Infosec 716, which is an informal group that meets monthly to discuss the latest security news and typically features a speaker presenting on a particular information security topic. Their goal is to create an accessible, noncorporate event for people interested in information security. They also have in-person social events roughly every quarter such as happy hours, grabbing tacos or other local food, without the technical component as a means of encouraging interaction and strengthening the local community. More information on Infosec 716 can be found here: www.meetup.com/Infosec-716.

Burbsec

Chicago, Illinois, has multiple chapters of a local meetup called Burbsec, such as Burbsec Prime, Burbsec North, and Burbsec East, among others. Burbsec is the Information Security Meetup Network for the Chicago area. This meetup is open to anyone in the technical field, even those not directly in the security space, such as system administrators, developers, and students. All meetings are social meetups with a focus on networking rather than formal presentations. The goal is to bring people together from all walks of the technical life who can each bring their own experiences to the mix. Each chapter meets once a month in a particular location, typically a pub, at the same time to make it easy to know where and when to find them. More information can be found here: https://burbsec.com.

#misec

Michigan has an information security group called #misec. Their mission is the continued professional and personal development of people in Michigan's IT and IT security community. They have regional chapters in Ann Arbor, Detroit, Grand Rapids, Jackson, Lansing, Marquette, and Southfield. Most chapters have regular monthly meetups that feature a speaker and networking as well as monthly social meetups focused on fostering community as well as the enjoyment of each other's company. In addition, they put on a conference in Detroit called Converge, and sometimes they also run BSides Detroit. More information can be found here: https://misec.us.

Makerspaces

Another place you might find offensive security professionals is in makerspaces. Makerspaces are informal, collaborative workspaces for making, learning, exploring, and sharing that are typically open to anyone interested in getting involved. Because the idea of a makerspace grew out of a mindset of creativity and invention, it should not be surprising to find people with the hacker mindset in them. They can incorporate a variety of tools, such as 3D printers, laser cutters, CNC machines, sewing machines, and soldering irons as well as computing equipment.

Some makerspaces can be found within public libraries and are open to their patrons and the public. Others might be in a privately owned space rented by a group of people interested in encouraging the exploration of creation, collaboration, and learning. Still others might be owned by organizations that have more structured rules and require membership.

DEF CON Groups

Popular with offensive security professionals are the various regional chapters associated with DEF CON known as DEF CON Groups (DCGs). A logical extension of the annual DEF CON conference, they provide a way for people interested in information security to continue to meet year round for discussions about technology and security topics. As of 2019 there were 270 DCGs found across about half the US states as well as over 20 countries.[vi]

They are open to everyone, regardless of level of skill, age, gender, job, ethnicity, culture, and so on, to encourage a free exchange of ideas and research. What brings these folks together is a collective interest in technology.

DCGs are run by a variety of people, including defensive security professionals and offensive security professionals as well as students. Some of these people are the same individuals who help run DEF CON each year, so they can be useful contacts to know if you have any interest in attending DEF CON or getting more involved. More information about DEF CON groups can be found here: `https://defcongroups.org`.

2600 Meetings

2600 is a reference to a magazine called *Hackers Quarterly*, which has been around since 1984 and served as a technical journal as well as highlighting legal, ethical, and technical debates about hacking. The goal of 2600 meetings is to provide an informal setting to bring together anyone interested in learning about security. They are places where people can meet to share information, ideas, and technical information with a group of interested folks. 2600 meetings take place on the first Friday of each month and can be found in multiple cities in the United States and around the world. For more information on 2600 meetings, please see `www.2600.com/meetings`.

Online Security Communities

Even if you are unable or unwilling to attend a physical meetup, there are online ways to interact with folks from the offensive security community! While there are many of these online spaces and they can change regularly, one place to find a good, curated list of useful online communities can be found on the GitHub page of Johnny Xmas, a well-known offensive security practitioner. The list is called "Infosec Discords with Useful Activity" and it's found here: `https://gist.github.com/johnnyxmas`. In the coming paragraphs, I'll provide some insight about the variety of online communities that are available and what to expect within them.

Several of the meetups previously mentioned, such as #misec and Infosec 716, also have online communities in platforms such as Discord or Slack. In addition, several security companies have set up their own online communities, such as TrustedSec, Black Hills Information Security, and GRIMM. Furthermore, conferences often have an online platform to continue engagement with their communities outside of the conference throughout the rest of the year.

DEF CON CircleCityCon, BSidesROC, and Wild West Hackin' Fest are just a handful of examples of conferences that have an online presence. There are even online communities that tie into well-known hands-on learning platforms such as TryHackMe and Hack The Box. More information on these platforms will be provided in Chapter 3, "Offensive Security Engagements, Trainings, and Gathering Intel," where we discuss places to obtain offensive security trainings.

Still other online opportunities exist with a particular focus, such as interacting with people new to the industry and those who just want to enhance their existing skills. One great example of this community is the Republic of Hackers Discord. They offer a welcoming community for those learning cybersecurity, regardless of existing level of knowledge or skill. Another one is DeadPixelSec, which started as a team of players for a CTF but has now grown into a full-fledged collaborative community on Discord.

Within each of these online communities are typically multiple channels, each with its own focus. Some have dedicated channels for security subdomains such as defensive or offensive security. Others are broken down by interest, chapters, education, or employment opportunities. There may even be channels for hobbies or interests outside of security, such as cooking or pets. Participants are usually given access to a variety of these channels and encouraged to participate in whatever interests them.

Generally speaking, these communities offer some fantastic networking opportunities for anyone interested in security and, in particular, often can provide a way to engage with the offensive security community for those who might not feel comfortable doing so in person.

Another online place to interact with the offensive security community is Twitter. However, determining who to follow can be a challenge. As a result, it's often easier to build up a list over time as you get to know offensive security professionals in other ways. While I will discuss Twitter more in terms of a place to obtain intel in Chapter 3, I thought it was worth mentioning it here as well, because certainly it is one place that you can interact with all kinds of information security professionals, including those who participate in offensive security.

Traditional Security Communities

While it might seem counterintuitive, you can sometimes find offensive security professionals who attend meetings of traditional security organizations such as the Information Systems Security Association (ISSA), ISACA, or the Open Web Application Security Project (OWASP). Keep in mind, this is extremely location-dependent. In some places, there is significant overlap between offensive security practitioners and those who are considered traditional security professionals. However, in other areas they are very segmented. In other words, don't rule out attending meetings of a security organization just because you might think their typical attendees are not offensive security practitioners.

An Invitation

Now that you generally know how to find us, I wish to extend a personal invitation to anyone reading this book to not just read about it but actually join those of us in the defensive space who have found an amazing world in the hacking community, which is typically where one finds members of the offensive security community. Whether in person or online, there are so many fantastic opportunities to learn, grow, and just have fun while involved. You've already seen in Chapter 1, "What Is an Active Defender?" how engagement with this community can generally benefit defenders of all kinds to become better at their jobs. However, what I haven't yet discussed are the other reasons why you might want to get involved with this other side of the story.

For example, many events offer resume workshops in which volunteers sit down with folks who are job hunting to offer advice about their resume and tips for successful interviewing. In addition, the organization Hak4Kidz teaches young people about cyber safety, security, and ethics from leaders in the field by appealing to their natural curiosity and desire to play.[vii] They offer a variety of hands-on workshops from topics such as reverse engineering, Snap Circuits, and network security. Participants are encouraged to explore what interests them the most such that they can spend as much or as little time as they want doing each activity.

The hackers in this space also are willing to give back to more than just their own communities. Donations to help those less fortunate are often collected at hacker conferences. For example, at one hacker conference, unwanted swag backpacks were collected to be donated to local school children in need. In 2017, when Puerto Rico was devastated by Hurricane Maria, hackers turned an anecdote about a cockroach in a milkshake into over $4,000 in donations.[viii] In addition, the organization Hackers for Charities, a charity hacker organization that seeks to make the world a better place, sent a pallet of communications, power, and water filtration gear worth over $14,000 to Puerto Rico in order to start the process of rebuilding their infrastructure.[ix]

Another fantastic example of hackers supporting others is the Rural Tech Fund. Started in 2008 by Chris Sanders, this organization provides opportunities for students living in rural communities to not only be introduced to technology but also explore potential tech career fields. Typically, these students are less likely to be acquainted with technology than their urban or suburban counterparts and, as such, frequently are lacking the skills they need to obtain high paying tech jobs found in the field. The Rural Tech Fund's goal is to help reduce the digital divide between rural and non-rural areas such that these rural communities can remain economically viable and foster additional growth. As of June 2022, they've been able to help more than 150,000 students and over 800 schools with scholarships, technical education opportunities, and classroom technology resources. More information about this amazing organization can be found here: https://ruraltechfund.org.

While every group has people who are good and bad, I contend that overall, the hacker community is full of decent, passionate people who not only love to share what they know but also support other people in their community. Do not let a negative experience with a conference, group, or particular people, immediately dissuade you from investigating this space. By spending just a little bit of time asking around, you will no doubt find those who are likely to be welcoming.

I would encourage you to just keep searching for places where you feel welcome and comfortable. Villages and contest areas at conferences can be great options for new people to get acclimated. Because villages are focused, they tend to be lower-traffic areas than the main conference, making it easier and often more comfortable to meet new people. Contest areas always need participants, and the people leading them are usually excited to get people started. They may even help pair you up with others you might have otherwise not met.

Despite my first negative DEF CON experience, I still found a welcoming space in the Packet Hacking Village and will be forever grateful that I didn't just give up.

Summary

Defenders typically are either unaware of offensive security professionals or they choose to avoid them for a number of reasons, such as the media's pejorative view of hacking, the belief that one needs to be some kind of savant to participate with them, the contentious relationship they have with government entities, and a fear of not fitting in with them, among others. While these concerns are understandable, my experience, at least, has shown them to be unfounded. There are many different places to interact with those working in offensive security, including conferences, local meetups, and online communities, such that most people who want to can find a way to get involved, regardless whether their nature tends to be introverted or extroverted. For those needing an invitation to jump in, I not only offer a personal invitation but also provide some additional reasons why you might want to join us.

Notes

i. www.reuters.com/world/us/hackers-compromise-fbis-external-email-system-bloomberg-news-2021-11-13 (3/29/22)

ii. www.darkreading.com/endpoint/russian-speaking-hackers-hijack-satellite-links-to-hide-cyberspying-operation (3/29/22)

iii. www.infosecurity-magazine.com/news/missouri-governor-slammed (3/30/22)

iv. www.securitybsides.com/w/page/12194156/FrontPage

v. www.securitybsides.com/w/page/12194156/FrontPage

vi. https://forum.defcon.org/node/231249

vii. www.linkedin.com/company/hak4kidz

viii. www.gofundme.com/f/trevor-the-roach-memorial-fund

ix. https://hackersforcharity.org/puerto-rico/major-shipment-ordered-for-puerto-rico

Offensive Security Engagements, Trainings, and Gathering Intel

Being immersed in the offensive community to cultivate the hacker mindset is, as I've argued, the key to being a better defender. However, it is also important to have a basic understanding of what an offensive security engagement generally involves to use as a framework for making sense of the tools and concepts discussed later. Therefore, the following will be a very high-level overview of what these operations entail based on the work of Matthew Monte in his book *Network Attacks and Exploitation: A Framework* (Wiley, 2015).

Note that this discussion will not include how to actually accomplish an engagement such as a penetration test or an adversary emulation. There are already entire books designed to teach someone how to perform any number of offensive security operations. Instead, it will explore the overall, general steps that are taken during the life cycle of an engagement.

Offensive Security Engagements

Before beginning any kind of testing, a contract is typically signed that gives the offensive security professional permission to run tests. This contract lays out both the scope of what they're allowed to test and the time frame in which to do so, as well as any special conditions or other important details they need to know. A typical offensive security engagement, and likewise an attack, contains six stages: targeting, initial access, persistence, expansion, exfiltration, and detection. It is important to understand, though, that any one or more of these stages may remain ongoing throughout the life cycle of an entire operation rather than ending when the next begins. Furthermore, between the fact that the field of offensive security testing is extremely broad in nature and that each company operates a little differently, there can be significant differences in exactly how implementation occurs.

Targeting

Targeting involves both the selection of the target network and determining the particular attack strategies to be used and the tactics to exploit the network selected. Although this is the first stage, targeting remains continuous throughout an engagement because as new information is obtained, additional networks or systems may be identified as targets.

This stage includes gathering both technical and nontechnical information about an organization. Technical information might include whether they have a presence on the Internet, the software they have in use, or what brands of hardware are deployed. Nontechnical information could include names, titles, email addresses, and outside interests of employees. The strategies used and tactics selected will depend in large part on what is uncovered during the targeting phase. They may also evolve as the engagement continues and more information is collected about the organization.

Targeting may also be opportunistic. In other words, rather than selecting a particular network and then attempting to gain access, the operator might select a network because during a scan it was found to be vulnerable to a known flaw. In the real world, once a new vulnerability is discovered, an attacker might just begin scanning for any organizations with this flaw as a place to start. However, for the offensive security practitioner, the opportunity must present itself within the scope of what the engagement allows them to do.

Initial Access

With all of the information obtained during the targeting phase, offensive security practitioners will next attempt to gain initial access. Initial access involves obtaining a foothold into the environment to be able to run commands or other software on a target system. Selecting the particular tactics, techniques, and procedures to use will depend on whether systems can be accessed inbound from outside the network, outbound through a connection to outside of the network, bidirectionally, or not at all. Ultimately, the goal is accomplished by getting past defensive security measures via a variety of ways such as exploiting vulnerabilities, network misconfigurations, and social engineering. This stage is where successful phishing attacks or malware sent via email with the ability to bypass antivirus are frequently used. It is not uncommon for initial access to land on a target that has restricted users or seemingly unimportant content. While that may seem counterintuitive, these systems may be easier to directly exploit because of fewer controls in place. Once access to the network is achieved, it is often trivial to move to another more valuable target during the expansion stage, which will be discussed shortly.

Persistence

The goal of persistence is to move from the initial foothold to being able to secure future, recurring access regardless of normal usage on the system. In other words, even if the system is rebooted or there is a change in user, there needs to be a way to either maintain or automatically reestablish a connection. Persistence can be achieved through many mechanisms, such as editing registry entries, modifying the boot process of the machine, adding malicious web browser extensions, and creating a backdoor by adding malware to an application, just to name a few. This particular stage can require some ingenuity on the part of the offensive security professional and is, in part, why it requires someone with the hacker mindset. If an organization is fairly mature in its security posture, some of the common ways to obtain and maintain persistence may just fail. Gaining persistence can be challenging depending on the environment and sometimes requires nonlinear thinking to be successful.

Expansion

Once initial access has been obtained and steps are in place to stay connected, the goal becomes expanding access within the target network. As a result, the potential for greater persistence is increased, as is the ability to find and access any targeted data viewed as critical to the operation. Because initial access often lands the offensive security practitioner on a system used by someone with limited permissions or minimal access and not on a system with the keys to the kingdom, expansion becomes key to reaching the objectives of the engagement. This stage can be extremely time-consuming and often traverses multiple networks or multiple portions of a network to complete. Again, the hacker mindset is key here. In particular, the offensive security professional must have the ability to think through all of the relationships between systems as well as accounts discovered and then tie all this information back to the goal(s) of an engagement. The ability to ask "what if?" here can be crucial to finding the right combination of techniques to build a procedure that will do the trick. Furthermore, having the tenacity and inquisitiveness to keep trying even when any number of attempts fails is vital.

Exfiltration

With a firm foothold in the network and their various tendrils of access spread throughout the organization, the offensive security practitioner can now work to retrieve data from a network, which is known as exfiltration. It is often seen as the ultimate measure of success in an offensive security operation because it can prove not only that particular data was accessible but that it was able to be removed from the environment. That said, there may be instances, depending on the particular tests and the details of the contract, when exfiltration may not be requested or required. When it does occur, this stage is another one that is often ongoing as the engagement moves forward and new systems and data are discovered. To successfully exfiltrate data requires a careful balance of being stealthy enough to fly under the radar while still sending out a huge volume of data.

Detection

The final step in an offensive security operation is when the target uncovers what the offensive security professionals have been doing. This stage can be quite sudden or take a lengthy amount of time to occur depending on the skill of the defenders, the security maturity of the environment, and the proficiency of the team doing the testing. Once the operation is detected, it may either just signal the end of a particular series of tests or it may indicate the end of the engagement. The details in the contract typically dictate which way it plays out.

Offensive Security Trainings

Attending trainings in which offensive security methodologies are taught is a great way for defenders to continue to immerse themselves in this space. I will examine some places where this training can be found and provide some examples of the kinds of training typically offered. While good training does not have to mean expensive, it can be. I will cover a wide range of training opportunities from free or inexpensive to extremely pricey. Similar to the guide I provided for conference fees, I will use ($) to indicate that the cost of a training is about $50 to $100, ($$) to indicate a cost of about $101 to $299, and ($$$) to indicate a cost of about $300 $500. For trainings that are $500 to $1,500, I will use ($$$$) and anything over $1,500 I will list as ($$$$$). Furthermore, while I cannot cover every training opportunity, I will explore some of the ones that I've found to be particularly enjoyable and/or are particularly well-known and well-respected in the community.

Some classes will provide all the hardware and software resources necessary for the course. Others will require you to bring a minimum setup, such as a laptop running a particular OS, and provide additional resources such as a preconfigured virtual machine. In addition, any necessary prerequisites will be listed. Note that, regardless of what kind of training is offered, it is critical to pay close attention to what is communicated regarding any course requirements and prerequisites. If you are unsure whether you meet the prerequisites, it's a good idea to reach out to the instructor in advance for clarification whenever possible. Be sure to bring whatever hardware and/or software is required for the class and have the correct configurations completed in advance. Otherwise, you may spend the entire course trying to catch up with the rest of the class. Instructors will typically do their best to assist students who are having configuration issues but may have limited time to do so.

Conference Trainings

One of the places that training in offensive security topics can be found is at conferences. Many of the conferences that I've already described offer training either just before or during the conference itself. Sometimes training offerings are included for free with the cost of a conference ticket but require a separate, advanced registration. Others may require a separate, advanced registration but also require an additional fee. Overall, trainings associated with conferences tend to be significantly cheaper and the conference itself provides additional networking opportunities. One advantage of attending trainings at a smaller conference is that class sizes are likely to be smaller and more intimate with more individual assistance from the instructor. Larger conferences will often have larger class sizes leading to potentially less individualized attention from the instructor, but they may have more variety in terms of topics from which to choose.

Security BSides

As previously mentioned, many Security BSides events offer some type of trainings, often referred to as workshops. Some have trainings the day before the main conference. For example, BSidesROC, held in Rochester, New York, typically has training that occurs on Friday with the conference itself held on Saturday. Others may have trainings during the conference itself, such as BSidesLV held in Las Vegas, Nevada. BSidesLV is a two-day conference and has a half day of training on each of the two days. A separate registration, completed in advance, is often required and classes are available on a first-come- first-served basis.

The cost of training varies with the specific Security BSides event, but most are either low cost ($) or included as part of the regular conference ticket price. Class length can vary between a half day and a full day or more. Because Security BSides events tend to be smaller, training classes are as well. Common topics that could be covered include Open Source Intelligence (OSINT), web app testing, malware analysis, and wireless hacking.

DEF CON

DEF CON also offers training in the form of numerous workshops that occur during the conference. These workshops are free with the purchase of a ticket to DEF CON ($$$) but require a separate registration. They are offered on a first-come-first-served basis, and as a result, it can be difficult to obtain a ticket. An announcement is usually made as to when registration will open both on the DEF CON website and on Twitter. If you really want to attend a workshop, be ready to claim your seat the moment these separate tickets become available or you may lose your chance. While there are sometimes opportunities to grab a ticket after the fact from someone who had to drop out at the last minute, these workshops are extremely popular, and seats do go quickly.

Workshops are usually half-day in length. Class sizes can be fairly large, ranging anywhere from 50 to 150 seats, although there can be a few much smaller ones for niche topics with around 15 to 20 seats. While instructors will do their best to assist students, the large class size means that individual assistance will typically be more limited than in smaller environments. Topics can include wireless attacks, network analysis, writing malware, web security topics (SQL injection, cross-side scripting), Bluetooth hacking, bug bounty hunting, and buffer overflows among many, many, more.

Also of note is the fact that many of the villages (e.g., specialty areas) at DEF CON also offer free or low-cost training options for which it can sometimes be easier to acquire a ticket to attend. However, most of the time these trainings require a separate registration in advance and they too can fill quickly.

GrrCON

GrrCON offers training workshops during the conference, but registration and payment for both GrrCON ($–$$$) and an additional training ticket is required. The cost for this training ticket is nominal (not even $), typically only a few dollars in order to ensure that people who sign up actually attend. Attendees with a VIP ticket are eligible to attend training for free but must make arrangements for workshop tickets in advance.

GrrCON typically sells out completely and seating is limited for the workshops, so both purchasing a ticket to the conference and obtaining a workshop ticket should be done as soon as possible to avoid disappointment. Topics such as Android APK reverse engineering, OSINT, and IDS/IPS testing have been covered in past workshops.

Thotcon

Thotcon offers mini-workshops during the conference; they are two hours in length. They are free to attend with any ticket to Thotcon ($–$$$). However, unlike workshops at many conferences, these mini-workshops are a mixture of hands-on workshops and longer, more detailed talks that take a deep dive into particular subjects. No additional registration is required, but seating is often limited as this is a smaller conference.

Hands-on topics will generally require bringing a laptop at a minimum. Topics covered in the past included Thotcon badge hacking, hacking software defined radios (SDRs), reverse engineering application-layer protocols, and Linux kernel exploitation.

CircleCityCon

CircleCityCon offers community-led training classes that are free with the purchase of any conference ticket ($–$$). Seats are available on a first-come-first-served basis. However, if you want to guarantee a seat in a particular training class, a separate, advanced registration for a nominal fee of a few dollars is required. That said, a block of seats is always made available for walk-ins on the day of the conference.

Keep in mind that as a smaller conference, seating will be limited, but there will be more opportunity for individual assistance. Topics covered at previous conferences included exploit development, ethical hacking, and forensics as well as modern web application firewall (WAF) bypass techniques among others.

Wild West Hackin' Fest

Wild West Hackin' Fest offers two-day training classes prior to the conference. Classes and access to the conference are available virtually as well as in person. The price varies depending on which option is selected, but these trainings tend to be priced higher ($$$$) than the previous options discussed. However, they are each two full days of training, unlike many other conference options.

Courses at this conference are offered through a partnership with its sister company Antisyphon and includes 12-month free access to the Antisyphon Cyber Range, which is a hands-on training environment meant for anyone from a beginner to an advanced professional. Attendees select the course they'd like to attend at the same time they register for the conference. Thus, no separate registration for training is necessary.

Black Hat

Black Hat is an internationally recognized cybersecurity event series that offers training prior to its major events in the United States, Europe, and Asia and prior to SecTor in Toronto, Canada.[i] Courses are either two or four days, and while often taught by well-known experts in the field, they come with a much higher price tag than all previously mentioned conference trainings ($$$$$+). Class sizes vary with the average between 40 and 100 students. Because these trainings come with such a high price tag, most of the attendees work for fairly large companies and these events tend to have a very corporate feel.

Security Companies

Another place training in offensive security methodologies can be found is through individual information security companies that offer classes directly.

Offensive Security

Offensive Security is an information security company that specializes in penetration testing and digital forensics.[ii] Founded in 2006, it is perhaps best known for its pen testing certification, Offensive Security Certified Professional (OSCP), and the penetration testing Linux distribution called Kali. However, this organization also offers a full range of offensive security training options, including web application testing, exploit development, and additional penetration testing courses as well as additional certifications based on these courses.

Considered a gold standard in offensive security training, these courses do cost more than most of the conference options ($$$–$$$$$), but it does have several options for discounts, including subscription models. In addition, it offers both free and paid training lab environments to test one's skills. Cost for the paid environment is either a monthly or an annual fee ($–$$).

TrustedSec

TrustedSec is an information security consulting company that provides a variety of services, including cybersecurity testing and analysis as well as cybersecurity incident response and forensics.[iii] It also offers a handful of online live security courses as well as live training at conferences from time to time. Some of these trainings can be helpful to both offensive and defensive security professionals because they illustrate the behavior on both the adversarial and detection/ defensive side.

These courses have a fairly high price for a single individual ($$$$) compared to many previously discussed. However, some of the cost can be mitigated if attending as part of a group. Furthermore, TrustedSec training found at a conference can sometimes be offered at a discount. Class sizes, while not tiny, are typically manageable enough to get some individual assistance from the instructor(s) when needed.

Antisyphon

Antisyphon is the sister company of Black Hills Information Security (BHIS), which focuses specifically on providing information security training to people of all levels.[iv] It offers both live and on-demand training classes in many different information security areas. While its training courses can be found in conjunction with conferences such as Wild West Hackin' Fest as you've seen, it also offers classes independently, often including 12-month access to its Cyber Range for additional hands-on virtual learning opportunities.

Classes specific to offensive security include attack emulation tools, web app penetration testing, offensive development, red teaming, and windows post-exploitation. The price of a course varies, based in part on the length of the class, but for an individual it's roughly mid-range in terms of what has been previously discussed ($$$–$$$$). In addition, it also offers a pay-what-you-can model for certain classes in an effort to help more people get started with an information security career, even if they ordinarily could not afford it. This model literally allows you to pay as little as $30 for a course, depending on your circumstances. Classes tend to be of a manageable size, regardless of in person or online, still allowing for some individualized attention when needed.

SANS

SANS is an information security company that focuses on cybersecurity education.[v] Perhaps best known by defenders for its courses in both security fundamentals and advanced defense operations, SANS also offers coursework in penetration testing, both at a general level and specialized areas such as cloud, wireless, and mobile.

While it offers world-class training, the cost of this training can be overwhelming ($$$$$+). One option available to make it slightly more affordable is its Work-Study program in which you do work for the conference as an in-person facilitator or online monitor. In this role you are responsible for monitoring the classroom/virtual training platforms and communicating with SANS support teams as well as distributing and processing student evaluations in exchange for a training ticket at a significantly reduced price. However, even at this reduced cost, it is still significantly more than Antisyphon's full-price offerings.

Online Options

Other types of training in offensive security skills include online challenges that individuals can work through at their leisure, CTF events, and YouTube videos. For example, sites like hackthebox.com (HTB), tryhackme.com (THM), and hackthissite.com (HTS) each offers a legal, safe, hands-on, gamified way to learn the skills of an offensive security practitioner. There's something for people at all levels, from beginner to more advanced challenges for someone with more experience. These online platforms not only offer training through active participation, they also often have their own communities, another way to engage with others interested in learning the same skills.

Hackthebox

HTB has a multitude of different learning options from capture-the-flag (CTF) contests, real-time multiplayer gamified environments, professional labs that simulate real-world scenarios, and full online training courses. Resources include a knowledge base, blog, forum, meetups, and Discord server in order to connect with other members of their community. HTB offers three tiers of pricing from free to a modest monthly charge (less than $) for VIP or VIP+ or, if paying annually, even slightly cheaper.

Tryhackme

THM offers small, hands-on, interactive training modules on a variety of topics including Introduction to Web Hacking, Introduction to Offensive Security, and Introduction to Pentesting. For a more guided education, it has what are called "learning paths," which ties a series of these modules together to help the learner build knowledge of a higher topic progressively. For example, the learning path Jr. Penetration Tester includes 64 hours of instruction, beginning with Introduction to Offensive Security.

Learning paths are available for both beginners and those who are more advanced. Students who finish an entire learning module earn a certificate of completion. A gamified series of challenges to further test these abilities is also available for individuals to compete against themselves as well as for small groups.

A THM community exists to connect with others interested in learning these skills and includes a forum and Discord server. Access to THM involves purchasing a subscription for a nominal monthly fee. Subscriptions are available from a single month (< $) to two years ($$).

Hackthissite

HTS is a continuously evolving project that offers a less structured learning environment that includes a variety of interactive learning challenges and CTFs as well as some traditional modes of learning such as lectures and articles. In addition, it offers a variety of ways to connect with others in the community working through the material, such as an IRC channel, Discord, and forum. Although the offerings for HTS are completely free, the project is completely volunteer run and donations are welcome. In addition, participants are encouraged to contribute their own articles, lectures, and ideas to help others learn.

CTFs

CTF games can be found within the learning environments mentioned previously, at many of the conferences already discussed as well as others, and independently online. One of the best known online CTFs is the Holiday Hack Challenge that SANS makes available each year for free in conjunction with its virtual hacking conference, Kringlecon.[vi] A new competition with a different theme is offered each year, but previous years' challenges are always readily available to play. Going back as far as 2002, the answers to these older challenges along with the winning entry are also available. A Discord is also available to allow people to team up via text or voice channels and work together through challenges, whether current or past.

Some independent CTFs are topic specific. For example, there is a CTF specific to web hacking skills that can be found here: `https://ctf.hacker101.com`. One place to find a wide variety of CTFs is `https://ctftime.org/event/list`. This site provides a long list of upcoming contests from online options to in-person ones.

YouTube

YouTube is another place where training material about offensive security skills can be obtained, generally for free.[vii] However, as with anything found on the Internet, caution is warranted: be sure to seek out high-quality material from a known trainer with a positive reputation. For example, Ippsec offers a variety of vulnerable VM walk-throughs and presentations on different tools. Other reliable offensive security material can be found on the YouTube channels of John Hammond, LiveOverflow, and The Cyber Mentor. One way to find additional material is by asking trusted contacts made at conferences or reading articles from reliable sources.

Higher Education

Higher education at certain institutions offers students some unique opportunities for learning about offensive security. Some schools have specific classes, independent studies, or student clubs that focus on learning this tradecraft.

One of the more innovative and unique ways to learn about offensive security in higher ed is the Global Collegiate Penetration Testing Competition (CPTC), which was started by a professor at the Rochester Institute of Technology (RIT). [viii] Each year a new immersive mock organization is built with the help of volunteers and sponsors. This organization is said to be looking for penetration testing services and provides a request for proposal (RFP), which is a formal bid for the job. Students from their respective institutions register as a team to play the role of a consulting firm to provide these services.

As part of the registration process, teams are asked to respond to the RFP to demonstrate that their teams have the appropriate qualifications to provide these services. Teams are evaluated on the quality and timeliness of the RFP. The best ones are selected to compete at regional events. At these events, teams are asked to provide presentations to company management and recommendations on the vulnerabilities found as well as other deliverables. Scoring is based on the vulnerabilities discovered and the professionalism of the team as well as their communication skills.

The nature of the competition makes it stressful as it involves limited resources and short timeframes. The scenario is tailored to be close to a real experience working as an offensive security professional for a consulting firm. However, many students rise to the challenge and can return with their teams for multiple years until they graduate. There is no direct cost to the student associated with registering or participation in CPTC, but travel expenses might be required.

Gathering Intel

Regularly visiting places where offensive security practitioners obtain the intel they use for an engagement is another way for defenders to practice immersion. These spaces include social media platforms as well as other useful online spaces. The key to these locations is that while each has everyday uses, offensive security practitioners often view them in a different light. The following discussion will organize intel into two categories: intel about organizations and intel about tradecraft. Tradecraft generally can be defined as the skills acquired through experience in a trade. Specifically, in terms of offensive security professionals, it involves all of the offensive security skills and methodologies learned through experience, which includes much of what we've been discussing. By understanding what kinds of information these locations generally contain, the objectives by the offensive security professional for obtaining that information, and how it can be used for an operation, the defender can gain better insight into the activities an attacker might similarly perform.

Tradecraft Intel

There are several common places where offensive security professionals seek out intel about methodologies they can use during their engagements. Visiting specific websites that include security research information or information obtained through certain social messaging platforms can be exceptionally useful for this purpose.

Project Zero

Project Zero is a team of Google's security researchers who focus on zero-day vulnerabilities in a variety of hardware and software systems.[ix] The purpose of this research is to work toward getting serious vulnerabilities patched, a better understanding of exploit-based attacks, and long-term improvement of the Internet for everyone. The team shares its research via a web blog, posting new information once a month. Offensive security professionals can refer to the information provided here to give them ideas for attack strategies in a particular engagement.

AttackerKB

`Attackerkb.com` is similar in concept to the site provided by Google's Project Zero team, except that it is created and maintained by security researchers at Rapid7.[x] It brings together pen testers, researchers, consultants, and others from the security community to share their insights so that others can make informed decisions about the vulnerabilities away from the hype that is often shared on social media. The goal is to assess the level of risk and set a priority for each vulnerability by focusing on the conditions and characteristics that make it useful to attackers. Each entry in the feed contains an indication of whether it has been exploited in the wild, any alerts that might have been written, and ratings based on attacker value and exploitability. In addition, some entries also have a full technical analysis.

Offensive security practitioners can use the information in this site to determine whether a particular vulnerability might be worth using during an engagement. In particular, it will help them gauge how difficult it would be to exploit and whether it might be worthwhile to exploit. They can also determine whether there might already be existing exploits or patches available. Note, however, that this site is just one of many that offer tradecraft intel about vulnerabilities/exploits. Furthermore, it would be a mistake to consider any one of them complete sources of this information. In other words, just because something isn't listed in one of these sources doesn't mean it's not vulnerable, and useful attacks still may exist for it.

Discord/Slack

Discord and Slack are both social messaging platforms that allow for real-time interaction between users through voice, video, or text chat. As previously discussed, these spaces can be great locations for generally engaging with offensive security professionals, especially when in-person options are not available, and to continue to connect with other individuals after a conference. These platforms can also be particularly useful to the offensive security practitioners for connecting with each other and share research or other tradecraft material that they may not want to make publicly available. However, be aware that because of the sensitive nature of some of the material being discussed, some Discord and Slack channels have very specific sharing restrictions and have a vetting process for who can join them.

Twitter

Twitter is currently the primary social media platform of the offensive security community.[xi] This social media platform allows the user to post a short, no more than 280-character message to their followers. However, users can also choose to post what is known as a thread, which is a series of connected Tweets that make up a longer post. It is ideal for real-time, immediate notifications from individuals and organizations, new research, and technical tips and tricks as well as job opportunities, training and conference information, and of course, cute animal pictures.

Twitter acts a unique space for this community because it serves multiple functions. Not only does it allow members to directly interact with each other, often in real-time, but they can often find information useful for an engagement, in terms of both tradecraft intel and organization intel. For example, offensive security professionals may find Tweets discussing vulnerabilities published by software and hardware vendors as well as those that might have been reported to the vendor but subsequently ignored. However, they can also follow accounts relevant to an engagement they might be working to obtain organizational intel, such as corporate accounts or individual accounts by employees.

The trick with Twitter is finding the right accounts to follow such that the information gleaned from this site will be useful to the defender. There is, unfortunately, no magical right way to go about curating a good list, especially if you are new to this side of the world. However, one way to begin is to start by either following people you know and trust or by researching organizations or speakers that interest you to determine if their content is likely to be reliable. Conference presenters often reference material from other people by their Twitter handle, which can be a good way to begin to follow someone new who is doing work that interests you. Ideally, a good list includes diverse spaces that are connected in a variety of different ways.

Note that although Twitter is the social media service of choice today, that is subject to change at any time. The need for continuous communication has always been the case in the hacker community, which emerged around online bulletin boards but later migrated to Internet Relay Chat (IRC) and Usenet. If Twitter no longer meets the needs of the hacker community as technology continues to evolve, another service will likely rise up and take its place.

Organizational Intel

Organizational intel includes information that offensive security practitioners can uncover about an organization and its employees. A great deal of this information can be gleaned by some basic OSINT searches, looking at accounts found on social medial platforms. Furthermore, web repositories such as Pastebin and GitHub can contain additional valuable information about an organization as can message boards, internal wikis, and other sites. Let's examine a few of them now.

LinkedIn

LinkedIn is a business- and employment-related social media website that is predominantly used for professional networking and career development. Users post any number of work-related things such as their employment history, indicate if they're looking for a new opportunity, promote upcoming presentations or conferences, announce professional accomplishments such as new certifications or promotions, or publish/promote articles about topics relevant to their line of work.

The reality is that for good or ill, people post everything related to their employment from their entire resume to photos of corporate badges. As a result, offensive security professionals can use this information to their advantage on an engagement, typically for reconnaissance. For example, certifications and specializations held by employees can be indicative of what tools or software packages are used at a particular organization, making it easier to look for vulnerabilities to exploit. Employee names and titles could be used to create a social engineering pretext as part of a phishing campaign. Some of the email addresses needed for a successful campaign can be gained directly through LinkedIn. Additional email harvesting may be possible by knowing the names of certain employees and the format of the address used by the organization. Furthermore, ID badge photos can provide enough necessary information to successfully complete a physical penetration test, which involves assessing physical security controls to gain access to a network.

Pastebin

Pastebin is a website where users can save and share plaintext-based content publicly in real-time, such as bits of source code, on sites called pastes.[xii] While Pastebin can be used for legitimate purposes such as code review and collaboration, it is also used regularly by attackers to share breach data and other sensitive information. From these sites offensive security professionals can gather intel such as user or system credentials, credit card numbers, proprietary source code, or any other organizational data in a paste that might be useful to reach their goals during their engagement. They might even discover some code examples not specific to the organization but that could be used to help achieve their goals. In addition, some developers may use Pastebin to share corporate-owned code and data with contractors because they are frustrated by existing data sharing restrictions.

GitHub

GitHub is website and cloud-based repository that assists software developers in managing and storing their code. It provides version control using Git. Git is a distributed open-source version control system, which means that it helps developers track changes to the code they are writing. While GitHub offers both private and public code repositories, the former is typically what organizations use to manage software development projects securely. However, it's not unusual for some developers to occasionally use a public code repository to share code or for some information in the private repository to accidentally become public. During an operation, offensive security practitioners can then use that intel to their advantage to access restricted company assets or uncover a software vulnerability to exploit. They may even combine information they uncover from a place like Pastebin to access a private repository.

Message Boards

Message boards, such as discussion forums, are another place that can house a fair amount of intel. Most message boards require registration to post questions or information but not necessarily to read what is there. They can be hosted by manufacturers such as hardware or software vendors, collaborative learning spaces such as Stack Overflow, or social sites like Reddit. People typically visit these kinds of sites to, for example, exchange information, get assistance with a problem, and develop new ideas. Through the lens of the offensive security professionals, on the other hand, the goal is to seek out sites that can provide useful intel for an engagement. For example, technical support questions posted by staff members at an organization could provide some detailed insight about the versions of software or hardware products in use, which could then be used for exploit purposes. Personnel information posted such as names and titles of those posting could also be used to determine email address formatting, organizational structure, or other useful details.

Internal Wikis

Internal wikis are websites that are only accessible by the employees of an organization. Most of them are meant to be central repositories for information that an employee might need to facilitate some aspects of their job or find resources related to their employment such as benefits and general organizational information. For example, these sites might contain information such as policies, procedures, or organizational structure. Offensive security practitioners, on the other hand, view internal wikis as treasure troves of information that could be useful in an operation. For example, they often contain information about platforms and software used by the organization as well as information about organizational structure, which can be valuable as they form a picture of how an organization is put together, as well as information about server/network architecture, which can reveal new attack paths or suitable targets during the engagement.

Haveibeenpwned

`Haveibeenpwned.com` is a website that allows people to check whether their account information has been compromised in a data breach. Typical visitors check their email addresses to see if they were involved in a known breach and what services were impacted. The site only contains the email address or username and a list of sites where it appeared in breaches, but not passwords. However, with this same information, offensive security professionals can cross-reference against password dumps they may have encountered for particular breaches, such as those found on Pastebin or other locations. Because password reuse is common, they may be able to gain initial access with this information.

While some commercial repositories exist that contain the original passwords and other breach data, there can be legal ramifications for using these services. Some of them, such as the popular site RaidForums, have been shut down for having credential storage repositories. Always seek independent legal advice before potentially obtaining any data of this nature.

Summary

By immersing the defender into the offensive security space, they gain a greater understanding of how offensive security professionals operate and, by extension, how an attacker operates. This chapter provided a very high-level overview of an offensive security engagement to assist the defender in gaining a better sense of what offensive security practices look like as well as what occurs during an attack in a very general way. Attending training classes can further facilitate defenders' appreciation for how these stages are implemented. Therefore, the chapter also covered places to find offensive security training classes at a variety of different price points. Finally, some common places where offensive security practitioners gather their intel for testing purposes were explored. In the next chapter, we'll explore many of the common tools they use as well.

Notes

i. www.blackhat.com

ii. www.offensive-security.com

iii. www.trustedsec.com

iv. www.antisyphontraining.com

v. www.sans.org/cyber-security-training-overview

vi. https://holidayhackchallenge.com

vii. www.youtube.com

viii. https://cp.tc

ix. https://googleprojectzero.blogspot.com

x. https://attackerkb.com

xi. https://twitter.com

xii. https://pastebin.com

Understanding the Offensive Toolset

Beyond getting to know the people working in offensive security, having a basic understanding of their toolset can be extremely instructive to the defender. The goal here will be to help you familiarize yourself with a variety of these tools at a basic level, not to walk through using each one as there are plenty of existing resources out there for that purpose. As a defender, you should understand how, why, and in what circumstances these tools can be used as well as how to mitigate their use by a threat actor.

While there is no way to cover all tooling and many offensive security professionals do write custom tools, having a basic understanding of the following tools should provide a useful foundation. Most of these tools have been around a very long time and will likely remain in use for years to come. Note that if proper permission is obtained from their organizations, defenders can run most of these same tools to determine how susceptible their environments are to them.

The mitigations provided for each tool are preventive controls, not detective ones. They are geared towards keeping hosts on an organization's network from being adversely impacted by the tool in the first place, but are not intended to detect tool use by an attacker. While there are some specific methods that can be used to detect the use of these tools on a network, most of these tools are easily customizable such that they can easily avoid such detections. Therefore, it's extremely ineffective for a defender to focus on the detection of a particular tool. Instead, a better approach is to spend time to craft behavior-based detections.

We'll discuss this topic further and in more detail in Chapter 7, "Building Effective Detections."

In addition, to help explain why these tools are commonly used in offensive security engagements, I will provide a connection between each tool and one or more top-level categories represented in MITRE ATT&CK.[i] In total, there are 14 categories:

- Reconnaissance
- Resource Development
- Initial Access
- Execution
- Persistence
- Privilege Escalation
- Defense Evasion
- Credential Access
- Discovery
- Lateral Movement
- Collection
- Command and Control
- Exfiltration
- Impact

My goal is not to try to directly operationalize MITRE ATT&CK in some way. I specifically chose these categories because they do a nice job of carving up many of the post-exploitation goals that offensive security practitioners (and likewise attackers) typically wish to achieve but with which defenders are often unfamiliar.

It is important to note that while the rest of the MITRE ATT&CK framework can be very valuable, it is not really relevant to this discussion. Therefore, I will not be delving further into it in this book.

Each of the categories represents the overall goal for the actions that an offensive security professional might take during an engagement. For example, the purpose of Reconnaissance is to gather information for future operations, while Resource Development involves resources being established to support the engagement. Initial Access is what it sounds like: first attempts to access the network in question, and Execution involves attempts to run malicious code. The purpose of Persistence is to maintain a foothold once already in the network, whereas Privilege Escalation involves attempts to gain higher-level permissions either on a system or generally within the network. Defense Evasion involves taking steps to avoid being detected on the network by the organization. Credential Access is when someone attempts to obtain usernames and passwords to utilize, while Discovery involves trying to figure out the environment being tested. The purpose of Lateral Movement is to move throughout the environment, beyond the initial landing point. Collection involves further gathering of data relevant to the goal of the engagement, while Command and Control involves trying to communicate with compromised systems to control them. Finally, Exfiltration is the unauthorized extraction of data and Impact involves trying to manipulate, interrupt, or destroy systems or data.

All the tools examined have the capacity to help achieve one or more of these goals. However, I will not be able to cover a tool for each category, nor will I be able to describe every single category a tool can cover. Regardless, understanding both something about commonly used tools and the goals that offensive security practitioners are trying to achieve through their use can help develop greater insight into how these operators (and by extension attackers in general) accomplish their goals. This level of understanding is what enables defenders to better perform their duties. Keep in mind, too, that permission to run any of these tools should be obtained before doing so, whether by the offensive security practitioner or by the defender.

An important caveat: all the tool explanations and connected categories provided in the following sections make two basic assumptions. First, they assume that the local area network (LAN) is protected from unauthorized access of any kind. In other words, it assumes there are security controls to prevent someone from just plugging something into a network jack or connecting to the wireless network. Second, they also assume that testing of the organization is not being done with insider threats in mind. Many networks, including those of organizations like hospitals, educational institutions, and retail facilities, have easily accessibly physical network ports. If an offensive security professional can access the network directly, then any tool that is capable of remote code execution can be automatically categorized as Initial Access.

Nmap/Zenmap

Nmap and its graphical counterpart Zenmap are powerful free open-source scanning tools used for network discovery and auditing.[ii] They can be used to determine what hosts are live on the network. In addition, they can determine what services are open and available on the host, including application name and version number, any packet filters or firewalls in use, what operating system is running, what OS version is employed, and even the identity of a process owner in some cases. Using Nmap or Zenmap to test a system is fairly straightforward in that you run the nmap command at the command line (as shown in

Figure 4.1) or fire off the GUI for Zenmap, provide the particular options that you want to employ, and kick off the scan. The power in these tools lies in the different types of scans that are possible, many of which enable the operator to get past some of the traditional mitigations in place.

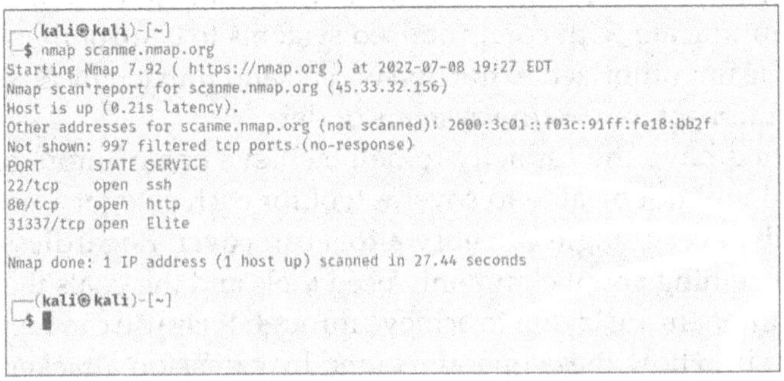

```
┌─(kali⊛kali)-[~]
└─$ nmap scanme.nmap.org
Starting Nmap 7.92 ( https://nmap.org ) at 2022-07-08 19:27 EDT
Nmap scan report for scanme.nmap.org (45.33.32.156)
Host is up (0.21s latency).
Other addresses for scanme.nmap.org (not scanned): 2600:3c01::f03c:91ff:fe18:bb2f
Not shown: 997 filtered tcp ports (no-response)
PORT      STATE SERVICE
22/tcp    open  ssh
80/tcp    open  http
31337/tcp open  Elite

Nmap done: 1 IP address (1 host up) scanned in 27.44 seconds

┌─(kali⊛kali)-[~]
└─$ ▮
```

Figure 4.1: Screenshot of Nmap

The initial use of Nmap can be to achieve Reconnaissance. As we've discussed, Reconnaissance involves gathering information to plan for the next steps in an engagement. By scanning the network with Nmap, regardless of whether directly inside or outside of the network, you obtain results that can be extremely valuable to the offensive security professional in determining exactly what resources will be tested and give them insight as to how best to approach the tests. For example, it can determine things like whether a host is on and accessible, its OS version, some software versions, what services are running, what ports are open, and it can even find certain vulnerabilities. As a result, it should provide the operator with a decent sense of what systems have potentially vulnerable hardware or software as well as what services could gain them additional entry points. Because potential adversaries often begin in this same manner, these actions are why defensive practitioners are told to have an inventory of their software and systems. Keep in mind that Nmap is not the only scanning tool that could be used, but it is one of the most common tools in the offensive security professional's toolbox.

To mitigate the use of scanning tools, be sure that firewall and IDS rules are set to detect and block the scans being used by any of these tools. All unnecessary ports both at the network edge and at the individual host should be blocked and limited to only necessary traffic. These mitigations should be set for all hosts on the network, regardless of whether it's a workstation, server, or other network device. In particular, network devices such as routers and firewalls must be configured to prevent being bypassed by these scans and be updated to their latest hardware releases. Some of these devices have a feature that can explicitly be enabled to block port scanning. Furthermore, removing server banners that include versions and rate limiting of traffic are also steps that can be taken to prevent successful use of scanning tools. Keep in mind that you must take steps to prevent scanning of not only IPv4 but also IPv6, because a service that is blocked on IPv4 might still be allowed via IPv6. Furthermore, unless it is explicitly disabled, IPv6 is accessible from inside the network.

Burp Suite/ZAP

Burp Suite and Zed Attack Proxy (known as ZAP) are tools used for application security testing. Burp Suite, a commercial product by the company PortSwigger, has a variety of versions from a free community edition up to a paid full enterprise product.[iii] See Figure 4.2. ZAP is a free, open-source product created by the Open Web Application Security Project (OWASP).[iv] Both of these tools provide an integrated way to map and analyze the attack surface of a web application as well as test and exploit its potential security vulnerabilities.

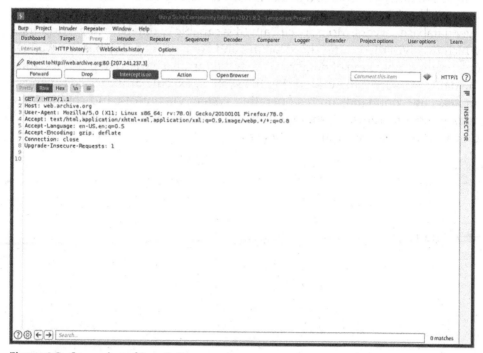

Figure 4.2: Screenshot of Burp Suite

Web application security tools are typically tied to the category of Initial Access because offensive security professionals can use them to gain a preliminary foothold into the environment. These tools can exploit weaknesses in Internet-facing applications and cause unintended or unanticipated behavior that may lead to access of the underlying system, regardless of whether they're cloud-hosted or on premises. In addition, the information acquired through these initial tests, such as company data residing in a database, may be used to achieve another category, such as Exfiltration.

Perhaps the most obvious mitigation against web application security testing is to make sure that the code written when building applications takes into account the most common programming flaws. Known as the OWASP Top 10, these known security risks include broken access control, which allows for a user to act outside of their intended permissions; cryptographic failures, which leads to sensitive data exposure; and injection, such as in a case where user data is not validated properly, among others.[v] Although the order of OWASP Top 10 changes annually, many of the core vulnerabilities remain constant.

sqlmap

sqlmap is a free, open-source tool that is used for testing databases. See Figure 4.3. In particular, it is used to detect and exploit SQL injection flaws as well as take over database servers. More specifically, it is capable of database fingerprinting, which involves discerning the structure and contents of a database as well as determining what kind of database it is, and it can also be used to pull data from the database, access the underlying file system, execute arbitrary commands, and execute commands on the operating system via out-of-band connections among other features.[vi] Although there are many other tools that have similar functionality, it is one of the best known.

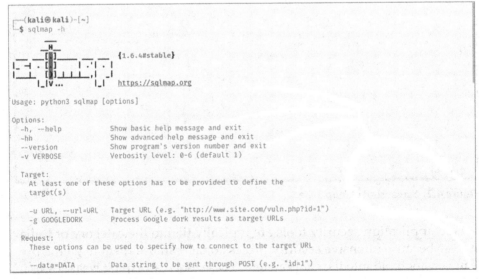

Figure 4.3: Screenshot of sqlmap

Database testing tools, just like web application security testing tools, are typically connected to Initial Access. The difference here is that these tools are focused on applications that specifically contain a backend database of some kind. Offensive security professionals will test initially to see what they can access. Once the type of database and structure have been determined, they may also test the ability to upload and/or download files, determine usernames, obtain password hashes, discover user roles, and execute code. Therefore, this tool can also fall under the categories of Exfiltration, Credential Access, and Execution.

There are a number of steps that defenders can take to mitigate against database testing tools. Much as with web application tools, it is important to make sure the applications used to access databases follow best practices such as mitigating injection attacks and ensuring accounts operated with least privileges. Prepared statements should be used rather than dynamic SQL for all database queries. Furthermore, query sanitization is critical and should be employed rigorously. Both the database accounts that the apps use and the database system accounts should follow the principle of least privilege. This principle says that the account should only have the specific privileges needed to complete its task and nothing more.

Wireshark

Wireshark is a powerful free, open-source protocol analyzer that allows for the examination of network traffic from the command line or a GUI.[vii] See Figure 4.4. It can be run on many operating systems and allows for deep packet inspections of hundreds of protocols and even has support to decrypt a number of them. This tool can read either existing captures of network traffic or live data from a variety of different types of networks as well as create network packet captures that can be read offline.

While often thought of by defenders as an investigative or operational tool, Wireshark and other protocol analyzers can also be used by offensive security professionals in a variety of different ways. In particular, this tool is generally associated with the category of Discovery, because it can assist in passively enumerating and mapping the network to provide details like the protocols in use and communications between hosts and to provide a sense of the general patterns of operation. Based on the information obtained, plans can be made for testing next targets. For example, this data might offer insight as to when a good time to run tests might be and what additional vulnerabilities can be explored. If a specific application is being tested, the data acquired can help to see which systems communicate with it as well as the protocols being used and the encryption levels. If the commands that are being sent by the person testing are unsuccessful, this data may provide some insight as to why as well as a suggestion for other protocols that could be used instead.

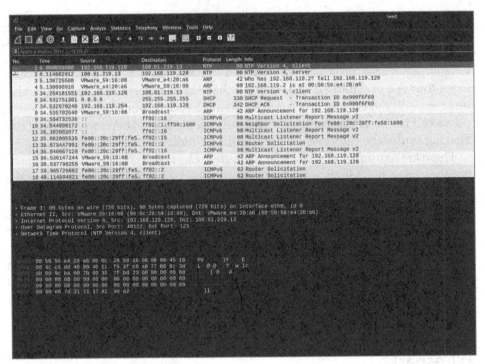

Figure 4.4: Screenshot of Wireshark

Defending against the use of any protocol analyzer, including Wireshark, is not particularly easy in part because threat actors typically monitor the network after gaining initial access as a way to gain information useful in lateral movement. They can use native tools such as `netsh trace` on Windows or `tcpdump` on Linux to create a packet capture for them. Keep in mind that at this point, testing is being done within the network in question and not externally. Therefore, any protections at the perimeter to prevent a view into the network are no longer relevant. All mitigations will require preventing any hosts that should not have access to the network from being able to connect to the network. Having some form of network access control (NAC) to prevent unauthorized systems from connecting to the network as well as manage what systems are allowed on certain segments can be valuable for this purpose.

Doing mitigation properly against something like Wireshark really requires implementing network segmentation, moving away from insecure protocols such as Telnet, FTP, SNMP v. 1/2, and so on throughout the network and implementing VLANs, all of which could require significant restructuring of the network. In addition, monitoring for anonymous traffic is something that should also be performed. Once network segmentation is in place, network captures should be run regularly to get a handle on what the traffic looks like in each of these different spaces. For example, a VoIP VLAN will look very different from a VLAN that contains an Active Directory server environment.

Metasploit Framework

Metasploit Framework is a tool used to test systems for security vulnerabilities against a remote target machine.[viii] See Figure 4.5. There are two versions currently available. The Metasploit Framework edition, which is free, and a Metasploit Pro edition, which is offered through Rapid7.[ix] Both tools provide a command-line interface, the ability to import a network data scan, over 1,500 exploits, the ability to do manual exploitation and brute forcing of credentials, and hundreds of payloads. It also provides the ability to build new exploits as new vulnerabilities are discovered. The Pro version adds additional automated functionality such as direct network discovery, automated brute forcing of credentials, and dynamic payloads to evade leading antivirus software.

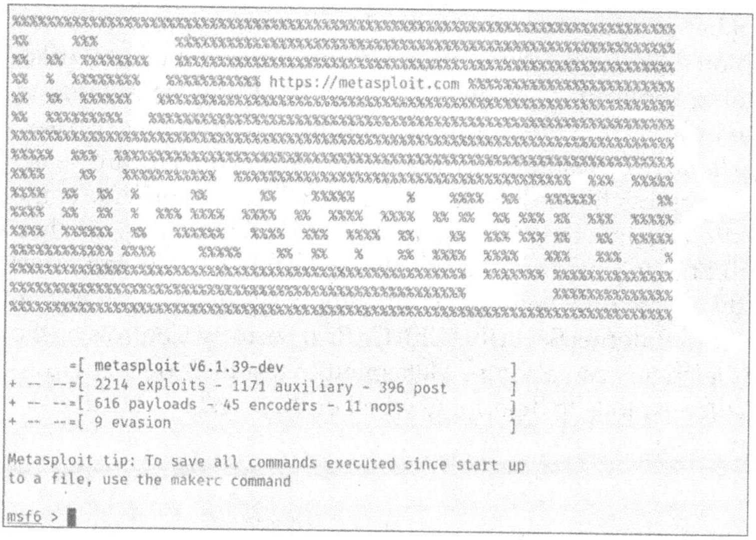

```
                                   https://metasploit.com

        =[ metasploit v6.1.39-dev                      ]
+ -- --=[ 2214 exploits - 1171 auxiliary - 396 post    ]
+ -- --=[ 616 payloads - 45 encoders - 11 nops         ]
+ -- --=[ 9 evasion                                    ]

Metasploit tip: To save all commands executed since start up
to a file, use the makerc command

msf6 >
```

Figure 4.5: Screenshot of Metasploit

Perhaps the best-known way that offensive security professionals can use Metasploit against a target involves selecting and configuring a particular exploit for a host, such as a vulnerability in the operating system. Next, they select and configure the payload such as a specific exploit, remote shell, or VNC server; select the encoding technique used; and then execute the exploit. Its flexibility comes from the ability to pair any exploit with any payload.

The diverse functionality of Metasploit means it can be associated with several categories. Because it can scan for vulnerabilities, one category that Metasploit can be connected to is Reconnaissance. It can also be tied to Initial Access because it can use exploits against a public facing, vulnerable service. In addition, it has auxiliary modules that can be used to execute online password attacks against public facing services or generate malicious scripts or executables that can be used indirectly to obtain this access. Furthermore, because of its ability to run malicious code, it can be connected to Execution. Under the category of Credential Access is Metasploit's ability to dump passwords from the target system. It's connected to Lateral Movement because after gaining access to one host, it can be used to pivot across the network to exploit vulnerabilities on other hosts. Privilege Escalation is another category with which Metasploit can be associated, because of tools that can gain SYSTEM-level privileges, not to mention Persistence because it can leave behind a backdoor even if the system is rebooted. Furthermore, Meterpreter can also be listed under the category of Defense Evasion because it contains payloads that run only in memory and are hard to trace with forensic tools.

There are a number of mitigations that defenders can use to protect against the use of Metasploit. However, most of them involve fundamental best practices such as running applications or processes with least privileges, limiting network access to only trusted hosts, running a fully configured host-based firewall blocking all but necessary ports, running some form of malware detection, and employing egress filtering where possible, which can provide some substantial protection against the ability to access one machine from another. Make sure that all known vulnerabilities in the operating system and other software and hardware are fully patched. Most of these system controls can be found in the Center for Internet Security (CIS) Critical Security Controls or the OWASP Top 10.[x] Defenders can also use Metasploit to test their own environments with particular exploits to determine whether their systems are at risk.

Shodan

Shodan is a specialized search engine that provides the ability to query for Internet-connected devices via a web interface, a command line, or its API.[xi] See Figure 4.6. It regularly scans the Internet looking for vulnerable Internet devices that are publicly accessible. These devices are either not protected at all or have minimal protections. For example, open webcams, printers that can be controlled remotely, and servers that have services available on open ports (such as web servers, FTP servers, and mail servers) are just some of the things that you can find here. To be clear, Shodan does not do anything nefarious with this information, such as decrypting or otherwise attacking the services to make them available. It only adds them to its database and makes them available to search. Accessing Shodan is as simple as going to the website: www.shodan.io It does allow for some free searches, but with restricted capabilities such as returning a limited list of results. For full functionality, users must register an account and pay a fee.

Figure 4.6: Screenshot of Shodan

Typically associated with the category of Reconnaissance, offensive security professionals will search Shodan for targets belonging to the organization they are testing. This tool focuses specifically on infrastructure vulnerabilities. Searches can be specific to a particular vulnerability across an organization's domain or IP space, look for any vulnerabilities across all devices in a single domain or IP space, or look for all devices with a particular open port, among others. The results include vulnerabilities impacting the host, open ports, and banners for open ports, which can be downloaded in a free report that is available in a variety of formats. This information can be useful in crafting a variety of tests, depending on the goals of the engagement. Shodan can also be listed under the category of Discovery because of its ability to also provide insight into what services or software might be running in an organization.

To mitigate Shodan scans, and thus limit the data they acquire about organizational resources, requires blocking the ability for scanners to access devices inbound, typically via a perimeter firewall and/or a host-based firewall on each host at a minimum. While defenders can actually request to opt out of

Shodan's scans for their organization, this decision may hinder their visibility into what devices are open to the Internet. Defenders can also regularly search Shodan for any devices they are responsible for protecting to see what might be unintentionally exposed. In addition, Shodan offers a network monitoring service to regularly provide information about devices they are responsible for that are open to the Internet.

Social-Engineer Toolkit

The Social-Engineer Toolkit (SET) is a free, open-source tool that is used to test an organization by social engineering its employees.[xii] See Figure 4.7. *Social engineering* is a term that encompasses a number of techniques, all involving human social interaction. Tests are performed by manipulating individuals to try to gain confidential information, such as banking accounts, social media accounts, email accounts, or even access to a target computer. SET has a bunch of custom vectors that can be used for testing, including spear-phishing attacks, website attacks, and SMS spoofing attacks, among many others. The spear-phishing module is used to perform targeted email tests with malicious attachments against an organization, whereas the website attacks can be used to specifically harvest credentials or deliver malware. SMS spoofing attacks allow someone to spoof the phone number an SMS text comes from in order to deliver a link to a website that can harvest credentials. Each of these tests can be used individually or together as a more comprehensive experience.

SET can be associated with the category Initial Access because it involves a variety of ways to obtain an initial foothold into a target system. For example, some form of phishing might be used for credential gathering, which also means this tool falls under the category of Credential Access. The offensive security professional either uses the built-in email templates or creates their own and sends specially crafted email messages written in such a way as to encourage the recipient to open them. If the goal is strictly credential gathering, the message may contain a link to a clone of a well-known site that has a username and password field, such as gmail.com, with the goal of harvesting all the information posted to the website. Instead, the message may contain an attachment that appears to be something of interest to the recipient such as "baby pics" or "computer issue" to encourage them to open the attachment. In reality, these attachments are payloads, which can be built with the ability to potentially bypass antivirus and create open connections back to the individual doing the testing, ultimately providing full access to the system in question. Because the user clicking on this file results in the payload running, this tool also can be seen to fall under the category of Execution. Furthermore, SET is affiliated with the category of Defense Evasion because of its ability to bypass antivirus and the category

Command and Control because it can send a payload as an attachment capable of creating a direct, interactive connection to the target system.

Figure 4.7: Screenshot of Social-Engineer Toolkit

Protecting an organization against something like SET is one of the most difficult tasks defenders face, in part because it requires the employees of an organization to understand the inherent risks in their day-to-day duties. These duties likely include opening email attachments and clicking links. Technical controls such as those that prevent email spoofing (e.g., SPF, DMARC, and DKIM), URL inspection, file download inspection, and EDR can be useful, as can security awareness training for employees that teaches them to be wary of unsolicited messages, attachments, and links.

Mimikatz

Mimikatz is an open-source tool that is capable of obtaining plaintext Windows account logins and passwords, along with many other features.[xiii] See Figure 4.8. It can be used to grab passwords as well as hashes, PINs, and Kerberos tickets from system memory. It is often coupled with or built into other tools and frameworks to facilitate more complex testing of systems. The functionality this tool offers is also available in another framework called PowerSploit (PowerShell Post-Exploitation Framework), which allows the operator to load Mimikatz completely into memory without writing it to disk.

```
C:\Users\jake\Desktop>mimikatz

  .#####.   mimikatz 2.1.1 (x64) built on Dec 19 2017 01:16:28
 .## ^ ##.  "A La Vie, A L'Amour" - (oe.eo)
 ## / \ ##  /*** Benjamin DELPY `gentilkiwi` ( benjamin@gentilkiwi.com )
 ## \ / ##       > http://blog.gentilkiwi.com/mimikatz
 '## v ##'       Vincent LE TOUX        ( vincent.letoux@gmail.com )
  '#####'        > http://pingcastle.com / http://mysmartlogon.com   ***/

mimikatz # privilege::debug
Privilege '20' OK

mimikatz # sekurlsa::logonpasswords

Authentication Id : 0 ; 90750 (00000000:0001627e)
Session           : Interactive from 1
User Name         : jake
Domain            :
Logon Server      : DC-01
Logon Time        : 6/24/2022 1:11:56 PM
SID               : S-1-5-21-1252044151-2136097517-1496704971-1787
        msv :
         [00000003] Primary
         * Username : jake
         * Domain   :
         * LM       : 6f59ad55de3e78e2358f4be2befbcf0f
         * NTLM     : acbfc03df96e93cf7294a01a6abbda33
         * SHA1     : 203e6de3293ae80f4910839cb306f36c8568875d
        tspkg :
         * Username : jake
         * Domain   :
         * Password : Summer2020
        wdigest :
         * Username : jake
         * Domain   :
         * Password : Summer2020
        kerberos :
         * Username : jake
         * Domain   :
         * Password : Summer2020
        ssp :
        credman :
```

Figure 4.8: Screenshot of Mimikatz

The goal of the offensive security practitioner in using this tool is typically to perform credential harvesting from Windows machines. Thus, we can see that there's a clear connection to the category Credential Access. Mimikatz can obtain this credential information from the Local Security Authority Subsystem Service (LSASS) process, which lives in memory in order to facilitate single sign-on capabilities. The data obtained includes Kerberos tickets, Windows New Technology LAN Manager (NTLM) password hashes, potentially LAN Manager (LM) password hashes in older OSs or those re-enabled in newer ones, and even cleartext passwords.

Once these credentials are obtained, the operator can use some additional modules to perform a variety of attacks including, but not limited to, pass-the-hash, which allows for password reuse to access additional systems without cracking the hash itself; pass-the-ticket, which allows for Kerberos ticket reuse on another system; and Kerberos Golden ticket, which obtains the ticket for the hidden root account called KRBTGT that provides domain admin access on any computer on the network. As a result, we can further associate this tool with the category of Privilege Escalation as well as Lateral Movement. Using legitimate credentials makes it harder to detect the test being performed and may provide an opportunity to create additional accounts to facilitate the operator's goals.

To prevent systems from being susceptible to Mimikatz, there are a number of specific things a defender can do. First, be certain that WDigest caching is disabled. WDigest is an older authentication protocol that retains a copy of the user's plaintext password in memory, which could be left open. By default, it is disabled starting with Windows 8.1 and Windows Server 2012R2, but it could be easily re-enabled by someone with the proper access.

Next, ensure that the Local Security Authority (LSA) Protection is enabled, which involves causing LSASS to be a protected process. This setting is the default beginning with Windows 8.1 and Windows Server 2012R2, but it could become disabled. Also, it is wise to disable the ability for the local administrator to use the debug mode on systems via the local security policy wherever possible, because this permission is crucial to how Mimikatz functions. Keep in mind, however, that any threat actor with permissions to run Mimikatz can also enable any setting that has been disabled. However, having these settings in place means that they have to take longer to gain the access they want, creating more opportunities for detection in the process. If the time for an attacker to gain access increases, it is possible the defender may have enough time to detect and evict them.

Furthermore, be sure to disable storage of plaintext passwords in AD (which is a legacy setting called Reversible Encryption), enable restricted admin mode, enforce the setting Enable Restrict Delegation Of Credentials To Remote Servers, enforce Network Level Authentication (NLA) for RDP sessions, and put administrative accounts into the Protected Users group to force Kerberos authentication. It's also a good idea to restrict service and other admin accounts to specific systems and set long, complex passwords on them.

Finally, ideally change the password caching policy on systems to cache 0 recent passwords instead of the default, which is 10. However, this setting may be problematic for laptops or other devices that are not able to directly communicate with domain controllers. Instead, you could use a setting of one or two to accommodate this scenario. In addition to making these changes, consider logging any modifications of the WDigest Registry key and review audit logs of WDigest use. More great details about Mimikatz mitigations can be found in this fantastic SANS post from handler Ryan VanderBrink: `https://isc.sans .edu/forums/diary/Mitigations+against+Mimikatz+Style+Attacks/24612`. A great general introduction to Mimikatz can be found here: `www.wired.com/ story/how-mimikatz-became-go-to-hacker-tool`.

Responder

Responder is an open-source tool that can obtain credentials and possibly even remote system access on Windows systems.[xiv] See Figure 4.9. It can be used to grab credentials and a password hash or cleartext passwords by sending poisoned requests of one of the following name services: NetBIOS name service (NBT-NS), link-local multicast name resolution (LLMNR) protocol, or multicast domain name service (MDNS).

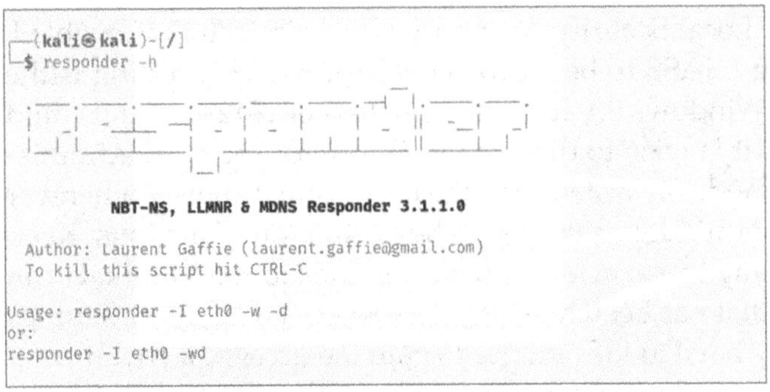

```
┌──(kali㉿kali)-[/]
└─$ responder -h

  .__                 .__  _____ ___ ____  ____ 
  |  |    _____|  |/  ____/   _   |/    |
  |  |  _/ __ \_  __ \  |   __\  |   |   |    |
  |  |__\  ___/|  | \/  |  |    |   |   |    |
  |____/ \___  >__|  |__|__|    |___|___|__  |
             \/                             \/

         NBT-NS, LLMNR & MDNS Responder 3.1.1.0

  Author: Laurent Gaffie (laurent.gaffie@gmail.com)
  To kill this script hit CTRL-C

Usage: responder -I eth0 -w -d
or:
responder -I eth0 -wd
```

Figure 4.9: Screenshot of Responder

These protocols work similarly in that they do machine name to IP resolution without using a DNS server. NBT-NS translates Windows NetBIOS names to IP addresses specifically on the local network via requests on UDP port 137. LLMNR, the successor to NBT-NS, sends out a multicast packet to port UDP 5355 to the multicast network address, asking all listening networks to reply. MDNS is a protocol predominantly implemented on Mac and Linux machines but is also used for printer discovery in Windows. Like LLMNR and NBT-NS, it also multicasts name requests but does so directly to all the clients in a network. In Windows, when a query is sent for a particular hostname's IP address, each host on the network will first check in its DNS cache. If the IP address is not found, the request will be sent to a DNS server. If it's still not found, the request is sent to the LLMNR and then NBT-NS protocols. Similarly, MDNS broadcasts are used to find IP information for hostnames.

Unfortunately, none of these protocols do any host authentication and, as a result, it's easy for one host to impersonate another one. Responder takes advantage of that functionality and simply replies to these requests with fake responses. Responder can also prompt users for credentials when certain network services are requested, resulting in cleartext passwords, as well as perform pass-the-hash style attacks and provide remote shells.

Responder is connected to the category of Credential Access. Once offensive security practitioners have established initial access to the network, this tool provides the ability for them to quickly and easily collect or relay authentication information by spoofing an authoritative source for name resolution. Once a host is tricked into communicating with the system running Responder, either by interacting with one of these protocols or when a search is done for an incorrect UNC share name, Responder will reply to the request and then grab the username and hash information and log it. The hashes can then be cracked with well-known password cracking tools or relayed in real time to another host.

One additional protocol that can be taken advantage of by Responder is the Web Proxy Auto Discovery (WPAD) protocol, which is used by web browsers for automatically retrieving proxy settings. When a user attempts to surf the web, the browser will broadcast a request using WPAD looking for a configuration file that contains the information for a web proxy on the network. The host running Responder replies as if it's the proxy web server with basic authentication, providing a login prompt back to the user, which can be used to capture credentials in cleartext and log them as well. This setup allows for the monitoring of all web traffic to/from the victim machine as well as the modification of the outgoing requests and responses, thus providing full control over the traffic. In other words, it acts as a machine in the middle (MitM) attack.

Defenders have several options to protect their environments from Responder. Host-based firewalls can be used to block broadcast traffic inbound and/or outbound. Ideally, disable broadcast traffic wherever possible. However, disabling these protocols can break functionality for some networks, so testing will need to be done to understand the implications of this change. Other steps that can be taken are to disable WPAD and to add in a hard-coded DNS entry on the internal domain. Because DNS is the preferred resolver, this will prevent LLMNR or NetBIOS requests for WPAD from ever being performed.

In addition, enabling SMB signing can be used to prevent relay attacks by digitally signing the data transferred, although there can be performance hits as a result. If disabling or blocking these protocols is not possible, consider monitoring traffic on UDP port 5355 and 137, event IDs 4697 and 7045 in event logs, as well as changes to the DWORD value of EnableMulticast. This value can be found under HKLM\Software\Policies\Microsoft\Windows NT\DNSClient\EnableMulticast in the Registry.

Cobalt Strike

Cobalt Strike is a tool that can simulate adversary activities and provides a large variety of testing options.[xv] See Figure 4.10. While the main version of this product requires a paid license, there is a free community edition called Community Kit.[xvi]Although the name Cobalt Strike can be used to refer to the malware payload the tool can deploy or the backdoor it can execute, this name is specifically meant to refer to the actual command-and-control (C2) application. It has two main parts: the client and the team server. The team server is the C2 application that accepts connections from clients, callbacks from the malware payload called BEACON, and regular web requests. BEACON is the backdoor itself. The team server supports a number of different kinds of listeners, which run on the team server to accept connections from particular protocols such as HTTP/HTTPS, DNS, and SMB. Beyond these basics, there are also additional customizations called the Cobalt Strike Arsenal Kit, which is the framework used to build custom executables and DLLs.

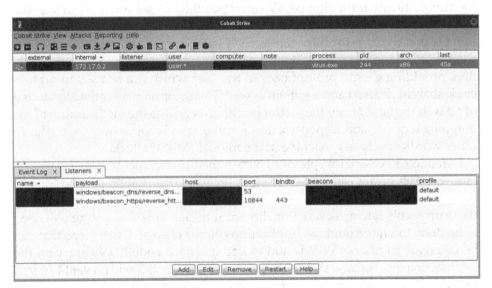

Figure 4.10: Screenshot of Cobalt Strike

Because this tool provides numerous testing options, its use can fall into multiple categories. For example, once an offensive security professional has gained initial access to a network, they can use its Discovery features, which are based on native Windows utilities such as `whoami.exe` and `nltest.exe`, to enumerate hosts on the network. Credential Access is another category that can be tied to Cobalt Strike, because of its ability to retrieve credentials and hashes from memory. It can also be used for Lateral Movement via a number of different methods such as pass-the-hash (which involves taking a known password hash and feeding it to a different system), using SMB/WMI to execute payloads, connecting through Remote Desktop Protocol (RDP), or utilizing remote service execution. The category of Execution is also relevant, because Cobalt Strike can create a temporary process, use `rundll32.exe` to inject a malicious DLL into it, execute this code, and then return the results via the C2 environment via named pipes.

What I've just described is something known as process injection, which can make Cobalt Strike particularly difficult to detect. These payloads can be deployed in memory without having to drop a file on disk, making it far more difficult for defenders to track. Thus, this behavior supports the category of Defense Evasion. Cobalt Strike also falls under Privilege Escalation, because it can be used to obtain system-level privileges by using the `elevate` command to either drop an executable that creates a service to run under SYSTEM or attempt to create a new process as a non-privileged user using the stolen token of an existing elevated process. Naturally, it can additionally be filed under Command and Control, as that is the basic backend infrastructure that allows for all of the communication that occurs between this tool and the devices being tested. The C2 application uses GET and POST requests via HTTP or HTTPS to facilitate its communications to the backend. However, DNS, SMB, or raw TCP can also be used as C2 channels to communicate with the C2 server to hide its traffic.

Defending against Cobalt Strike is particularly challenging. Traditional tools looking for known malicious files or certain behaviors, such as antivirus or anti-malware, are unlikely to detect this tool. Instead, following recommendations such as command-line monitoring, in-memory scanning, dynamic/static binary analysis, investigation of the lineage of an abnormal process, and creation of a baseline for the frequency of the internal use of reconnaissance commands is advised.[xvii] Furthermore, having Sysmon installed is also beneficial. Without it, or tools like it, defenders will be hard pressed to detect any of this activity in the logs of their machines. Sysmon is a tool that can extend the logging capabilities of a Windows or Linux system to capture more than traditional logging provides.[xviii] With Sysmon installed, evidence of process creation—including the file that gets created to run as a service, the creation and tampering of the service itself, and any Registry values that get set—can be revealed.

Important to keep in mind, though, is that there will be different indicators for different feature use, which means understanding the implication of different collections of log entries and other evidence is critical. For example, the event IDs and evidence one must look for in conjunction with something like process injection and that of, say, lateral movement will be different. Regardless of what detections are in place, most of these detection methods can easily be bypassed with configuration changes to Cobalt Strike, which is why additional active defensive steps like threat hunting are so important.

Impacket

Impacket is a collection of tools that provide low-level programmatic access for working with network protocols within custom scripts or directly via the command line.[xix] See Figure 4.11. Packets can be built from scratch or pulled out from raw data. The protocols supported include, but are not limited to, IP, TCP, UDP, ICMP, IGMP, ARP, NMB, SMB1, SMB2, and high-level implementations of SMB-3.

```
┌──(kali㉿kali)-[~/impacket/examples]
└─$ python3 secretsdump.py book-test:password@192.168.19.130
Impacket v0.10.1.dev1+20220719.115410.d923c00f - Copyright 2022 SecureAuth Corporation

[*] Service RemoteRegistry is in stopped state
[*] Service RemoteRegistry is disabled, enabling it
[*] Starting service RemoteRegistry
[*] Target system bootKey: 0x196c46029591c93937ad4cc2f4b2e826
[*] Dumping local SAM hashes (uid:rid:lmhash:nthash)
Administrator:500:aad3b435b51404eeaad3b435b51404ee:8846f7eaee8fb117ad06bdd830b7586c:::
Guest:501:aad3b435b51404eeaad3b435b51404ee:31d6cfe0d16ae931b73c59d7e0c089c0:::
DefaultAccount:503:aad3b435b51404eeaad3b435b51404ee:31d6cfe0d16ae931b73c59d7e0c089c0:::
WDAGUtilityAccount:504:aad3b435b51404eeaad3b435b51404ee:e6f845b03753611d977d018081b4c1ad:::
User:1000:aad3b435b51404eeaad3b435b51404ee:31d6cfe0d16ae931b73c59d7e0c089c0:::
book-test:1001:aad3b435b51404eeaad3b435b51404ee:8846f7eaee8fb117ad06bdd830b7586c:::
[*] Dumping cached domain logon information (domain/username:hash)
[*] Dumping LSA Secrets
[*] DPAPI_SYSTEM
dpapi_machinekey:0x176abd7452bfea40dc00607fd092ff40a461d989
dpapi_userkey:0xa3cc8420bb75ae63c5d79306d7e325e9f3eb1404
[*] NL$KM
0000   B4 75 F3 FF D2 40 DB 89  AB 94 BE 3B 74 E0 99 9D   .u...@.....;t...
0010   09 8A 96 FD 6E 1B C0 7C  74 E0 8B AC F6 7C 50 30   ....n..|t....|P0
0020   F6 E4 D0 BB 39 41 63 25  71 C0 CA DB F1 A9 32 06   ....9Ac%q.....2.
0030   4A 55 AE 9E 8E 4C 06 EF  83 1C 16 03 DE BE 8A 3F   JU...L.........?
NL$KM:b475f3ffd240db89ab94be3b74e0999d098a96fd6e1bc07c74e08bacf67c5030f6e4d0bb3941632571c0cadbf1a932064a55ae9e8e4c06efb31c1603debe8a3f
[*] Cleaning up...
[*] Stopping service RemoteRegistry
[*] Restoring the disabled state for service RemoteRegistry
```

Figure 4.11: Screenshot of Impacket

This compilation of tools falls under a number of categories much like Cobalt Strike because of the diverse functionality it employs. For example, it falls under Execution because there are scripts that provide offensive security professionals with the ability to execute code on a remote system through the native Windows SMB functionality, the task scheduler, and Windows Management Instrumentation (WMI) or via semi-interactive shells. In addition, because it has basic packet sniffing functionality, it can also be used for Discovery. It also has Credential Access capabilities and can acquire remote registry information without requiring any agent running on the system, as well as grab NTLM hashes, Kerberos keys, and, if available, cleartext credentials. Even if a service is disabled, such as Remote Registry, the script provided can restart it. Privilege Escalation and Lateral Movement are made possible through its many available scripts to create, acquire, or manipulate Kerberos tickets. Impacket has Collection abilities in that it can collect information about remote users and groups as well as shares and files. Furthermore, it has Exfiltration functionality with the ability for an unauthorized user to directly download files from a system.

Like many of these tools, Impacket can be used legitimately by offensive security professionals and defenders. Defenders use it for administration and as part of vulnerability-scanning applications, including tools built on Linux used to scan Windows environments. Therefore, determining whether the usage is malicious or benign can be challenging without additional context and requires having a baseline of legitimate usage in the particular environment in question. That said, the best ways for a defender to protect from Impacket is to limit inbound communication. In particular, restrict all incoming RPC, SMB, and WinRm connections to only those few systems with which the host needs to communicate. On servers in particular, also limit egress control to prevent them being used as another mechanism for lateral movement.

Mitm6

Mitm6 is a tool that can spoof replies to IPv6 DHCP requests and subsequently DNS queries on Windows machines.[xx] See Figure 4.12. When a Windows client requests an IPv6 configuration via DHCPv6, this tool will reply to that request by assigning it a link-local IPv6 address as well as assigning the IP of the system running the tool as the DNS server. However, no gateway is advertised. Furthermore, even if there is an IPv4 server, Windows clients will always prefer the IPv6 DNS server. As a result, these hosts will not attempt to communicate with anything outside of the local network and go to the machine running mitm6 for all DNS requests. Most importantly, because these machines are dual-stacked, meaning they have both IPv6 and IPv4, they will always try IPv6 first, which will only have the attack traffic, but then fail over to IPv4. As a result, the host retains IPv4 functionality, which means there is often no visible indication to the end user that anything is wrong.

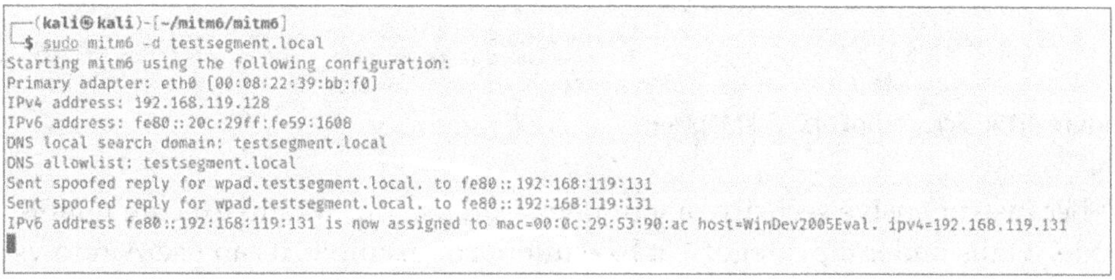

```
┌──(kali㉿kali)-[~/mitm6/mitm6]
└─$ sudo mitm6 -d testsegment.local
Starting mitm6 using the following configuration:
Primary adapter: eth0 [00:08:22:39:bb:f0]
IPv4 address: 192.168.119.128
IPv6 address: fe80::20c:29ff:fe59:1608
DNS local search domain: testsegment.local
DNS allowlist: testsegment.local
Sent spoofed reply for wpad.testsegment.local. to fe80::192:168:119:131
Sent spoofed reply for wpad.testsegment.local. to fe80::192:168:119:131
IPv6 address fe80::192:168:119:131 is now assigned to mac=00:0c:29:53:90:ac host=WinDev2005Eval. ipv4=192.168.119.131
```

Figure 4.12: Screenshot of mitm6

Offensive security professionals will use mitm6 for Credential Access by obtaining credentials through essentially coerced authentication and then potentially relay them to another system. These credentials can then be used for other types of further testing.

The best mitigation for mitm6 is to disable IPv6 on endpoints that don't explicitly use it. However, you can also block DHCPv6 at the host firewall level if IPv6 is not in use. Although if it is in use, the only option is to monitor the network for rogue DHCPv6 servers.

CrackMapExec

CrackMapExec is an open-source tool that can be used to test large Active Directory environments.[xxi] See Figure 4.13. Running purely from Python scripts, it does not require any external tools to function. It relies on a number of features and protocols that are built into AD natively such as SMB, HTTP, and MSSQL, which can make it exceptionally stealthy. If configured correctly, it can also evade most endpoint IDS/IPS protections. Furthermore, it includes a database that logs all credentials that are obtained. It also correlates what admin credentials are relevant to a particular host and vice versa.

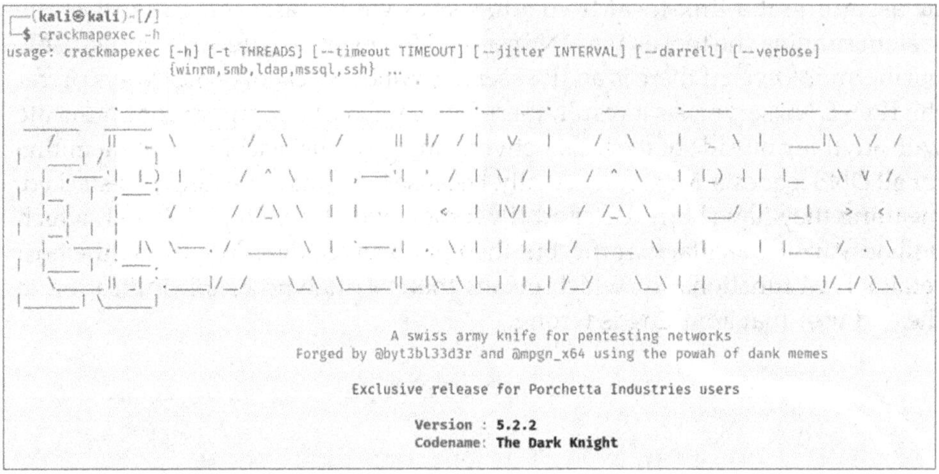

```
┌──(kali㉿kali)-[/]
└─$ crackmapexec -h
usage: crackmapexec [-h] [-t THREADS] [--timeout TIMEOUT] [--jitter INTERVAL] [--darrell] [--verbose]
                    {winrm,smb,ldap,mssql,ssh} ...




                        A swiss army knife for pentesting networks
               Forged by @byt3bl33d3r and @mpgn_x64 using the powah of dank memes

                        Exclusive release for Porchetta Industries users

                                Version : 5.2.2
                                Codename: The Dark Knight
```

Figure 4.13: Screenshot of CrackMapExec

Because offensive security practitioners can use this tool to execute remote code, it falls under the category of Execution. For example, it can use Windows Management Instrumentation (WMI) to create a semi-interactive shell on the Windows host. In addition, it can do Credential Access through extraction of hashes from a number of places such as the Security Account Manager (SAM) and the Local Security Authority (LSA), as well as through password spraying and dictionary attacks. There are additional modules that allow CrackMapExec to work in conjunction with other tools, such as Mimikatz. It can also be used for Reconnaissance by scanning an entire domain, subnet, or network to discover what hosts, shares, and/or sessions are available. Furthermore, it provides the ability for Lateral Movement because of the information it is able to obtain from its other functions.

Mitigations for CrackMapExec are similar to several of the tools previously discussed. Limit inbound access for all ports and protocols, especially RPC,

SMB, and WinRM, and limit outgoing connections whenever possible, especially on servers.

evil-winrm

evil-winrm is a tool written in Ruby that takes advantage of a built-in Windows protocol, WinRM.[xxii] See Figure 4.14. This protocol allows systems from a variety of different vendors to be able to access and exchange management data across an IT infrastructure over ports 5985 (HTTP) and 5986 (HTTPS). In Windows versions prior to Windows 7, it ran on port 80 and 443. While evil-winrm can be used for legitimate purposes, its function is to be able to load shellcode or DLLs into memory of a target where it can be executed. As a result, it's possible for the operator to execute arbitrary code like PowerShell and .NET apps.

```
Evil-WinRM shell v3.3

Usage: evil-winrm -i IP -u USER [-s SCRIPTS_PATH] [-e EXES_PATH] [-P PORT] [-p PASS] [-H HASH] [-U URL] [-S] [-c PUBLIC_KEY_PATH
] [-k PRIVATE_KEY_PATH ] [-r REALM] [--spn SPN_PREFIX] [-l]
    -S, --ssl                          Enable ssl
    -c, --pub-key PUBLIC_KEY_PATH      Local path to public key certificate
    -k, --priv-key PRIVATE_KEY_PATH    Local path to private key certificate
    -r, --realm DOMAIN                 Kerberos auth, it has to be set also in /etc/krb5.conf file using this format → CONTOSO.CO
M = { kdc = fooserver.contoso.com }
    -s, --scripts PS_SCRIPTS_PATH      Powershell scripts local path
        --spn SPN_PREFIX               SPN prefix for Kerberos auth (default HTTP)
    -e, --executables EXES_PATH        C# executables local path
    -i, --ip IP                        Remote host IP or hostname. FQDN for Kerberos auth (required)
    -U, --url URL                      Remote url endpoint (default /wsman)
    -u, --user USER                    Username (required if not using kerberos)
    -p, --password PASS                Password
    -H, --hash HASH                    NTHash
    -P, --port PORT                    Remote host port (default 5985)
    -V, --version                      Show version
    -n, --no-colors                    Disable colors
    -N, --no-rpath-completion          Disable remote path completion
    -l, --log                          Log the WinRM session
    -h, --help                         Display this help message
```

Figure 4.14: Screenshot of evil-winrm

This tool falls under the category of Execution because of its ability to execute code on a target. Once an offensive security professional is able to run code, they are able to gain remote access via a shell connection. With that connection in place, they can do just about anything else to the target. For example, they can stage additional payloads like Cobalt Strike or BloodHound. If the target is running WinRM natively such that port 5985 or 5986 is already open to the world, then it can also fall under the category of Initial Access because the operator is simply exploiting a public-facing application at that point.

Mitigating against evil-winrm involves either disabling the service where possible or limiting access so only authorized endpoints can access it. These changes can be done in the Windows firewall and the WinRM configuration. While WinRM does not have a listener on by default (e.g., the ports open with something listening), many software management packages enable it by default when they are installed. Also, be aware that using WinRM with the `/quickconfig` option will open these ports up to the world.

BloodHound/SharpHound

BloodHound is an open-source tool that uses graph theory to provide an analysis of Active Directory domain security in terms of its rights and relationships.[xxiii] See Figure 4.15. There is also a version that can collect data for BloodHound from a Linux system, OS X system, or Windows system that has Python installed; it's called BloodHound.py.[xxiv] This tool, which can be installed on Windows, MacOS, or Linux, can reveal hidden and often unintended connections that could allow an attacker into the environment in some unexpected ways. In particular, it highlights the potential for escalation of privileges in Active Directory domains by uncovering hidden or complex attack paths that can compromise security of a network. For example, service accounts that are used for automated maintenance may be able to be leveraged for lateral movement and spreading of malware if they have access to critical assets such as domain controllers, mail servers, or database servers.

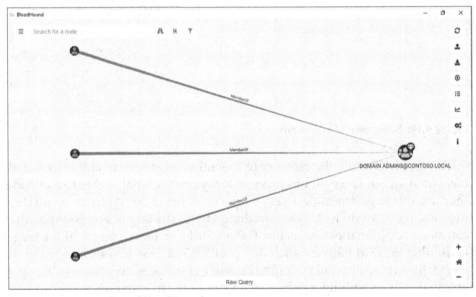

Figure 4.15: Screenshot of BloodHound

To obtain useful information from BloodHound requires first running Sharp-Hound, which is the corresponding data collection tool used to gather data about the environment by enumerating everything in AD.[xv] There is also a version of SharpHound that can provide information about Azure called AzureHound.[xxvi]

Once this data is imported into BloodHound's database, a map is generated of the objects in an AD, such as users, groups, and computers. By querying each of them, it can ascertain information about the relationships between these objects to discern those that may lead to privilege escalation or lateral movement capabilities. BloodHound contains a number of built-in queries that can be useful. "Find the Shortest Path to Domain Admins" and "Find Dangerous Rights for Domain Users Groups" are examples of some of the built-in queries available. However, custom queries also can be run. Note that though it is not recommended, it is possible to run SharpHound from a machine that is not a member of the domain with user credentials from that domain.

Using the information gleaned from BloodHound, the offensive security practitioner can begin to explore some of the possible relationships to exploit. Not only does it provide the relationships themselves, but it can give the operator the exact PowerShell commands necessary to pivot through or exploit a particular relationship, regardless of the level of complexity it has. Thus, this tool falls squarely under the category of Discovery. It even offers operational security considerations for the operator to potentially avoid detection. Running SharpHound can create a significant amount of noise in logs that can be used to obscure a real threat actor's activity. The same conditions are true if it is being run by a defender for legitimate purposes, which is unfortunate but important to understand. Thus, we see a connection to the category Defense Evasion as well.

There are no real mitigations specific to preventing running BloodHound / SharpHound aside from the standard recommendations for preventing unauthorized devices from accessing the network. However, limiting the number of accounts with administrative permissions on multiple machines is useful if you want to limit what BloodHound/SharpHound can discover. Block all unnecessary inbound traffic at the border and use some form of network access control. Employ network segmentation. Run a fully configured host-based firewall blocking all but necessary ports, run some form of Endpoint Detection and Remediation (EDR) software, and utilize egress filtering where possible.

Summary

Having a basic understanding of the tools used by offensive security practitioners can be enlightening to defenders who may be unaware of them. This chapter aimed to help educate defenders by offering a high-level explanation of various tool, what kinds of capabilities they have in terms of attacks, and any mitigations specific to the tool in question. While I focused on specific tools in this chapter, I did so to illustrate what kinds of tooling is out there and what actions can be taken with these tools to exploit an environment. The defender should try not to hyperfocus on defending from these tools specifically. Instead, it is important to think more broadly about defending an environment. To that end, finding some training to start putting some of the pieces together can be enormously valuable and that will be the subject to which we turn in the next chapter.

Notes

    i. https://attack.mitre.org/tactics/enterprise

    ii. https://nmap.org

    iii. https://portswigger.net/burp

    iv. www.zaproxy.org

    v. https://owasp.org/Top10

    vi. https://sqlmap.org

    vii. www.wireshark.org

    viii. https://en.wikipedia.org/wiki/Metasploit_Project

    ix. www.rapid7.com/products/metasploit/download/editions

    x. www.cisecurity.org/controls

    xi. www.shodan.io

    xii. https://github.com/trustedsec/social-engineer-toolkit

    xiii. https://github.com/gentilkiwi/mimikatz

    xiv. https://github.com/SpiderLabs/Responder

    xv. www.cobaltstrike.com

    xvi. https://cobalt-strike.github.io/community_kit

    xvii. https://redcanary.com/threat-detection-report/threats/cobalt-strike

    xviii. https://docs.microsoft.com/en-us/sysinternals/downloads/sysmon

    xix. https://github.com/SecureAuthCorp/impacket

    xx. https://github.com/dirkjanm/mitm6

    xxi. https://mpgn.gitbook.io/crackmapexec

    xxii. https://github.com/Hackplayers/evil-winrm

    xxiii. https://github.com/BloodHoundAD/BloodHound

    xxiv. https://github.com/fox-it/BloodHound.py

    xxv. https://github.com/BloodHoundAD/SharpHound

    xxvi. https://github.com/BloodHoundAD/AzureHound

CHAPTER 5

Implementing Defense While Thinking Like a Hacker

By now, hopefully you are starting to get a feel for the offensive security space and ways you can actively immerse yourself into it. As you continue down this path, you should start to have a better sense of what attacks are possible and, by spending enough time in that world, begin to develop a hacker mindset. As a result, ideally, you'll start to think about the implementation of defensive methods in very different ways. To assist in this progression, I want to turn some topics that are often thought of as strictly defense-centric on their heads and view them from an offensive security perspective to help guide this thought process. In addition, we'll revisit some proactive activities that can be particularly effective and examine what they look like when practiced by an Active Defender.

OSINT for Organizations

While we've already discussed some of the specific places that offensive security professionals find their intel for their operations, what we have not yet covered is the general idea of data gathering through OSINT, which stands for open-source intelligence. However, to help you understand OSINT, I will start with the notion of OPSEC, because it is something with which defenders typically are more familiar.

OPSEC

At a very high level, the defensive practice of operational security (OPSEC) is to both prevent sensitive information from winding up in the wrong hands and prevent innocuous actions that could generate information that could inadvertently be used against an organization. OPSEC was originally a military concept used for risk management, but like many military terms, it has moved into the information security space. For example, if a member of the military posted a photograph of themselves on a secret base to social media and it was discovered by the enemy, they could potentially use this photograph to locate the base and attack.

OSINT

In order to understand OPSEC from the offensive security perspective, one must first understand OSINT. As we've seen, one of the first steps in an offensive security engagement involves targeting and information gathering. While defenders often understand the concept of OPSEC, they are not necessarily familiar with offensive security practitioners use of OSINT, which is in part why OPSEC is necessary. OSINT is "any data you can find from publicly available, unhidden sources."[i] It is important for defenders to have an idea of what public data is available about their organization that could be used against them.

You may not realize it, but we've already seen a number of examples of how OSINT can be used as part of an offensive security engagement. For example, it was part of the discussion involving places where offensive security professionals obtain their intel in Chapter 3, "Offensive Security Engagements, Trainings, and Gathering Intel." LinkedIn, Twitter, message boards, and GitHub included what some of this OSINT was and how it could be used. In addition, we saw something similar in Chapter 4, "Understanding the Offensive Security Toolset," during the discussion of some tools they use, such as Shodan. Beyond what was already mentioned, other places that can be useful for OSINT are job boards and career sites, and other social media platforms like Facebook and Instagram.

Furthermore, a publicly traded company is required to file documentation demonstrating that the company is compliant with the rules of the US Securities and Exchange Commission (SEC) and the law. In particular, the SEC Form 10-K, which is the company's annual report, contains financial information and any concerning risks as well as the names of some of their key executives. All of these documents are freely available to the public, making them a useful source of OSINT.[ii]

Social Engineering

As with any intel, OSINT is continually gathered throughout an engagement. It can be particularly useful for the offensive security practitioner, and likewise an attacker, to use in social engineering campaigns. Social engineering is "any attack that leverages human psychology to influence a target, making them perform an action or provide information." Phishing, the sending of fraudulent emails in order to entice the user to provide credentials or other personal information, click links, or open attachments, is perhaps the best known social engineering tactic. However, there are others, including pretexting, which involves impersonating someone else whether physically or virtually; vishing, which is like phishing but entails calling the target on the phone rather than sending email; SMSishing, which involves phishing via text message; and good old-fashioned dumpster diving, which involves collecting trash from the target organization and taking it off site to explore for useful information.[1]

Although it can be utilized at any time during an engagement, social engineering is often leveraged as a mechanism to obtain initial access to an organization. The most innocuous information left in a publicly accessible space can be used to build social engineering campaigns. For example, discovering employee names and titles, email addresses, and format, or photographs with useful details like badge and system information, can all be useful in an engagement with a business. The available OSINT might also contain details specific to the business such as what software is employed at the target, who its vendors and customers are, specifics about its operations, or locations.

Not only can OSINT be gathered from social media or public documents, but it can also be discovered using a number of other platforms, such as Crunchbase, or command-line tools such as Recon-ng and theHarvester. Some of these tools can even pull metadata such as email address or username formats from online documents. Crunchbase offers both a paid tier and a free tier and, depending on which you select, can provide details such as the address of the corporate headquarters, the full corporate history including acquisitions and mergers, financial information, and details about critical employees, among other things.[iii] Recon-ng and theHarvester, both found in Kali Linux, have a number of modules that can also be used to gather this information.[iv]

Looking at these spaces with the eye of an offensive security professional, rather than that of the traditional defender, can provide significant insight as to what information out there could be leveraged against your organization. While many companies regularly employ a variety of security awareness programs, few consider also regularly monitoring what OSINT is readily available. Tools like Shodan can not only be queried manually but set up to provide real-time notifications when something new appears. Keep in mind that although it is

---

[1] Note: It is unusual and could be potentially problematic for an offensive security engagement to include personal devices in scope, unless the client agrees to it and/or has an existing BYOD policy, which is rare. Because very few organizations provide cell phones to their staff, SMSishing is rarely employed by offensive security professionals. However, I mention it because it is still a common social engineering practice by attackers about which defenders should be aware.

possible to run an OSINT and reputation monitoring program in-house, it must be scoped very carefully. Content shared privately or between friends should remain out of scope. It may be better to outsource this function as a means of alleviating ethical concerns and potentially prevent the possibility of stalking or harassment accusations.[v]

Actively Defending

The Active Defender not only should be aware of the OSINT available about their organization and employees, but, when possible, should also implement some additional proactive data security practices that involve the use of OSINT to better defend their organizations. I've discussed the use of OSINT and reputation monitoring earlier in this chapter, but there is a more comprehensive method: Attack Surface Monitoring (ASM). As part of ASM, account takeover (ATO) prevention should also be employed.

ASM

The purpose of ASM is to regularly discover, monitor for, evaluate, prioritize, and remediate an organization's external attack vectors. Unlike traditional vulnerability scanning, this assessment is performed from the perspective of an attacker and does not just involve a single point in time. In other words, it entails both OSINT and real-time monitoring to provide visibility into the vulnerabilities, weaknesses, and misconfigurations of any system and discovered assets that make up the attack surface of an organization.

The attack surface includes anything that involves an entry or exit point on public interfaces of the network that attackers can target to gain unauthorized access to the organization, regardless of location. The pieces of an organization's attack surface that should be regularly monitored include, but are not limited to, cloud environments such as Storage as a Service (SaaS); Infrastructure as a Service (IaaS); SaaS applications; domain names and SSL certificates used by the organization as part of interacting with customers or employees; as well as web applications and services, including APIs used for email. It also should include all systems connecting to the network regardless of whether the device is owned by the organization or BYOD (including IoT devices) as well as code repositories. In addition, as part of ASM, ATO prevention should be implemented.

ATO Prevention

ATO occurs when attackers gain control over a user" account by stealing their credentials. As a result, the attacker obtains access to the data and privileges associated with the account. This access is then used to commit identity theft and fraud, enabling other types of attacks.

OSINT is directly related to the methods attackers often use to obtain these credentials in the first place. As you've already seen, public information about employee names and titles as well as email addresses and format can be used in phishing scams. Other company information, such as financial data, corporate risks, employee accomplishments, or specific company verbiage (e.g., referring to employees as "associates" or "staff members"), can be used to craft these messages. The more information that is available, the easier it is to build a convincing phishing message that someone will want to click on. Much of this same information can also be used to guess passwords as well.

ATO prevention is used to thwart these actions. There are a number of proactive steps that the Active Defender can take to establish ATO prevention, including educational awareness programs, two-factor authentication, and account monitoring.

Educational Awareness Programs

Perhaps the most obvious and well-known is some form of educational awareness program for everyone within an organization. I won't spend a ton of time on this element since it's so common, but I will highlight the pieces that I think are often mishandled and provide some overall recommendations.

Any awareness program should be an ongoing company-wide initiative that grows to become part of company culture. It should focus on recognition and reporting, rather than 100 percent prevention, especially with regard to phishing exercises. Ideally, this program should not be punitive in nature; it should instead focus on the success of someone notifying the appropriate people rather than accidentally making a mistake. Encouraging positive behavior rather than punishing bad behavior is significantly more effective when the goal is behavior change. Employees must feel comfortable reporting what they encounter, regardless of whether they clicked something potentially dangerous. For most people, opening email messages, clicking on links or attachments, and having pleasant conversations with co-workers or other people is a significant part of their job. They need to understand how and where to report any form of social engineering attack.

Help employees, regardless of technical proficiency, understand why their help is needed to thwart attackers. Make them partners in safety rather than creating an antagonistic situation where they see you as the enemy. Be sure to communicate awareness information such that it is accessible to the listener and such that they can relate to it. In particular, I've found that any messaging that teaches people how to stay safe online regardless of whether they are home or at work can be particularly effective, since most people are more interested in protecting their own information rather than that of the organization. I also typically emphasize looking for specific language in the message that indicates urgency or potential financial gain (greed), which are common methods for building social engineering attacks.

Two-Factor Authentication

Having multi-factor authentication (MFA) in place for all accounts can significantly reduce the potential for ATO. One of the biggest problems with a traditional username and password is that people often use the same credentials on multiple accounts. As a result, if their account is compromised in one place, attackers can use that information for ATO in other places.

While not infallible, because there are ways for attackers to get past it, adding MFA substantially increases the chances that the person logging in with an account is who they claim to be. It requires more than one authentication factor in order to access an application or system. These factors typically include information the user knows, like a password; something the user has or owns, like an authentication app on a phone or a hardware token; or something that the user is, such as biometrics including fingerprints and retina scans.

Account Monitoring

The Active Defender has a multitude of resources for account monitoring. If you can prove that you have ownership of a particular domain, alerts can be set up for data appearing in sites such as haveibeenpwned.com and Pastebin, both mentioned in Chapter 3. In addition, practices like comparing breached credentials from haveibeenpwned.com with new user credentials can be useful. Furthermore, alerting users when their credentials have been discovered in a compromise, whether or not these credentials are specific to the organization, and asking them to reset the associated password can also be beneficial.

Benefits

Because the focus of ASM is from the attacker's perspective, the defender should have an easier time prioritizing what to address first. They will understand what would likely get targeted by attackers first. Furthermore, ASM tools can provide insight into not only devices an organization knows are on the network but potentially rogue devices, systems, or software misconfigurations, as well as uncovering shadow IT that might have been put in place. In addition, they can uncover these weaknesses in an environment at the time when they're introduced instead of waiting until the next point-in-time scan is completed. Likewise, defenders gain visibility into vulnerable applications outside of standard patching cycles.

Types of Risks Mitigated

There are several risks that can be mitigated with ASM tools, such as ports unintentionally open to the world. They can also find vulnerable software, including operating systems, as well as vulnerable firmware. In addition, as mentioned, they can detect misconfigurations, such as databases or cloud instances that are not properly secured, which could lead to data leakage or exfiltration. Furthermore, ASM tools can help prevent domain hijacking performed through brute force attacks on administrative passwords.

Keep in mind that that while there are a plethora of ASM and ATO prevention vendors, they are not created equal. Each of them takes a different approach to solving the problems at hand. Consider the applicability and efficiency of the solutions offered in relation to the organization in question. Remember that they do not have to be expensive to be effective.

Threat Modeling Revisited

In Chapter 1, "What Is an Active Defender?" we discussed the general idea of threat modeling, formal approaches that can be taken, and how there are a number of ways we all practice it informally. But what does threat modeling look like for the Active Defender? To answer that question, we need to consider what it might look like from an offensive security perspective. In other words, the Active Defender must continually consider what is needed by the offensive security practitioner, or likewise an attacker, to determine the technical and nontechnical controls in place in order to make some decisions about the best way to approach each step in an engagement. Rather than just starting threat modeling at the beginning of a project or engagement, they must essentially continuously reverse engineer the organization's threat model while moving throughout the operation.

Framing the Engagement

First steps of reverse engineering any engagement will typically entail framing it through the lens of the business type. Understanding something about the nature of the business in question helps inform the offensive security professional where to focus their efforts and make testing more valuable for the client. In particular, they will often seek out what assets are viewed as critical to an organization's revenue stream. For example, if testing a bank, one of the considerations would likely involve the systems that are responsible for managing money. If testing a manufacturer, considering how to access and potentially interrupt the production line might be the focus instead.

Scoping in Frame

The objective(s) of an offensive security engagement will vary greatly depending on what is requested by the client and who the client happens to be. For example, the goal(s) will be radically different if the client is an entire business unit within an organization that needs elaborate testing rather than one that needs testing for a particular application or system.

In addition, considerations will need to be made for whether the testing requested is meant to be transparent or opaque—in other words, whether or not the offensive security practitioners are given much insight into the environment they're testing. In an opaque test, they are given as little information as possible, such as the company name and maybe the domain of its main web presence. In contrast, a transparent test is meant to simulate already having some form of access into the environment, such as a normal user account, typical imaged laptop, or something to simulate a piece of stolen hardware.

Motivation in Frame

Likewise, how an attacker approaches an organization will vary depending on their goal(s). The Active Defender must remember that attackers are human and thus have a wide variety of motivations for their actions, which can significantly impact their approach. Some attackers are motivated by money. Others, like nation states, are motivated by intelligence gathering. Some may be motivated to see what they can access or just for kicks. Part of what differentiates an average offensive security professional from one that is extraordinary is the ability to both understand and emulate these different motivations during testing where appropriate.

The Right Way In

As defenders, we are often told that an attacker needs only one way in to compromise a network and thus we must defend all the things. However, the reality is that they not only need a way in, but they need the *right way in*: the one that will get them the right access, specific to the goal(s) they have in mind. For example, if an attacker gets access to the domain admin account of an organization's Active Directory, but the goal involves obtaining source code located on an independent Linux box sitting on a completely separate network segment, their access may prove to be useless in this quest.

Experienced offensive security practitioners not only recognize this distinction but take it into consideration when planning out their attack chains. Furthermore, much like their defensive counterparts, they typically have a limited amount of time and resources available to achieve their objective(s). As a result, they are required to be as efficient as possible while still being effective.

Reverse Engineering

With an eye to what the business would most want to protect, the offensive security professional can then begin to build an attack chain. Rather than consider what could possibly go wrong to allow an attacker access as a defender would, they instead begin the process of evaluating what protections are or might be in place and how to evade them.

Targeting

The initial targeting phase is perhaps the easiest to reverse engineer, because there are typically few if any controls in place to prevent OSINT gathering. Through OSINT, some controls that could be determined initially include operating system version and patching levels; administrative tools in use such as Dameware, VNC, or RDP; or the particular helpdesk software the organization utilizes. If any specialized hardware or software is uncovered, such as a mainframe, enterprise resource planning (ERP) software it would also be useful to know. Since targeting continues as the engagement unfolds, there may be a need to determine what protections are in place around other services or accounts required at a later time as more is uncovered.

Inbound Access

As they enumerate what systems they might be able to use for initial access, the offensive security practitioner will investigate whether they will have to subvert inbound or outbound blocks, or perhaps both. Inbound access is typically restricted by controls like a password, VPN, security key fob, or physical location, which can each be circumvented. If there is nothing easily accessible from the outside in, the next option is to look for a way to get someone inside to initiate an outbound connection. Since most users are allowed to connect outbound to browse the Web, the easier initial access often involves gaining access through a phishing email or website hijack.

Persistence

Once inside the environment or system, the goal of the offensive security professional is to determine what controls are in place that might prevent them from either maintaining that connection perpetually or allowing for recurring access and then figuring out how to subvert those. For example, they have to determine whether they have the appropriate level of access on the system where they initially landed to be able to create a backdoor. Perhaps, instead, they have to find a way to elevate privileges to obtain that level of access. In addition, they have to determine whether there is some kind of detection system in place that might further hinder these activities.

Obtaining access to a single account or system, unless they get exceptionally lucky, is unlikely to be enough to meet the objective(s) of a typical engagement. Therefore, certain portions of the process repeat as necessary to pivot to the system(s) or account(s) that will ultimately help them reach their goal(s).

Egress Controls

Just as important to the offensive security practitioner as setting up persistence is uncovering the existence of any egress controls an organization has in place and finding a way to work around them. The ability to exfiltrate information from a network can be critically important, both to provide proof of engagement success, as previously mentioned, and to allow for certain testing mechanisms that could be helpful even where data retrieval is not required or requested.

They must work to uncover whether something like endpoint detection and response (EDR) software is deployed or sandbox technology is in use. EDR software is meant to provide rapid investigation and containment of attacks on endpoints. Sandboxing provides an isolated environment on a network that mimics the operating environments of the average user in which unknown files can be automatically detonated and their behavior examined before being allowed to reach the end user.

Each of these controls could prevent the default functionality of certain tools or methodologies as well as tip off other defensive detection mechanisms. However, once the offensive security professional is aware of them, there are typically workarounds that are available. Other controls that could be employed include, but are not limited to, the interception and inspection of encrypted Internet traffic, DNS blocks, arbitrary ICMP blocks, and other protocols that might be protected.

LOLBins

Just as we explored how OPSEC is in part a response to OSINT and how threat modeling for the Active Defender is a practice of reverse engineering defensive controls, we can also look with a unique perspective at some of the legitimate utilities, libraries, and other tools that are native to a particular operating system. Ordinarily, the presence of these files would be considered safe and their occurrences benign, and as such, the typical defender would not think twice about them. However, from the vantage point of the offensive security professional, they are often viewed as LOLBins (Living Off the Land Binaries).

To "Live Off the Land" in this context means to use what is readily available in a way that goes beyond the original purpose. In other words, these legitimate system utilities and tools can be used to execute payloads as part of engagement. Because they are native to the environment and thus trusted, any nefarious use more easily blends into regular network activity, making it much more difficult to detect.

The main benefit of the offensive security practitioner using LOLBins, and likewise an attacker, is that they are readily available on a system, thus negating the need for specialized tooling. In addition, unless the system is running endpoint security tools that specifically inspect scripts or monitor process behavior, these files are essentially invisible. In other words, they can easily bypass detections and aid in the delivery of hidden code execution. It is critical that the Active Defender be aware of the alternative uses of these files. In addition, they must understand what child processes a LOLBin normally invokes in order to recognize when they're calling for something unusual as well as what the expected parent processes of the LOLBin itself are.

Although technically LOLBins exist in most operating systems, the best-known ones are Microsoft signed binaries. They can be used for a wide variety of activities, including, but not limited to, executing code; performing file operations such as upload, download, or execution; lateral movement; maintaining persistence; or exfiltration. One of the best places to learn about these Microsoft LOLBins is the LOLBAS website at `https://lolbas-project.github.io`. Its goal is to "document every binary, script, and library that can be used for Living Off The Land techniques."[vi] For each of the 166 files listed, its functions, type (e.g., binary, library, or script), and ATT&CK techniques are documented. I'll examine five of the most commonly used ones in the following sections to provide a feel for what alternative functionality they hold: `rundll32.exe`, `regsrv32.exe`, `msbuild.exe`, `cscript.exe`, and `csc.exe`.

Rundll32.exe

`Rundll32.exe` is a native Windows binary file that is ordinarily used to execute dynamic link library (DLL) files. However, it can be used by a normal, unprivileged user to execute other, potentially malicious DLLs as well as alternate data streams. Alternate data streams are special attributes found in New Technology File System (NTFS) files that can hold additional data in such a way that the original size and functionality of the existing file is preserved. This feature allows someone to hide malicious data in order to evade detection.

Regsvr32.exe

`Regsvr32.exe` is a native Windows binary file that is typically used to register and unregister DLLs on Windows systems. However, even by a normal, unprivileged user it can also be used as a workaround to bypass AppLocker or other application controls. Furthermore, because this particular LOLBin can interact with the network and proxy settings of the operating system, it can use a URL pointing to a file on an external web server as a command-line parameter during execution. In other words, it functions like `wget` or `curl`, which are command-line tools that enable data transfer over various network protocols. As a result, `regsvr32.exe` can be used to retrieve a malicious script from wherever it is hosted, which can then be executed.

MSbuild.exe

`MSbuild.exe` (Microsoft Build Engine) is a native Windows binary that is used by Visual Studio for building applications. However, Visual Studio is not required to be installed to use it. A default installation of Windows 10, for example, includes the .NET framework which contains `msbuild.exe`. It can be used to indirectly compile and execute code by passing it a maliciously constructed XML file. Thus, even a normal, unprivileged user can use it as a workaround to execute arbitrary code and bypass AppLocker or other application controls.

Furthermore, because the code is compiled in memory, no permanent files exist on the disk, and various methods can be used to obfuscate the payload, it is much more difficult to detect. Most endpoint security software will likely be completely unaware of this technique. However, there may be limited need for this binary in an organization, so consider blocking all instances except those actually required.

Cscript.exe

`Cscript.exe` is a native Windows binary that can be used to execute VBScript or JScript. However, it can also be used by a normal, unprivileged user to execute scripts hidden in an alternate data stream. Thus, it can be used to evade detection or hide as a mechanism of persistence.

Csc.exe

`Csc.exe` is a native Windows binary that can be used to compile code written in C# stored in a `cs` file, which is a C# source file. Much as with `msbuild.exe`, it does not require anything else to run. A default installation of Windows 10, for example, includes the .NET framework, which contains `csc.exe`.

Because files can be compiled on-the-fly, they can often evade detection by endpoint security software. Once the file is compiled, it can be invoked by any method that can run an executable. Unless it is used for development purposes, `csc.exe` should normally not run as the System account.

Legitimate Usage?

To know whether any of these files are being used in a nefarious way requires examining several potential places for indications of misuse. First, examine the path from where the file is being launched. Some will have a default location, such as `C:\Windows\System32`, whereas others can be launched from any independent location. Be aware of the default locations for those that have one and be on the lookout for unusual ones like `c:\temp`.

Next, investigate any command-line activity related to the instance being used by looking for instances of Event ID 4688 found in the Windows security logs. Event ID 4688 with command-line logging captures when a new process is created as well as the arguments that were passed to the process when it was started. However, neither these events nor the command-line logging feature are logged by default and must be in enabled in advance. Furthermore, keep in mind that if you see a DLL being called by one of these LOLBins, it may not be the DLL it appears to be. Malicious DLLs often have a valid name, so it's important to check the hash of a DLL being passed, which can be captured with Sysmon or an EDR solution.

In addition, monitor the execution of any processes that appears to be a parent or child of the LOLBin in question in conjunction with another process. For example, instances of `rundll32.exe` running from an unusual parent process such as `lsass.exe` or `winword.exe` or `regsvr32.exe` in conjunction with another unrelated process, such as a Microsoft Office application (e.g., Winword, Excel), are common indications of malicious usage. Furthermore, look for any reaching out to the Internet that you wouldn't normally see. Many of these scripts make calls to external systems to pull down malicious files or code.

Threat Hunting

We previously discussed the general purpose of threat hunting, what overall value it brings to an organization, and some fundamental guidelines in Chapter 1. By this point, hopefully you are starting to grasp why automated detections are not always successful at discovering the various ways a network can be infiltrated and thus why threat hunting is necessary. Now we'll explore what threat hunting specifically looks like as an Active Defender. As you may expect, it is greatly influenced by the hacker mindset and by understanding the offensive security practitioner's methodologies.

Begin with a Question

According to some guidance provided by prominent threat hunter Neil Wyler, the best way to begin to start threat hunting is with a question rather than an indication of compromise—for example, "How would I get in from the outside?" He also recommends having a plan for what you're trying to find but remaining flexible based on what is uncovered. Tool selection for the search will vary and depends greatly on what you are trying to find.

Be aware that the process of threat hunting can take many twists and turns and may not arrive at an expected destination. It may also lead to an incident response, so be prepared for that possibility. Furthermore, be sure to document your process and what you find so that you can share it with others.[vii]

The Hunt

The hunt itself should take a layered approach, starting with something small like focusing on process creation. Begin searching collected logs for indications of process creation, which as we discussed is Event ID 4688 in the Windows security logs. Take time to examine any parent/child relationships around what is uncovered. This direction should seem obvious, especially given what we just discussed about LOLBins. Look for unique processes that have been executed only a couple of times within a 24-hour period and investigate them by checking that the hash values match those of known executables.

Other related indications of maliciousness may include processes that are missing the company name or version number, processes that are named something similar to but not exactly the same name as a legitimate process, or processes starting from an unusual location. Getting a feel for the legitimate use of scripting LOLBins such as `cscript.exe` by specific hosts or administrators can help narrow down which instances need investigating. Also, keep an eye open for encoded commands and consider who might be using them and for what purpose. In addition, monitoring for users being added to privileged groups could be a sign that something has gone awry.

From here, there are a number of other associated oddities that you can seek out during your hunt. For example, you can search for the execution of commands that are normally only run by administrators but are suddenly being run by end users or even administrative tools that typically are not used at all in your environment. In addition, investigate whether logs have been unexpectedly cleared or manipulated. Examine whether there are new scheduled tasks or unplanned changes to existing ones as well as whether there have been any changes to the Registry. Don't overlook logs from antivirus, either. Information from these logs can help correlate other events being observed.[viii]

Applying the Concepts

Let us return again to the scenario introduced in the Introduction but expanded further in Chapter 1. Threat hunting could have been extremely useful to detect the attacker's use of `rundll32.exe` with `comsvcs.dll` to dump memory and capture passwords. In addition, it could be used to potentially detect lateral movement and the secondary C2 connection that was used to exfiltrate data. To see how, we'll follow the advice provided earlier, with the assumption that appropriate logging has been implemented and the hunt is being conducted within 24 hours of the attack. Keep in mind that there are often multiple ways to locate the same information, so if you are unable to locate something initially, keep digging. For example, logs can be removed or get overwritten, but you may still be able to find what you're looking for, just somewhere else.

Dumping Memory

First, we start with a question as recommended. In this case, the question might be something like, Have there been any unusual executions of LOLBins in our environment? In order to hunt for the answer to that question, we now know that we should be looking for evidence of process creation in the Windows security logs by searching for Event ID 4688. To narrow down the search, we will look back for only 24 hours and specifically for only processes with a unique configuration that have been executed only a couple of times. Because we understand how these files can be used maliciously, we will focus our attention on location of invocation, any command-line arguments being used, and DLLs being passed.[ix]

Ideally, the informed Active Defender would recognize the usage of `rundll32.exe` with a command line that includes a call to something unusual such as `comsvcs.dll`. Consequently, they would begin to dig into what `comsvcs.dll` is as well as what the implications of that combination might be. The time stamp of the LOLBin execution, together with the time stamp of the AV logs indicating that someone attempted to run Mimikatz just prior to when `rundll32.exe` was called, should be enough of a pattern to recognize that an attacker was looking for and likely succeeded in obtaining passwords.

At this point it is critical to remember that the attacker is a human being and as such is influenced by their own motivations. Therefore, keeping potential motivations in mind can help guide an Active Defender's next steps. It is unlikely that the end goal of the attack was to obtain passwords. Given the organization and the nature of its business, what might motivate an attacker to act? The answers to that question should help lead them to know what to do next.

Lateral Movement

Knowledge of offensive security methodology and its parallels to attacker operations should inform the Active Defender at this point that they should be hunting for additional information. For example, the system where initial access is obtained often has limited permissions or access. Therefore, although evidence of malicious process creation and potential password theft on one machine was discovered, it is likely that the adversaries' actions would next involve pivoting to additional systems.

Knowing something about the nature of the business can be illuminating here because we know that is in part how the decision is made about where to go next. If, for example, the business involves banking, looking for ways to pivot to the system controlling the money may be key. Thus, the next steps for the Active Defender should involve a new question: Has there been lateral movement from the system that was originally targeted?

To answer that question requires considering how lateral movement might be possible in that particular environment. From the system that was targeted, inbound and outbound connections and logins should be examined as well as any outbound communications to unusual or unknown domains, looking for the possibility of suspicious or beaconing activity. One of the easiest outbound connections to spot is remote access via Remote Desktop Protocol (RDP). On the system in question, typically, connections are made via TCP port 3389, if the system uses a standard configuration. There are, of course, other ways to move laterally, such as Secure Shell Protocol (SSH) or SMB shares. However, with the scenario in question, the Active Defender would have indeed observed traffic heading to another machine on port 3389.

On the system running RDP, connections are logged in Terminal-Services-RemoteConnectionManager/Operational logs with Event ID 1149. If, instead, users connect to remote desktops through the Remote Desktop Gateway, the user connection logs in the Microsoft-Windows-Terminal-Services-Gateway log will provide evidence of Event ID 302. However, despite the description "User authentication succeeded," each of these logs only indicates a successful network connection has been established to the server from the user's RDP client, not whether authentication was successful. To find successful login sessions, look in the Windows security logs for Event ID 4624 with either a logon Type 7 or Type 10 with the description "An account was successfully logged on." The Terminal Services Local Session Manager/Operational log will also usually contain an Event ID 21 for a successful logon. From there, it should be easy to see what credentials were used.

Secondary C2

With evidence of a LOLBin being used as password stealing tool and lateral movement obtained, the Active Defender would likely be aware that at some point that another goal of the attacker would be to exfiltrate data of some kind and pursue a new hunt. While there's a significant chance the specific data itself may not be visible because it is encrypted, it's still worth exploring because it provides more of the story. Therefore, this hunt would begin by asking the question, Is there evidence of a connection that could have been used to exfiltrate data?

Answering this question starts with examining both the machine where initial access occurred and any systems that were pivoted to for strange processes as well as inbound and outbound connections or beaconing activity. In reviewing outbound communications, pay particular attention to DNS requests by looking for unusual names (e.g., seemingly random), the use of dynamic DNS, and the possibility of DNS tunneling. Requests to a large number of subdomains can signify the use of slow exfiltration. A large number of requests to a single domain from just a few machines is another potential indication of data being stolen. In addition, beware of requests to .onion addresses or browser processes that are not specific to the Tor Browser.[x]

Remember that the very presence of a C2 connection does not guarantee that any data was exfiltrated. The ability to detect actual exfiltration is extremely difficult. However, because it absolutely *could* be used for that purpose among other illegitimate activities, tracking down connections of this nature is critical. Furthermore, in this particular scenario, by uncovering the second C2 connection, you can examine the other systems involved, leading to a more thorough and complete investigation.

Proof of Concept

From this example we have seen how valuable threat hunting can be, especially if an Active Defender who understands offensive security methodologies is involved. As a result, unlike the traditional defender, ideally the first system would not have been immediately reimaged, leading to a loss of critical evidence. Being able to find nefarious LOLBin usage, lateral movement, and ultimately both C2 connections would have gone a long way to provide a more complete picture of the attacker's activity.

Attack Simulations

We briefly discussed the topic of attack simulations and the general purpose they serve in Chapter 1. However, we still need to explore the difference between attack simulations and attack emulations as well as why testing in general is so critical. Furthermore, we will discuss the special insight the Active Defender brings to the use of these tools and what this testing looks like under their direction.

Simulation vs. Emulation

The distinction between attack simulations and attack emulations, at least for the purposes of this discussion, is that an attack simulation involves demonstrating something that is similar to an attack, whereas attack emulation involves actually performing an attack the way an adversary would with their intentions in mind.

Using tools that can test a checklist of independent individual techniques against an environment is a form of simulation. In the real world, an attacker performs a particular technique with a reason in mind and that informs their next steps. If you are chaining multiple tests collectively in the way that an attacker would approach their end goal, that would be emulation. One is an approximation of an attacker's activity, and the other is meant to mimic the actual activity.

There are hybrid examples as well that combine elements of simulation and emulation. For example, if you set up an attack chain the way an adversary would with the goal of data exfiltration, but instead of exfiltrating actual data you exfiltrate fake data for the exercise, you wind up with a combination of both. The steps up to the exfiltration would be considered an emulation, but the last step is a simulation.

Why Test?

Employing an attack simulation involves using a proactive testing methodology to determine whether a particular attack mechanism would succeed in a given environment. Without testing, we can believe that the defenses put in place whether to prevent or detect are working, but we cannot really know whether they are. Note that creating effective detections is too complicated a topic to discuss here, but one we'll return to in Chapter 7, "Building Effective Detections."

The need to actively practice and test goes well beyond the technical realm. In the fire service, regular preparations for an incident include a ton of hands-on practice, known as drills, which are paramount to a successful outcome. These drills are how firefighters test their tools, gear, and knowledge before an incident occurs such that when the time comes, they are ready to engage. They do not just assume that their masks will hold an air-tight seal, a saw will start, or a pump will help supply a sufficient amount of water pressure, despite the fact that their gear and tools are physically inspected regularly. While mistakes can still happen and tools could still fail, there's a much less likely chance if practice and testing is performed consistently.

Many traditional defenders focus their resources on preventing attacks, and certainly prevention should be an integral part of an organization's security. However, how do we know if the preventative measures in place will work as expected? In addition, we have seen that initial access is often fairly trivial. Active Defenders understand both how controls designed to keep out attackers may not work as intended and how even seemingly benign things that don't seem like vulnerabilities (e.g., LOLBins) can be used against an organization. Therefore, the ability to detect an attacker once they have successfully circumvented any controls in place is also essential. It is for these reasons and more that a variety of testing mechanisms must be used to validate any controls that a business believes to be in place.

Risky Assumptions

Organizations that rely on passive solutions without some form of testing often come to regret this decision later. For example, consider disaster recovery teams who rely heavily on backups during an incident. Backups are passive in the sense previously discussed in the introduction: they typically lack regular human interaction. Many teams naively assume that if there have been no obvious errors, their backups not only completed successfully, but the appropriate data was also backed up. Furthermore, they believe that upon attempting a restore, this necessary data will be recoverable. Without testing, however, they may find out the hard way that these assumptions are irrevocably wrong and restoring critical data is no longer a possibility.

Likewise, companies often take great pains to put security protections in place such as blocking particular protocols with perimeter firewalls, performing patch management, or maintaining least privilege access wherever possible without properly testing these protections. Configuring these defenses typically relies on following instructions provided by vendors, such as Cisco or Microsoft; trusted partners, such as a managed security service provider (MSSP); information sharing and analysis centers (ISACs); or third-party cybersecurity companies, such as Mandiant or CrowdStrike. If the steps are followed correctly and no errors occur, there is often an assumption that these safeguards will work as designed. Defenders may even run vulnerability scanners in an attempt to confirm this assumption. Unfortunately, vulnerability scans are passive in the same way as backups and they, too, can have flaws. When traditional defenders rely exclusively on the output from these tools, they risk missing something significant.

The way most vulnerability scanners work is to check for something like the hash of a file, the file version, or perhaps Registry settings to determine whether a patch has been properly applied. However, it is not uncommon for one tool to indicate that all necessary patches were applied properly but scanning with a secondary tool suggests otherwise. As most organizations cannot afford the monetary investment or person-hours it would take to use multiple tools, it is not uncommon for organizations to wind up with a false sense of security from the tools they do have.

There have also been instances where a patch is applied but a vulnerability still exists either because the underlying issue was not addressed in the fix or because the patch only modified a portion of the code but additional vulnerabilities were not addressed. A well-known example of this situation is the Apache Struts vulnerability that was used in the Equifax breach in 2017. Although an initial patch was issued that addressed one threat vector, it did not actually fix the underlying issue. In 2020 a second patch was released addressing another threat vector, although incompletely, that exploited the same underlying problem as the first vulnerability. In 2022 a third patch was needed to address the rest of the code problems not fully resolved with the second patch.[xi]

Practice Is Key

Assumptions can be dangerous, and the Active Defender knows as much. They realize that to solidly support the claim that a system is not vulnerable to a particular type of attack requires practicing some form of active testing, not just a passive scan. Remember that for the Active Defender, *security* is a verb and that excellence in security involves regularly practicing proactive behavior. Thus, for each control that is in place, they recognize not only that the phrase "trust but verify" is applicable, but that the verification must be of an active nature. An attack simulation is one option that takes this next step and allows the Active Defender to mimic attacks against particular vulnerabilities to gain access to an environment. Let's examine a specific, recent example.

In December 2021, a severe vulnerability was discovered in Apache Log4j, which is a widely used Java-based logging utility.[xii] However, because of the way Java apps are packaged, a simple file system search for Log4j was not sufficient. Thus, additional methods were needed to determine if a system was vulnerable. While some vulnerability scanners did create plug-ins to check for this flaw, they were often equally as inadequate. Because they typically don't check every input with a web application and may not use authenticated scans, some form of attack simulation was needed to further validate whether deployed code was at risk.

Tools like FullHunt's *log4j-scan* acted as a form of attack simulation that could be used to validate a particular website.[xiii] This tool initially sets up a DNS callback server and then, when given one or more URLs by the operator, could be used to send a benign payload that would trigger the flaw if it was present on the system, cause it to call back, and then report the URL as vulnerable. Unlike traditional vulnerability scanners, this tool requires regular human interaction with knowledge of the environment and what sites require testing, thus making it a more active test that provides superior detection compared with traditional passive scanners. The simulation could also be run after patching to verify whether the patch was successful.

Tools for Testing

Now that you understand what an attack simulation involves and why it's so important, we need to explore some of the available tools that the Active Defender could use for this purpose. While I'm sure there are many tools that have been created to do attack simulation, I've chosen just a few well-known free or paid options to discuss. I am not necessarily endorsing or recommending any of them in particular, but I thought I should at least provide some familiar examples.

Microsoft Defender for O365

Microsoft offers an attack simulation platform as part of its Microsoft Defender for O365.[xiv] Note that an organization is required to have a higher level of licensing to have access to this feature. The focus of this tool is testing multiple social engineering techniques used regularly by attackers, including credential harvesting, malware attachments, links in attachments, links to malware, drive-by-url, and OAuth consent grant.

Credential Harvesting

This technique involves an email that contains a URL being sent to a recipient. When the recipient clicks the URL, they are redirected to a page asking them to log in with their credentials. The URL often mimics a well-known website that may seem more trustworthy, such as Microsoft, PayPal, or Facebook.

Malware Attachments

This technique entails an email sent to the recipient containing an attachment that runs some arbitrary code, such as a macro. In the real world, this code might infect their system or provide a mechanism for persistence.

Links in Attachments

Using this technique is another version of credential harvesting in which the recipient is sent an email with an attachment that contains a link. When they click the link, they are taken to a page where they are prompted to log in with their credentials. Typically, the URL mimics a well-known website which may seem more trustworthy, such as Microsoft, PayPal, or Facebook.

Links to Malware

This technique involves sending to a recipient an email that contains a link to an attachment on a file sharing site such as SharePoint Online, Dropbox, or Google Drive. When the recipient clicks the link, the attachment opens, causing arbitrary code, such as a macro, to run on their machine. In the real world, this code might infect their system or provide a mechanism for persistence.

Drive-by-URL

Using this technique, a recipient is sent a message containing a URL. When they click the URL, they're taken to a website that runs code in the background in the browser. This background code may attempt to collect information about the recipient or deploy additional arbitrary code to infect the system or provide a mechanism for persistence.

OAuth Consent Grant

In this technique, a malicious Azure application is created with the goal of gaining access to data. The recipient receives an email that contains a URL from the application. When they click the URL, a request for consent tied to the application asks for access to the user's data. Assuming the recipient accepts the consent, access is then granted via the application to that data.

Atomic Red Team

Red Canary offers a free, open-source library of tests called Atomic Red Team that can be used for attack simulation.[xv] Using these simple, focused tests, an organization can examine how the security controls it has in place perform in the face of specific adversarial techniques. For example, they can be run to validate visibility or prevent an attack. In other words, they can help verify whether the proper detections are triggered when a specific technique is used against the environment or whether the technique was prevented from succeeding altogether. By simulating an attack, these tests can also help a security team understand where there might be gaps in their operational security processes. In addition, they can even be used as a mechanism for comparing multiple security products or validating the claims that the vendors make.

Each available test is tied to the MITRE ATT&CK matrix and takes no longer than five minutes to execute. Many of these tests even come complete with an easy-to-use configuration and commands to clean up the test after it is performed. For each technique, there are often multiple tests, each tied to a particular procedure that can be used to achieve the goal. For example, under the technique of *OS Credential Dumping: LSASS Memory*, there are 12 different tests that simulate different ways an attacker could perform this technique, such as using either ProcDump, Mimikatz, or Windows Task Manager to dump memory. While not all MITRE ATT&CK techniques are covered for every platform, the community is continuously developing additional tests. Platforms include Windows, MacOS, Linux, Google Workspace, Azure AD, Office 365, IaaS (Infrastructure as a Service), SaaS (Software as a Service), and containers.

Caldera

Caldera is a free, open-source security framework that can be used for either simulation or emulation exercises, but here we will focus on how it can perform simulation. The Caldera server itself is a command-and-control point for agents deployed to the targets to be tested. Agents are available for Microsoft Windows, macOS, or Linux hosts. Like Atomic Red Team, these agents can be used to test individual ATT&CK tactic/techniques, which they call abilities. You can also combine these abilities to create an adversary profile, which is used to mimic the activities of a particular threat actor.

Once you log into the Caldera interface, you must first create a network, which is effectively the group of hosts that you wish to test. You then add any hosts running the agent to this network that you want to be part of the test. Next, you create the adversary profile by selecting what techniques you want to run on the network. Finally, you create and run an operation based on the adversary profile that you created. You can specify under what type of user this set of tests will run (e.g., active user, system, or logon user), what parent process it should run under, and whether or not to automatically clean up any artifacts the test created once it is complete.

SCYTHE

SCYTHE is a paid modular malware platform that can be used for testing post-exploitation techniques, either through simulation or emulation. As with Caldera, we will focus on its simulation capabilities here. Within SCYTHE's interface, you can create your own security test, which they call a campaign. Within the campaign, you can select from several pre-built tests in SCYTHE's threat catalog or build a custom one. Using these options, you can safely emulate all kinds of malware, including ransomware, which can be deployed on-premises or in a cloud environment because it does not require an active connection to the Internet.

If you build a custom test, you can select from a variety of network connections for command-and-control purposes, load some individual modules, which tell that malware what it can do, and then select what actions you want executed. In addition to or instead of choosing these individual options for a custom test, you can select from individual existing Atomic Red Team tests that use MITRE ATT&CK techniques, which will automatically add the modules needed to test that particular technique. Once you have either built a fully custom campaign or selected built-in options for one, the next steps involve downloading the malware in a format (e.g., EXE, DLL, x86, AMD64, etc.) and executing it on the system of your choice.

Summary

Thinking like a hacker while implementing defense involves focusing more on understanding what an attacker could do with what is readily available rather than checklists of steps to secure an environment. As a result, it requires turning some traditional defensive ideas on their heads. Instead of just worrying about hiding sensitive information with OPSEC, the Active Defender also considers the additional implications of OSINT and proactively seeks out what could be used against them. Furthermore, they recognize that threat modeling needs to be a continuous process involving the examination of the technical and nontechnical security controls from the perspective of an offensive security professional in order to capture how they might bypass each one. For example, the use of LOLBins makes it much easier to circumvent many built-in security controls. It is only with this information in mind that the Active Defender can truly understand and defend against threats to their environment.

Beyond this new mode of thinking about traditional strategies, there are also some proactive activities that the Active Defender should perform whenever possible and these, too, can be influenced by the hacker mindset. Threat hunting can provide great insights into the gaps left behind by our automated tools and with the hacker mentality provide a better understanding both of what these gaps might be and why they exist. Attack simulations further allow us to verify whether existing protections and detections we have in place work as designed and help give us insight into what we might need to change to be better protected.

Becoming an Active Defender, however, is not the end of their journey in security. Really, in some ways, this step just the beginning. Once someone reaches a point where they feel comfortable in the Active Defender role, there are additional steps they can take to become more advanced. It is to this subject that we will turn next in Chapter 6, "Becoming an Advanced Active Defender."

Notes

i. J. Grey, *Practical Social Engineering*. No Starch Press, 2022. p. 35.

ii. Ibid. p. 68.

iii. `www.crunchbase.com`

iv. `www.kali.org/tools/recon-ng` and `www.kali.org/tools/theharvester`

v. J. Grey. *Practical Social Engineering*. No Starch Press, 2022. pp. 141–142.

vi. `https://github.com/LOLBAS-Project/LOLBAS/blob/master/README.md`

vii. Neil Wyler, "Heads Up, Hands On II." Aug 2020. Microsoft PowerPoint presentation.

viii. Ibid.

ix. Ibid.

x. Ibid.

xi. `www.theregister.com/2022/04/13/apache_struts_bug_new_patch`

xii. `https://logging.apache.org/log4j/2.x/security.html`

xiii. `https://github.com/fullhunt/log4j-scan`

xiv. `https://learn.microsoft.com/en-us/microsoft-365/security/office-365-security/attack-simulation-training-get-started?view=o365-worldwide`

xv. `https://atomicredteam.io`

Becoming an Advanced Active Defender

Building a hacker mindset through immersion in the offensive security community takes time but, as you've seen, can be extremely valuable. As you make progress as an Active Defender, you likely will get to a point where, despite the knowledge you've gained and the mindset you've been cultivating, you may want to evolve to another, deeper level. That next level I am calling the Advanced Active Defender.

The Advanced Active Defender

The Advanced Active Defender is someone who is not only actively fostering the hacker mindset but is also capable of performing more advanced testing practices in part because they have a grasp on both the procedures and intentions held by offensive security professionals and attackers alike. They also know how to work with deceptive technology and often engage directly with offensive security teams in various ways to improve their own organization's security posture. Furthermore, they've taken steps to understand enough about the business and its people, processes, and policies to critically consider and appreciate the implications of a security incident in that environment. They also understand the benefits of potentially bringing in an external offensive security team for the right reasons. In addition, they know how to effectively work with offensive security practitioners. As a result, they can help educate management on how to select and scope an engagement to make the best of the time and resources available.

Automated Attack Emulations

Remember from our discussion in the previous chapter that attack emulation involves actually performing an attack the way an adversary would with their specific intentions in mind. Because the Advanced Active Defender's hacker mindset is further along in its development than the Active Defender's, they have the mental capacity to perform certain types of attack emulation within their organizations. By the time someone has reached this more advanced stage, they have a much stronger understanding of the intentions and procedures used by offensive security professionals and attackers alike. With this knowledge, the Advanced Active Defender should be able to learn how to build more specialized emulation tests using automated tools.

Some of the tools that we discussed in Chapter 5, "Implementing Defense While Thinking Like a Hacker," have the technical capabilities to perform either simulation via specific individual tests or emulation by chaining together a collection of tests. For example, we've seen that SCYTHE can be used to connect either a variety of Atomic Red Team tests or custom ones together. With Caldera, you can build an adversary profile to create a particular attack. However, what truly makes these collections into an attack emulation is not the particular set of tests being performed but having an operator who understands how to group the tests together in a way that a real adversary would approach their end goal. In other words, they know enough about the potential procedures used by an adversary to know what might make the most sense in their environment, not just the tactics or techniques. Therefore, it's the use of these tools specifically by an Advanced Active Defender that truly makes them attack emulations.

It is important to note, however, that while using a variety of tools to validate existing detections and/or create new ones is a critical step to proactively protect your environment, building effective detections can be quite challenging. We'll discuss this topic further in Chapter 7, "Building Effective Detections."

Using Deceptive Technologies

As we discussed briefly in Chapter 1, "What Is an Active Defender?" the goal of cyber deception is to make an attack more time-consuming to the threat actor, ideally to give the defender enough time to detect and evict them. However, more specifically, cyber deception involves augmenting existing security programs by using certain technologies to deceive attackers by placing decoys across an organization's infrastructure that imitate legitimate assets. The overall objective of these decoys is to detect malicious activity within internal networks that other types of tools may miss due to limited visibility. The more of these decoys that are deployed, the more likely an organization is to spot this dangerous activity early. If enough forethought is put into positioning them, ideally you will lead an adversary right to the deception techniques that have been employed.

The vast majority of the deceptive technologies that I will cover in the following sections do not require an organization to have a particularly advanced security maturity. In other words, even if they don't have some of the fundamental security settings or processes in place, deception can still be extremely valuable. With even some really basic logging and alert capabilities, many of these tools can be easily implemented and provide some great visibility into a network. I have postponed the detailed discussion of deception technologies until describing the Advanced Active Defender only because by now the reader should have a deeper understanding about why these tools are so effective.

Keep in mind that while these technologies are technically passive, like many of the ones previously discussed, they offer proactive insights that the Advanced Active Defender can use in an active defense capacity. Let's examine some examples to see how.

Honey Tokens

Honey tokens are a way to identify attackers within a network by helping to reveal critical information about who they are and the methods they use to exploit a system. There are a wide variety of honey token types, such as accounts, email addresses, database data, files, URLs, API keys, and other resources that are monitored for access. Each is deployed in a different way and can reveal some key information about the attacker and their attempt at penetrating a system. Ideally, as a result, defenders are notified when there's been a breach of the perimeter and the attacker is about to interact with these decoy assets. From the offensive security perspective, it's a land mine that cannot be detected. A common saying is that defenders have to be right 100 percent of the time to prevent attacks, whereas attackers only have to be right once to gain access. However, with this technology in place, that perspective changes. Instead, attackers only have to be wrong once to be found, followed, and ejected.

Decoy Accounts

A decoy user account is one form of a honey token. For example, fake Active Directory (AD) accounts can be created to prevent attacks such as Kerberoasting. This post-exploitation attack involves the offline, usually brute-force cracking of the password of a service account. Utilizing a user account with a service principle name (SPN), which is what ties a username to a service in AD, the attacker sends a request to access a service. What is returned is a ticket that contains a hashed password. Once the password is cracked, the attacker has the credentials to impersonate the owner of the account in question and obtain access to just about anything else on the network.

One fairly simple way to detect this type of attack is to create a decoy user account with an SPN that masquerades as a real one. The account should be one that is never actually used but mimics the format and feel of the real ones. An alert should be set up to trigger anytime this account is accessed, which is a dead giveaway that an adversary is attempting this form of attack and that the defender needs to take immediate action. Keep in mind that this action should not be to immediately shut down the attacker but to start collecting the relevant telemetry, monitor the attacker to find all of their C2 instances, and *then* shut them down. Otherwise, you risk the adversary just finding other ways to engage in post-exploitation compromise.

Generating a handful of fake standard AD user accounts that are not used by anyone can also be useful for attacks. If alerts are generated anytime someone attempts to authenticate with these accounts, then they can be used to detect techniques such as password spraying. Password spraying involves using some common passwords and trying them against multiple accounts. Adversaries will typically dump a list of accounts from an environment, which will include these decoys, and attempt this technique against them all.

Decoy accounts can be equally as useful in other operating systems. For example, on Linux/Unix, you can create an important looking fake account with a simple password in the /etc/shadow file. Attackers can grab this hash, crack it offline, and then use the results to attempt to access other resources. Set up an alert for anytime this account is used, and when it triggers, you have a reliable way to know you have an intruder in your network.

Email Addresses

A fake email address is a simple honey token that can be used for detecting attackers that have breached the perimeter. The idea here is to create a fake email address that is not actually being used within the organization and leave it inactive. If the account starts to receive phishing or spam messages, assuming the directory of email addresses is private, it is likely that an internal email or web server has been inappropriately accessed.

Database Data

Fake database data can also be used as a honey token; it can be either fabricated records with names created to look enticing to attackers within a fake database or fake data within an existing, legitimate database. If an attacker is able to access and retrieve this data, they will be stealing the honey token as well. If the attacker posts the data somewhere such that the organization is notified, the defender will have insights into how they got inside the network. Their methodologies might include a misconfiguration, other vulnerability, or possibly an issue with an administrative process.

AWS Keys

Amazon Web Services (AWS) keys are used to control access to specific areas within the cloud infrastructure. Placing fake AWS keys in strategic locations such as within text files, on desktops, or inside GitHub repositories can be particularly useful as honey tokens. With a real high-value key, such as that of an administrator, attackers can obtain access to sabotage portions of the network or reroute digital assets to their own systems. Even obtaining something with lower access could still allow them to steal other information, escalate privileges, or attack other portions of the network. Thus, offering up something to an attacker that appears to provide any kind of access can be extremely enticing. When they attempt to use the key, all activity is logged. Not only do the logs provide information to the defender, but they also allow them to monitor who is using the key and how they're being used without being detected. However, be aware that in practice, this form of deception will likely create a ton of noise, even within a private repository. Furthermore, it might interfere with bug bounty programs.

Canary Tokens

A canary token is a free type of honey token that provides a way to put a tracer into a variety of file types including, but not limited to, documents, websites, and folders to detect lateral movement or data collection. Creating a document called something like `passwords.docx` and leaving it around where it can be discovered can be very appealing to an attacker and yet provide an alert to the defender when the file is opened. URL tokens can be generated that detect when a particular website is accessed as well. These can be useful in situations where an attacker has screen scraped a logon page to use for their own nefarious purposes.

Honeypots

Honeypots are devices that mimic systems such as regular servers or user systems that host services that might be of interest to an attacker. Typically, they are located inside some portion of the network perimeter to detect post-exploitation activity, but external-facing honeypots are often used by research organizations to get a feel for what kind of exploits or other attacks are being used. Here, we will focus on internal honeypots.

These devices are not actually used for any real purpose except to entice attackers to explore them further. For example, having a honeypot that looks like a file server or a backup server running RDP on an isolated network along with some legitimate servers can be extremely attractive to an attacker. The idea here is to monitor these honeypot devices to see who might be trying to access them and what they are trying to accomplish. Alerts can be set up to trigger if anyone tries to access these systems, which creates an early warning to defenders that an attacker has gotten into the network. For an additional visibility, canary token files can also be placed on the legitimate servers to detect lateral movement.

Other Forms of Deception

As you've seen, honey tokens and honeypots typically are meant to deceive attackers once they've gotten past perimeter defenses and onto the network. However, there are some other deceptive measures that can be employed that can interrupt and potentially slow down an adversary even before they reach that point. As you know from the overview of an offensive security engagement described in Chapter 3, "Offensive Security Engagements, Trainings, and Gathering Intel," the targeting stage involves information gathering about the environment. But what happens when the information being gathered is wrong because the defensive team intentionally set it up to be misleading or inaccurate? Each of these next examples of deception technology illustrates exactly this kind of technique and how it can interrupt or slow down an adversary, whether the activity involves legitimate tests from offensive security professionals or attacks from criminals.

Web Server Header

One way to deceive potential attackers is to alter the header that is returned by a web server when it is being connecting to. By default, this header, also known as a banner, returns some standard information about what software the web server is running. In some cases, it might just return a simple string such as "Apache," but in other instances it might reveal both the name of the software and the version it is running, such as "Apache/2.4.54 (Unix)" or "Microsoft-IIS/10.0." In addition, this header can return information about additional software running on the server, such as the version of SSL or .NET that is installed.

Clearly, whether an offensive security professional or attacker, obtaining this information could be very useful in the targeting phase. However, as a deception tactic, the headers can be altered to either hide this information or return incorrect information, such as IIS and version information for a server that is actually running Apache. Attackers and some offensive security practitioners often rely on automated web scanning tools in order to determine what version and software type is being used and adjust their next steps based on the results. Obfuscating the header will likely just send them to start looking elsewhere for this information, which does cost them time, but the use of deception may also cause them to deploy the wrong scripts multiple times. Thus, there is a greater possibility of an attack or test being detected.[i] It is important to note, though, that this change can also cause issues with internal vulnerability scanners, so be aware of that side effect.

User Agent Strings

Specifying which user-agent strings are allowed to request information from a web server is another form of deception that can be useful. The user-agent string identifies the browser, its version, and the operating system on which it is running and that is requesting content from the server. For example, an agent-string might look like this:

Mozilla/5.0 (Windows NT 10.0; Win64; x64)
AppleWebKit/537.36 (KHTML, like Gecko)
Chrome/107.0.0.0 Safari/537.36

Websites can then use this information to determine which content will be returned, such as a full or mobile version of a site or perhaps an error if the browser is not compatible with the site in question.

However, this feature can also be used against the server in question. When targeting an environment, one approach the offensive security professional can take is to manipulate the user-agent string in order to find vulnerabilities that are only available to certain user agents. They can also use it to disguise requests to make them look like they're coming from a particular browser instead of some kind of script being used for testing. Attackers, of course, have the same capabilities and use them to their advantage whenever possible.[ii]

Fortunately, most web servers also have the capability to deny or allow specific user-agent strings requesting content from them, and the defender can use this feature to their advantage. Some web testing tools, such as Acunetix, put the name of the tool into the user-agent string, making it particularly easy to block requests from them if desired. In addition, some threat intelligence reports and feeds include lists of known user-agent strings used by attackers that can be used to automate some blocking.

Fake DNS Records

Another deceptive measure that can be effective involves a number of nonexistent DNS records. Offensive security professionals, and likewise attackers, typically spend time scanning and enumerating systems as part of the information gathering process during the targeting phase. Creating a large number of DNS records that point to IP addresses not in use causes the number of possible targets that need to be scanned and investigated to increase substantially. As a result, the enumeration process slows down. Note that these systems should only exist in the organization's DNS server. To make this form of deception successful, monitoring must be set up to detect any DNS requests that come in for these systems and either log and alert on or block the requests. While a few users who attempt a zone transfer or a reverse lookup may also trigger this behavior, most normal users will not, which should limit the activity this deception generates.[iii]

Working with Offensive Security Teams

At some point, the need for adversarial testing may either exceed the capabilities of the Advanced Active Defender or be required for compliance purposes. Another possibility is that someone in leadership has decided that they need to bring in some form of offensive security team. This decision may come because they have attended a conference, read some security literature, or been instructed by another member of leadership. It is not uncommon for executives in an organization to be convinced by a third party that they need a "pen test" or that they should hire someone to complete a full adversarial emulation engagement. Offensive security testing is also sometimes required to maintain a compliance certification, such as the PCI-DSS standard, which requires a penetration test twice a year. Some larger organizations even have their own offensive security teams that can perform full adversary emulation. However, given their knowledge of offensive security, the Advanced Active Defender can still be of immense assistance by being directly involved with any discussions about who should be brought in and what types of testing should be performed.

Whether bringing in an external offensive security team or just working with one internal to an organization can be an extremely beneficial endeavor. However, it requires some careful considerations, including both defense and offense having the proper attitude, selecting the right team to hire, and scoping the engagement properly to be effective. Let's explore some of these issues now.

But We Need a PenTest!

One of the most common problems with deciding to bring in an offensive security team, or even utilizing an internal one, is both understanding what the organization hopes to gain from an engagement and communicating this information to the team doing the testing. While the two main types of offensive security engagement have been mentioned, pen testing and full adversarial emulation, there are variations on these tests. These include transparent or opaque, which were discussed in Chapter 5, as well as internal or external. In addition, there are other types of tests, such as vulnerability assessments and purple teaming. Offensive security teams can even assist with automated threat simulations or emulations in cases where there may not be an Active Defender available to perform them.

Unfortunately, there is significant disagreement by offensive security vendors and practitioners over what each of these types of tests entail. What one organization may refer to as a pen test may be considered a vulnerability assessment to another. As a result, those requesting testing may ask for one kind and get something other than what they are expecting. Therefore, just knowing the name of what you think you want is not sufficient enough to be successful in this quest for assistance.

Renowned offensive security professional Joe Vest suggests focusing on what is being mitigated. For example, he views vulnerability assessments as testing that can identify flaws and when these flaws are mitigated, the assessments then become an effort in attack surface reduction. Penetration testing, he indicates, is a type of testing that is designed to identify the relationships between flaws, otherwise known as attack paths. Thus, once mitigations are put in place, pen testing also becomes about attack surface reduction. Threat-based testing, which he notes falls under multiple categories such as red team testing, adversarial emulation testing, and purple team testing, is scenario-based threat testing that assumes that a breach has occurred and emulates how an adversary would move through your network. Mitigations that address this kind of testing are about detection and response capabilities rather than prevention. That said, trying to define the exact nature of the tests may not be worthwhile. As Vest recommends, "Don't get into a definition battle." Instead, he contends that it makes more sense to discuss and understand the problem(s) being addressed, determine what the goal(s) of the testing are, and then map them back to the terms if necessary.[iv]

Potential Testing Outcomes

Organizations often have no idea what kind of test(s) they want done or what the possible goals of offensive security testing could be. However, it is really important to understand that the purpose of this form of testing should never be solely to determine if the offensive security team can gain some form of unauthorized access. The answer to that question will almost always be yes, making it less valuable.

While that perspective may seem disheartening, it overlooks a number of important ideas. First, just because someone obtains unauthorized access does not mean that it's game over for defense. It discounts the intent of an attacker who may be looking for something specific that requires a particular path in to get to it. Second, relying entirely on prevention is simply not a realistic goal. A good security program, even a minimal one, should prevent what it can as well as detect and respond to what was not prevented whenever possible.

With that in mind, we can return to a discussion of what the realistic objectives of an offensive security test might be, without using any of the terminology that adds to the confusion (e.g., vulnerability assessment, pen testing, red teaming, purple teaming). Instead, I'll just provide some of the outcomes that an engagement could provide, which effectively help identify the problem(s) the organization is trying to solve. By having this knowledge, the Advanced Active Defender can be extremely helpful in determining what might make sense to request. Let's examine some of the things that can be discovered by working with an offensive security team.

Vulnerability Identification

One area where offensive security teams can help is identifying security vulnerabilities. For example, they can help determine whether there are vulnerabilities on internal user workstations or servers that allow access from the Internet. These tests can be performed from either inside or outside the organization. Furthermore, scans can be either authenticated or unauthenticated. While there is a fair amount of nuance in terms of what and how the scanning is conducted, obtaining this outcome requires very little in terms of interaction with the organization and does not involve anything particularly complex on the part of the company who is hiring the team.

Vulnerability Exploitation

Another possible outcome that could be identified is whether or not, given a list of vulnerabilities an organization may have, any of them can be exploited. This particular outcome validates whether any of the vulnerabilities provided are truly problematic for the organization and what level of risk is involved as well as the efficacy of any compensating controls. As part of this outcome, the paths that attackers could take to abuse these weaknesses could also be potentially uncovered. Interaction at this level is a bit higher, since it includes a demonstration of impact, but complexity is still fairly minimal.

Targeted Detection/Response

Offensive security teams can also help an organization establish its existing level of ability to detect and respond to a particular type of attack, such as phishing, credential dumping, or a specific form of ransomware or other malware that may include lateral movement or data exfiltration. Obtaining this outcome is certainly more complex and does require more interaction with the organization.

Real Threat Actor

One of the most complicated outcomes that an offensive security team can offer is to help an organization understand its current abilities to detect a real threat actor that is actively trying to bypass existing security controls and evade detections in place. This objective is significantly more complex than any of the others and involves a higher level of engagement with the organization because there is likely to be operational impact. By operational impact here, I mean that defenders will ideally be actively engaged in responding to and attempting to prevent any attacks from being successful.

Detection Analysis

One additional outcome that can arise from an offensive security operation involves helping an organization both to determine whether their detection strategies are functioning as expected and find any gaps they might have in responding to alerts or other detection mechanisms. This objective is perhaps the most involved because it requires a collaborative engagement between defenders and offensive security professionals directly working together to improve security posture.

Scope

Not only does an organization need to select a type of outcome they'd like to test, but they also need to determine exactly which applications, users, networks, devices, accounts, and other assets should be tested to achieve the organization's objectives. Identifying vulnerabilities for an organization is a pretty wide-ranging goal. Therefore, it is important to identify if there are particular systems or network segments, for example, that should become the focus of this test or whether the hunt for vulnerabilities should be performed from the outside or the inside of the organization. Collectively, this information is known as the scope of the engagement. In addition to the scope, there are rules of engagement which are also required. These rules outline what type of actions are allowed by the offensive security professionals during the engagement. For example, it is important to know whether something like social engineering or brute forcing of passwords will be allowed.

Defining both the scope and the rules of engagement correctly in advance are critical to the success of the operation. Regardless of the specific objectives of the test(s), the underlying purpose in having testing done is to learn something about the environment that subsequently drives action to create improvement. If the scope of the engagement is so narrow that the organization learns nothing or so broad such that no real action can be taken, then any testing is a wasted effort. Thus, hopefully it is obvious that the answer to the question "What do you want to test?" should never be something vague like "I want to see whether our organization is vulnerable." Furthermore, the rules of engagement need to be discussed in detail and agreed upon before an engagement begins so that all parties are on the same page. Otherwise, the engagement runs the risk of either not fulfilling the required goal(s) or adversely impacting operations.

Scoping Challenges

Unfortunately, scope is an area that is easy to get wrong. Fear of what may be uncovered can cause an organization to select a scope that is too narrow. In addition, not recognizing the relationships between the system/application selected for testing and any dependencies may result in a scope that is too limited. Starting with too small a budget can result in the same problem, because it may not provide an appropriate length of time for testing. Not understanding what types of objectives are possible or the general underlying goal of testing can lead to too wide a scope. Too wide a scope can lead to excessive cost and potentially have a disproportionate impact on operations. In addition, scope can often be impacted by outside factors that can cause limitations. Be aware of operational issues such as known problematic infrastructure or any potential for fines over service-level agreement (SLA) violations that can also lead to scope limitations. Furthermore, contractual obligations around data access by third parties can be another challenge. Tests need to be scoped narrowly enough that they focus on systems or infrastructure of interest and use the most appropriate type of testing so that the owners of those specific systems can use the information to improve their security most effectively.

Additional Scope Considerations

Some other specific considerations for defining the scope of an engagement include an understanding of whether the systems are on premises or in the cloud, the existing security controls in place, existing known gaps in these controls, network and system configurations, the tolerance for these systems to be attacked, the sophistication needed to compromise these systems, and the overall security landscape of the organization. In particular, some cloud providers require special authorization to test while others will not allow it at all. Defining what types of systems are being tested tells the vendor, in part, what kind of experience is needed on their team for the testing. Having knowledge of existing security controls and the gaps in coverage can provide a sense of where testing should or could take place. Understanding the tolerance level and sophistication of attack necessary to compromise particular systems can play into preventing significant operational issues as well as creating the right type of tests needed to accomplish the goal(s) in question.

Building an accurate scope and developing a solid set of rules of engagement requires strong communication on both sides from the very beginning. Working with a vendor who is both knowledgeable and reputable to help guide this discussion is crucial. In addition, the Advanced Active Defender, who understands the goals of this additional testing as well as the challenges of the organization, is in the perfect position to be part of these discussions along with the other decision makers.

Decisions, Decisions

So how should an organization decide what outcome(s) might be useful to pursue? While most organizations may want to know the answers to the questions that each of these outcomes provides, they are often not in a position to select more than one at a time. The answer to where to start will depend on a number of factors. Some of these considerations involve the security maturity of the company, including staffing levels available for an engagement, existing security processes, and existing security architecture as well as leadership support for taking these steps, which often is tied to the funding allocation for the engagement.

Measuring Existing Defenses

Keeping those points in mind, one way to begin this process, according to Joe Vest, is to start with defenses that the org believes to be in place already. In other words, he believes that testing should be a measurement of what defenses are actually in place rather than what an organization believes should already be in place. Therefore, he recommends treating any claims of existing defenses as fact, and those facts are what should be tested to prove or disprove. For example, if a company claims that only privileged users have access to a particular server or chunk of data, test to see if that is really true. If it's not, it should be considered a gap and addressed. As a result, the assumptions in place get challenged and either validated or invalidated.[v]

Crown Jewels

Another way to begin is to consider what is fundamental to the business such that if removed or destroyed it could interrupt the revenue stream. It is critically important that both those making the request for testing and those asked to perform the tests understand what assets are vital to the existence of the organization. *Assets*, in this case, means anything owned by a business that is essential to business continuing, including but not limited to important data, intellectual property, physical objects, and network infrastructure.

The Advanced Active Defender can be particularly useful here, having enough knowledge of the business, its people, and its processes to contribute to the conversations about the identity of these assets, including some that perhaps others have not considered. For example, certain assets may not appear to be critical without recognizing their relationships to other ones. A great example of this would be the compromise of IT management software, such as SolarWinds, because it can interact with many other, essential systems. While an organization might easily survive if its management software became unavailable for a period of time, having numerous critical systems compromised as the result of attackers adding malicious code to an update of this software could be disastrous.

Selecting a Vendor

If selecting an external vendor for offensive security testing, there are numerous factors to consider beyond the obvious one, cost. For example, the reputation of the organization as well as its employees, their expertise and experience, the processes they use for testing, and how they handle company data are all instrumental pieces of information you should have before selecting a company to perform testing. Keep in mind that it's not feasible to cover all of the potential considerations here. However, because it is important that the Advanced Active Defender have at least some foundational knowledge, we will at least explore some of them now.

Reputation

One factor to consider is the reputation of the vendor in terms of both the organization and the people it employs. The company should be well-known within the information security space and have a good reputation for producing thorough results through ethical means that are communicated in a straightforward way. A good vendor will not simply try to sell you a particular type of test or upsell you something you do not need. Its employees should be equally as well respected in the security community, even if they're not individually well-known.

A reputable vendor should offer up front to discuss what goals the organization is trying to achieve by having this test completed, even if you request a test by name (e.g., pen test) because that is what the compliance documentation indicates is required. Consider, too, whether testing is based on an hourly rate or via a flat rate for a particular service. Pay attention to how the vendor communicates with you during those conversations. They should be regularly asking questions about your environment and share information about their processes. Do not forget that you can ask vendors for references, ideally from other organizations in the same industry.

Experience and Expertise

Consider the level of ability and background of the employees who will be performing the testing. Some points to ask about should include things like years of experience, industry certifications, the ability to hold a security clearance (where needed), and what additional training they do regularly to keep their skills current. In addition, it can be useful to find out whether their testers perform high-quality research through open-source contributions, published blogs, conference presentations, or techniques released.

Inquire if the vendor has any employees that specialize in obtaining the kind of outcomes your organization hopes to procure. For example, if you want information about both on-premises and cloud assets, you will need a company that has people who specialize in each or both types of environments. This question is especially important if you are asking for specific testing on an unusual system. Furthermore, find out if they have expertise doing testing in your particular industry. Testing for a bank will be very different than testing for a higher education institution.

It is also important to understand how employees are vetted and brought on board. Some vendors hire offensive security professionals as permanent, full-time employees. Others use contract employees that they only bring in as needed. As a result, the dynamics of a team can vary greatly. If it's a company that brings in contract employees, ask if they were vetted to the same standards as any internal ones and find out what those standards are. It may also be necessary to know where these individuals are physically located.

Processes

Ask about the processes involved for the kinds of outcomes being discussed. They should have some set of standard processes that they regularly use. For example, one standard they could reference is something called the Penetration Testing Execution Standard (PTES). This standard contains seven main sections: pre-engagement interactions, intelligence gathering, threat modeling, vulnerability analysis, exploitation, post-exploitation, and reporting. Each section defines the activities related to the topic being discussed. NIST also offers a standard called the NIST Special Publication 800-115, which provides the key elements of security testing, including methodologies.

By having detailed discussions of what a company wants tested and why the request is being made, the vendor should be able to articulate the processes they typically use to answer the questions asked. Additionally, find out whether they only use automated tools or whether they use manual testing methodologies as well. Some vendors will start with automated tools and then move to manual testing later. Automated tools may be appropriate for the particular questions your organization is trying to answer, but they have limitations and can potentially miss key areas if used in the wrong ways or for the wrong reasons. That said, because pure manual testing does not scale particularly well, most high-quality tests will involve a combination of manual and automated tests.

Data Security

Every test will result in information that an organization would like to keep from becoming public. Therefore, it's important to ask questions about what controls are in place to secure any data obtained through the test. While a reputable company will not disclose any customer information, nondisclosure agreements (NDAs) are common and can provide some additional reassurance in writing. Be sure to ask the vendor whether they carry some form of liability insurance.

Adversarial Attitudes

Regardless of the specific reasons for bringing in an offensive security team, it is extremely important that the relationship between the offensive and defensive teams do not start as nor become adversarial. As we saw in the introduction, traditional defenders often view engagements with offensive security professionals as another form of audit, thereby automatically setting up an antagonistic situation.

When selecting a vendor, it is crucial that the incoming team views themselves as contributing to the overall security posture of an organization rather than pursuing a goal of making the defensive team look bad or trying to prove some kind of point. There must be an immediate sense and underlying tone from these incoming testers that they want to collaborate and work alongside those defenders within the organization to ensure the testers are only ones who can find something rather than real attackers.

Ideally, having an Advanced Active Defender involved in these discussions from the beginning can help facilitate more positive attitudes going into the engagement. Not only can they advocate to bring in a positive collaborative vendor, they can explain to their fellow defenders that the purpose of the engagement has nothing to do with calling out or blaming defensive teams for mistakes or gaps in security. They can also take time to explain the benefits of bringing the offensive security team into the environment.

Results

One critical piece of information that should be obtained up front is what the organization expects to gain from the vendor when the testing is complete. The answer to this question should never just be "a report" but something more nuanced, explaining both what gaps exist in what was tested and actionable information to move forward. For example, references should be included for issues that are more complex to address as well as potential detection information where possible. Furthermore, any reports should explain not only what was accomplished but why it matters in the context of the organization and not just from a technical perspective.

The report must not only be well written, but whoever is writing it must consider who will be consuming the results of the test(s), what they care about, and how the results will be used. It should be created in such a way that it can help executives build confidence in their people, not criticize them. To that end, it should always include evidence of effectiveness of current defense mechanisms and detection methodologies, not just what weaknesses were discovered. If the scope is accurate and the right type of testing is selected, the offensive security professional will more easily be able to articulate the potential risk/impact of their findings and write a more useful and actionable report. Ultimately, it must provide a solid reference point for action moving forward.

Additional Considerations

Vendors that offer offensive security testing vary widely and include companies that perform a variety of auditing and consulting services beyond just security. For example, KPMG and Deloitte are both global, well-known, massive auditing firms that offer a broad range of services, including a business unit that provides offensive security testing. In comparison, companies like TrustedSec and Black Hills Information Security are smaller but exclusively security-focused. There are advantages and disadvantages to each, but it is important to have a feel for what kind of organization you are considering to even take those into account.

One of the most frustrating things that an offensive security team runs into with an engagement is when the organization that hires them is not prepared when the time comes. Most engagements require certain provisions to be in place before they begin. For example, IP addresses may need to be whitelisted, specific account credentials may need to be created, or a list of URLs may need to be provided for staging purposes. However, when these steps are not completed in advance, it cuts into the sometimes very tight time frame that has been allocated for testing.

Another important point about preparation is that organizations need to plan ahead when they will need to work with an offensive security team. Most established well-respected vendors have a lead time of a minimum of 60 days or more to schedule testing. Waiting until the last minute likely means they will be unable to schedule testing. In particular, the last quarter of the year is the worst time to make a request.

Finally, be sure to set expectations for your operational and defensive teams in terms of what to expect when testing takes place. Some forms of testing are meant to be stealthy, while others are not. If the defensive team detects testing that is meant to be stealthy, that can be significantly more important than if it is not. However, if the testing is not meant to be stealthy and the defensive team does not detect it at all, that could be equally problematic.

Purple Teaming – Collaborative Testing

The last topic we will cover in terms of working with offensive security teams is that of purple teaming. While I have avoided the using the *red team/blue team* terminology throughout this book because of the disagreement on what those words mean and the confusion they could generate, I will use the *purple team* nomenclature. However, I will provide a specific description to further clarify my usage.

Purple teaming is named after the idea of red (offense) and blue (defense) working together (red + blue = purple). It involves performing collaborative testing exercises in which defenders and offensive security professionals work closely together to achieve one or more goals, such as discovering and fixing gaps in detection capabilities, improving resiliency, and also providing a unique opportunity to train defenders by explaining and repeating attack activities as well as implementing new detections and/or preventions where appropriate. In addition, it fosters a collaborative culture within the security team. Let's take a look at what a purple team is and what an engagement might entail.

What Is a Purple Team?

A purple team is one that comprises people with a wide variety of information security skill sets. For example, a variety of defenders will likely be included, such as, but not limited to, people working in a security operations center (SOC), people who do threat hunting, people in the digital forensics and incident response (DFIR) field, and/or even those working for a managed security service provider (MSSP). Naturally, it also includes a team of offensive security professionals who are in charge of emulating adversaries and their TTPs. In addition, it may include cyber threat intelligence (CTI) teams who research and provide adversary TTPs. The mixture of people involved will depend greatly on the organization and the goals of the engagement. The engagement is managed by an Exercise Coordinator, who is the lead point of contact throughout the exercise. They are responsible for not only ensuring that all of the preparatory steps necessary for the operation to occur are completed in advance but also for providing the lessons learned document at the end. Together, they practice their specific specialties as part of a larger engagement to achieve one of the goals previously mentioned.

Purple Team Exercises

Purple team engagements bring all of the members of a purple team together to improve security in an organization. While there are a number of ways that purple team exercises could be performed, what I will describe here is based on the Purple Team Exercise Framework, created by the team at SCYTHE.[vi] While there are other security frameworks that could be followed for this purpose, it is one of the few specifically dedicated to purple teaming.

Usually, these engagements begin with the assumption that a successful initial attack from outside the organization has already happened. In other words, the scenario that teams begin includes the idea that a breach has occurred. Because initial access represents only a single point in time and a determined attacker is often able to achieve their goal given enough time, focusing on post-compromise detection and response capabilities typically provides a better return on investment in the end. Furthermore, it can take a significant amount of time, energy, and effort to test scenarios involving initial access attacks. Therefore, it makes more sense to spend time to test what happens after an attacker gets in rather than prevention. Focusing on detection and response better prepares organizations to handle real-world attacks.

A purple team engagement typically involves a full, transparent, hands-on assessment that has four steps: cyber threat intelligence, preparation, exercise execution, and lessons learned, which will be briefly described in the following sections.

Cyber Threat Intelligence

The cyber threat intelligence (CTI) step begins with the CTI team, which could be in-house or a third party, identifying an adversary that has the opportunity, intent, and capability to attack the organization. In other words, the adversary selected should utilize methods, tradecraft, and TTPs that are most likely to impact the organization doing the testing, those known to target the organization or their vertical. That adversary's TTPs will be extracted by the CTI team, specifically focused on the procedures, and relayed to the offensive security team participating in the exercise. The CTI team should also provide information about the tooling and host artifacts, such as registry keys or files, expected and used by the adversary being emulated.

Preparation

Once those core decisions are made, then the preparation step begins. This step includes multiple meetings, starting with one in which concepts of purple teaming are introduced and the goals and objectives are provided as well as a statement of value meant to help convince participants of the benefit of these exercises. Next, a meeting covering all the requirements outlined by the CTI group should occur to assign any action items to participants. In addition to these overall meetings, technical preparation and logistical preparations will need to be completed. The final meeting should ensure that all the preparation steps were completed and everything is ready to proceed.

Exercise Execution

On the day the exercise begins, first start with introductions if necessary. The Exercise Coordinator or the CTI team will begin the actual exercise by presenting information about the particular adversary that will be emulated along with the TTPs and technical details of the attack(s) used. Next, the Exercise Coordinator leads a tabletop discussion with all the teams involved in which each of the TTPs is reviewed. The teams should have conversations about which security controls should be expected for each TTP and what teams should have visibility into the TTP activity. Any TTPs that should be logged or alerted on should be specifically emphasized as areas where the exercise could provide some particular value. Threat hunters should be on the lookout for TTPs that are logged but don't alert. Those that do alert can be used to practice the processes SOC analysts use. Providing these expectations up front allows the exercise to validate or reject the assumptions that these teams have about their existing detections and processes.

Next, the offensive security team executes the first TTP while sharing their screens so that the rest of the teams are able to see the activity and learn what the attack actually looks like. They should provide all of the indicators of compromise they're using, such as the IP address they are utilizing to do the attack, the specific target being attacked, the exact time of their activity, and the steps they are taking to perform the attack itself. Meanwhile, defenders should follow their standard processes to identify the TTP within their expected time frames. Any metrics gained through this process should be documented. Screen sharing by the appropriate team should be initiated if any alerts fire, if threat hunting discovers the TTP in logs, or, if they are discovered through any other means of identification. If any additional short-term adjustments are identified that can be made to increase visibility for this particular TTP, they should be implemented and the offensive security team should repeat execution. Once the first one is complete, the offensive security and defense teams then repeat the same process with the next TTP.

Lessons Learned

The Exercise Coordinator should be taking minutes, notes, and action items and collecting any feedback. Feedback requests should be provided to all parties involved on the last day of the exercise to capture this information before it is forgotten. From this information, they should be creating documentation to be shared with all parties involved in the exercise no more than two weeks after the exercise is complete.

Purple Teams and Advanced Active Defenders

The Advanced Active Defender is uniquely primed to participate in a purple team engagement. With their knowledge of offensive security, they should already have an overall sense of what an attack from the team might look like and how the tools used in the particular TTP might impact visibility into detection. They have the background to act as a liaison if there are communication challenges between offensive and defensive teams. Furthermore, because of their knowledge of the organization and its existing detections and responses, they should be able to readily contribute to preparatory discussions as well as help implement changes after the lessons learned have been disseminated.

Summary

Working to become an Active Defender is an essential step toward understanding more about attacks and attackers, thereby making you better able to defend against them. However, there often comes a time in which diving even further into the offensive security world can be useful. Instead of just having a strong grasp of the tactics and techniques, the Advanced Active Defender also starts to recognize and understand the procedures that offensive security professionals, and likewise attackers, use. As a result, they are able to take the next step in learning to perform automated attack emulations to ideally test some of the defenses in place. In addition, they are able to learn and effectively deploy deceptive technologies such as honey tokens and honey pots, among others, to detect and respond to an attacker within the network more quickly.

Beyond having the knowledge to perform more proactive testing and adding deceptive technologies, Advanced Active Defenders also have a unique perspective on the kind of work that an offensive security team often executes. Therefore, when there is a need for additional assistance beyond what the Advanced Active Defender can do alone, they can help stakeholders decide how best to proceed. They can help determine the actual goals of the organization in doing this additional testing, in mapping out the right kind of engagement, and can help select the right vendor to make the most of the money and time designated for the project. In addition, they have the necessary knowledge to be particularly effective in working within a purple team engagement if it is selected.

Once an Advanced Active Defender starts working to test their defenses at this level, it is likely they will start to recognize gaps in the detections that are in place for their organization. However, to address those issues, they need to understand something more about successfully detecting attackers in an environment. Therefore, we will next move to a discussion about how to build more effective detections.

Notes

i. J. Strand, *Offensive Countermeasures: The Art of Active Defense*, 2nd Ed. 2017, p. 25.

ii. Ibid. p. 25–26.

iii. Ibid. p. 26.

iv. Joe Vest, Why We Red Team. Wild West Hackin' Fest, The RoundUp: Red Team. Aug 12, 2021. www.youtube.com/watch?v=XE9JZOC-SCE.

v. Ibid.

vi. Purple Team Exercise Framework 2.0 (2021). SCYTHE Inc. www.scythe.io/ptef.

CHAPTER 7

Building Effective Detections

Defenders often rely heavily on a variety of detections and alerts to indicate when an anomaly happens. In theory, the purpose of these signals is to provide a warning that an attacker either is attempting to or has already infiltrated resources they should not have the ability to access. Unfortunately, building effective detections is difficult at best. While this chapter will not teach you how to become a detection engineer per se, it will explore how offensive security practitioners, and likewise attackers, evade detections as well as some of the difficulties in properly validating existing detections. By understanding how offensive security professionals approach the problem of detection evasion, you will have a better grasp on why detection is so difficult to do correctly and learn how to avoid some of the basic pitfalls.

Purpose of Detection

In an ideal world, defenders would secure systems and networks in ways that prevent all malicious activities. However, as previously discussed, 100 percent prevention is not a realistic goal. Instead, we must rely on various forms of detection to supplement the prevention mechanisms that are in place. However, detection is just part of the larger overarching process through which we attempt to identify and remediate threats. Before we can talk about building effective detections directly, we need to first understand the larger process in which detection itself sits.

Funnel of Fidelity

To describe this larger detection and response process, we'll use the model that Jared Atkinson, chief strategist at SpecterOps, created called the Funnel of Fidelity.[i] The purpose of this model is to help an organization with limited resources more efficiently manage the countless events it receives. As a result, it will better be able to determine which ones are worthwhile to investigate and thus should be prioritized. There are five stages within this model: collection, detection, triage, investigation, and remediation. Atkinson asserts that the model was built by the actions of people involved in this process. It gets its name from the fact that as events move through it, the nonrelevant events are filtered out, allowing for a deeper level of analysis on what is left. This filtration process leads to an increase in fidelity, or reliability, of the remaining events. Most organizations perform these stages at least implicitly, whether they realize it or not. In other words, even if they have not considered the concept of remediation and how to implement a strategy around achieving that outcome, it still must be done. Without explicitly recognizing these stages, there could be significant deficiencies present.

Collection

The first step in this process is collection. Thus, our ability to detect properly starts by collecting the appropriate events that can be used to build detections. This stage involves the gathering of telemetry. Telemetry is the data provided by monitoring tools, including logs, network throughput, and other information that allows those who maintain the network to monitor its health and ongoing activity. Without collecting the right information, we cannot hope to build the right kinds of detections.

Detection

The second stage is that of detection. The purpose of this phase is to identify which of the events that have been collected are security relevant. The result is a reduction in the number of events that can be analyzed at the next stage. While some detection may occur as the result of threat hunting exercises or detection engineering, in production, automated detection logic is typically used for this purpose.

Triage

The triage stage is where defenders work to break the alerts detected into the following categories: known malicious, known good, and unknown. Known malicious events are recognized as incidents and immediately moved to the remediation stage. Unknown events require additional examination and are moved to the investigation stage. Unfortunately, it is at this stage where alert fatigue is prevalent. Defenders often do not understand the logic or relevant context or have the appropriate background in order to properly triage the alert. As a result, they mark malicious activity as a false positive. However, that result is less likely if one is an Active Defender since, as we have discussed, they often have a clearer understanding of the nature of the attacks in progress.

Investigation

During the investigation stage, additional context that was not previously available is gathered to help identify whether or not the events in question are malicious. This context might come from more labor-intensive examinations such as file system analysis or memory forensics. This scrutiny is feasible because the number of alerts being examined at this stage is fairly small.

Remediation

The final stage in the process is remediation, which involves determining the scope of the incident and removing the malicious activity from the network. Remediation is required any time an incident is declared.

Building Detections: Identification and Classification

With the larger process of identifying and remediating threats in mind, we can now begin to discuss creating effective detection rules. According to Atkinson, when building a detection rule, there are two main phases to consider: identification and classification. The identification phase involves identifying all events that should be subject to the particular detection rule. For example, in order to detect all malicious service creation, we must first be certain that we can observe all service creation. The classification phase, in contrast, looks at each instance of a particular behavior and, depending on the context, considers whether it should be an alert.[ii] Furthermore, it is important to think of classification not necessarily as "good" or "bad" but rather whether further investigation is warranted.

One of the big challenges with creating effective detection rules, Atkinson contends, is the overall lack of attention to the identification phase. More time must be taken to identify all of the possible related events before beginning classification. In many cases, identification requires a level of abstraction to account for all of these possibilities. In other words, you must take a step back in order to capture the big picture. Not only is this phase often overlooked, but identification and classification are often conflated rather than being viewed independently. As a result, some of the decisions made about classification ultimately affect identification. They wind up inadvertently excluding some of the relevant events from the start. Furthermore, because identification occurs so early in the process of building detections, small mistakes made there can wind up being considerably magnified later, including the creation of false negatives. A false negative is where you fail to identify the presence of a behavior that actually is present.

Another important consideration is what telemetry is available with which to identify the relevant events. As we saw, getting the collection phase right is critical to creating useful detections. If by taking that step back to see the big picture the correct telemetry is no longer available to do identification properly, some false negatives might be introduced. The benefit is that at least you would be aware of that limitation.

The classification stage has its own challenges. Atkinson points out that numerous variables exist that we cannot control. Furthermore, in some cases we may not even be aware of these uncontrollable variables.[iii] For example, the ability to perform a useful classification requires that you have enough context with which to successfully make a decision. If, during the collection phase, the alerts gathered contain only minimal information, such as a connection was made to a port, but not additional details (e.g., the user who made the connection, the process that generated the connection, etc.), it will be extremely difficult to make informed classification decisions. Furthermore, using a single feature to evaluate whether an event is malicious, known as a single variate analysis, is easily prone to errors.

Overall Detection Challenges

Beyond the specific issues with the phases of a detection rule, Atkinson identifies some more general challenges with building detection rules that must also be considered. He defines four areas in which it is easy to go astray when creating a detection rule: attention, perception, abstraction, and validation. We'll examine each in turn.

Attention Problem

The attention problem considers questions that involve where we should place our focus. At a very broad level, for example, we can ask, "Given the infinite number of things that I could choose to pay attention to, how do I know that what I'm looking at is the right thing?" At the collection stage of the Funnel, we might ask, "How do I know that the telemetry that I'm collecting is the best telemetry for the job?" More specifically, during the identification phase of detection, we might contemplate a question such as, What events should we attend to in order to capture the behavior we are interested in? During the classification phase, we might consider a question like, How do I know that the contextual details that I'm choosing to base my classification decision on are the most predictive features?

The process of building detection rules, like all parts of information security, does not come with unlimited resources. Therefore, it requires the allocation of finite resources as efficiently as possible. In other words, in order to capture the desired behavior, we must focus on only identifying the relevant events we want to be detected. Just because the telemetry exists does not mean that what we have is useful for the purpose of creating a particular detection. If our attention is in the wrong place, it can cost precious resources that can be few and far between.

One example of the attention problem is the tendency for detections to be built around tools. However, the reason we typically want to detect a tool is because of the actions that it performs. For example, the reason for detecting something like Mimikatz is because of the actions it performs. Focusing on those actions instead of the tool itself provides a broader scope and more resilience. We'll examine the topic of tool detections later in the section "Tools." In addition, this discussion will include some false assumptions that surround them.

Perception Problem

The perception problem attempts to grapple with questions such as these: if a product tells me that it's able to observe and/or log when a service is created, how do I verify that it will do what it says? How do we know that what we actually see in the telemetry is what we should see? The ability to identify the events that should be subject to a detection rule is greatly dependent on having knowledge of what is collected in that first phase of the larger process. In other words, the ability to build effective detection rules relies on accurately perceiving what telemetry is collected and will be available to you. Unfortunately, detections are often crafted with assumptions about the level of telemetry coverage of a particular activity, which in fact does not actually exist.

For example, consider the topic of service creation. According to Microsoft's documentation, the Event ID 4697 should appear in the Windows security event log when a service is installed on the system.[iv] The assumption is often made that every instance of a service being installed will generate this ID. However, it turns out that services can also be installed by writing to the Registry directly.

As a result, Event ID 4697 is never generated, which means detections based on this identification method have an inherent gap that will result in false negatives.

Another example might be a situation in which a detection rule for a particular activity relied on the presence of an initial LDAP query, such as what happens initially with most Kerberoasting attacks. For this detection to work as expected, that LDAP query must generate an event. However, if the adversary finds a way to obtain the information they're looking for without generating that query and subsequently generating that event, they will evade this piece of telemetry and avoid detection. Anytime there is a discrepancy between the telemetry that we think we will see and what we actually see, an adversary can and will use that gap to evade detection.

Vendor-provided protections often suffer from the same problem. They made assumptions both about what telemetry will be available and what telemetry is needed to identify the relevant events. Therefore, assuming that these detections will work as expected and always provide the proper alerts is equally problematic. We've already seen how some of the tools that offensive security professionals and attackers work with are legitimate built-in LOLBins. As a result, in some cases they won't be detected at all, and others may generate a ton of false positives. Additional context is required in order to detect the specific instances where they are used in nefarious ways. Furthermore, while some EDR products can alert on LOLBin usage, they may only do so under very specific circumstances. The outcome of this limitation ultimately restricts the scope of coverage. Therefore, you might assume that you have solid LOLBin detections in place only to discover that you have rules that never fire.

Abstraction Problem

As mentioned earlier during the discussion of identification and classification, identification requires a level of abstraction to account for all the possible related events before trying to build a detection rule. Abstraction, here, specifically refers to the layers that hide the complexity of the inner workings of a detection rule. To determine how far back that abstraction needs to go requires considering questions such as these: What level of analysis is appropriate for performing identification for a given detection? What are the necessary and sufficient conditions needed to build the right detection? However, answering those particular questions requires a technical understanding of the different layers of analysis. Having offensive security professional knowledge can be key here.

Atkinson provides, as an example, a rule that is supposed to detect anytime a malicious service is created. The way the rule was written, though, it only detected a subset of when malicious services are created—specifically those that were created using the command `sc.exe`. Ideally, by having some knowledge of offensive security tradecraft, you would know that there are many other ways to create a service, regardless of whether it's malicious. The fact that this existing rule does not account for these other methods should be a red flag. Therefore, in order to produce a rule that takes into account all the possible ways in which a malicious service could be created first requires a means to identify when *any* service is created. Taking that step back to account for those possibilities is critical and is an example of the kind of abstraction Atkinson has in mind. Once you've identified all of these possibilities, you can then consider the classification step to distinguish between the ones that might require an alert (e.g., are malicious) or do not (e.g., are benign). It should be obvious then that if identity and classification are not treated as separate processes, a number of malicious services could easily wind up classified as benign because they are not identified up front.

The abstraction problem becomes especially apparent when examining detection rules related to tools. Building detections for tools tends to focus on how something is being detected instead of what is being detected. We'll return to this subject later within the discussion of the Pyramid of Pain and detection rules.

Validation Problem

The validation problem asks, How do I evaluate whether I've (or a vendor) made the correct decisions when answering the questions about identification and classification? In other words, how do I know that, for the detection rules I'm relying on in my organization, the correct events were identified and captured and that the appropriate context was available to make an informed decision? Essentially, you must somehow verify that the detections that you have in place, whether vendor built or homegrown, are detecting what you believe they should. Furthermore, you need to determine whether or not detection rules in place are calibrated to capture the full threat and not just some portion of it, because as we know, just because a rule claims to detect an action such as Kerberoasting doesn't guarantee that it actually captures all of the ways that Kerberoasting can be accomplished.

The best way to validate detection rules is to test them. We've talked about using tools such as Atomic Red Team to test detections in place. Unfortunately, it turns out that a tool that includes tests that claim to detect a particular technique may only capture some of the related events but not all of them. We'll dive deeper into the subject of testing and its challenges later.

The Pyramids Return

The stages of detection and their challenges play a part in why, at specific levels of the Pyramid of Pain or the TTP Pyramid, it can be difficult for the defender to detect an adversary.

If you recall from Chapter 1, "What Is an Active Defender?," the Pyramid of Pain and the TTP Pyramid can be useful in rating how difficult it is for an attacker to maintain their activity without being caught as well as how difficult it is for the defender to detect the attack in question. Let us return to these ideas now, but within the context of specifically creating effective detections keeping the offensive security perspective in mind.

Lower Levels

Figure 7.1: Pyramid of Pain[v]

As you can see in Figure 7.1, the first four levels of the Pyramid of Pain from the bottom up respectively are hash values, IP addresses, domain names, and network/host artifacts. It is relatively easy for a defender to look for evidence of each of these items on their network. Likewise, building detections for them is pretty straightforward. The identification stage essentially only points to all events that involve the IP address, hash value, domain name, or artifact in question. There are no other possible events. Therefore, we can move quickly onto the classification stage and ask whether these events are something that need further investigation.

However, these indicators are not terribly reliable because an adversary can easily change them. Therefore, any detections created for them are of limited use. For example, picking a different IP address or domain name used in an attack process is exceptionally straightforward. Hash values of files can be effortlessly changed by adding or removing a single character to the file itself. If they are discovered, changing HTTP User-Agents or Registry keys, which are examples of network/host artifacts, can take a tiny bit more time and effort because configurations or tools may require changes to continue the operation. Regardless, the offensive security professional, and likewise an attacker, can easily continue without much effort.

At these lower levels of the pyramid, the offensive security professional or attacker generally has little difficulty moving forward with their processes toward whatever goal they have in mind. However, at the higher levels, we begin to see them faced with a more substantial challenge because significant changes would be required to maintain their course of action if discovered. Unfortunately, being able to create effective detections at this level also requires more effort, which we'll discuss next.

Tools

At the next level of the pyramid is the category of tools. Tools in this case refer to the pieces of software used by the offensive security professional, and likewise an attacker, to accomplish their goals. For example, this software could include utilities designed to create backdoors, establish C2 connections, or crack passwords. Tools can be really helpful because they expose you to a technique conceptually. Unfortunately, they're not a great choice for a detection point directly. Creating detections for tools has some challenges that we'll explore next.

Wrong Viewpoint

The overarching problem with creating detections for tools is the impression that they will be a significant remedy for attacks. Furthermore, there is often an assumption that the adversary will typically use specific tools and use them in the same way each time. As a result, defenders often focus solely on tool detections. Unfortunately, concentrating on detections for tools alone is deeply misleading. Instead, it's crucial to remember that the offensive security professional, like the attacker, views the world as software interactions that can be leveraged to achieve goals rather than as a collection of tools. The tool is merely a means to an end, not the end itself. It is important that the defender reset their view to be in sync with what they are trying to defend against.

One way to think about this issue has been highlighted by Andy Robbins, product architect of BloodHound Enterprise at SpecterOps. He notes that when thinking about what an attack path looks like, it can be tempting to view the environment they exist in as a maze with one entry and one exit because of the step-by-step narrative that is created after a breach has occurred.[vi] However, the reality is that because the adversary focuses on the goal they're trying to achieve, it really should be thought of more as a map or graph. One potential path may use a certain tool, but another one could use a different tool or a completely different process. Having a knowledge of offensive security tradecraft means that if one route does not work as desired, they just pick a different one and try again. However, it is important to note that this evolution of tradecraft is not random. There is intelligence being applied to decision-making based on what they learn about the environment. Therefore, we come back to the importance of the idea that attackers think in graphs, or relationships between systems. Robbins asserts, "This is why victims of a breach will often ask, 'If we had blocked this one attack, would we have been safe?' The uncomfortable answer is no."[vii]

It is important to note, however, that organizations will likely still want to have tool detections. They can be useful, especially if an adversary uses a tool as is without any changes. Therefore, it's not the case that we should forgo tool detections but rather that we should not rely entirely on them alone and realize that a tool is simply a single selection in the attack process.

Bypass Options

One assumption involving the detection of adversarial tools is to believe that whatever security products an organization has in place to detect the use of these tools will always be running, functional, work as expected, and always provide the proper alerts. For example, analysts often assume that they will receive timely critical alerts from their security products if these products are configured properly. However, if the critical path for the alert is broken, such as when a slack or email integration stops working, there could be a multi-hour delay. Furthermore, adversaries typically know a number of ways to deactivate security products, whether an antivirus or a full EDR product, and of course, as a result no alerts get created. Defenders rarely alert on the deactivation of their security tools, making it that much easier for an adversary to get away with it.

Having a tool detected can be a headache for the offensive security professional, or attacker, but it is not usually a showstopper. Because some offensive security engagements involve specifically testing in such a way that it avoids detections or alerts, it is common for offensive security practitioners to have additional knowledge in this area. Attackers, naturally, have experience in this space as well, but obviously for different reasons. Tools can often be altered to bypass existing detections, which though sometimes time-consuming, can also be as simple as adding a line break in the code turning one line into two. At a more fundamental level, another way to evade tool-based detections is to rewrite the tool to use a different function to achieve the same outcome. Functions are concrete methods of interacting with the operating system. We'll explore that idea further in the section on testing later in this chapter.

Unfortunately, it is common for defenders, including security vendors, to view attack techniques through a functional lens. As a result, they build their visibility, detection rules, or preventative controls around an exact pattern of functions rather than considering the goals for which the tools are used. Because they aren't approaching the problem from the perspective of the adversary, what they build won't account for these additional possibilities. Furthermore, it should be obvious that having knowledge of the functions involved is necessary, but not sufficient. You also have to understand the goal that they are trying to achieve, which is much easier if you have a grounding in offensive security knowledge.

Higher Levels

We have now arrived at the top of the Pyramid of Pain. If detections at the lower levels are problematic, perhaps we can find an answer up higher. However, as the Pyramid of Pain does not break these top levels out, we must now shift gears to the TTP Pyramid in order to examine them more closely.

As we can see in Figure 7.2, at the bottom level we find tactics, which represent the strategic goal or objective of the adversary, such as "Credential Access." However, as author Christopher Peacock notes, there isn't much to act on at this level because of its imprecise nature.[ix]

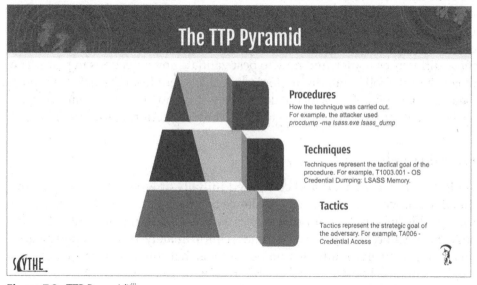

Figure 7.2: TTP Pyramid[viii]

At the next step up, though, we find techniques (and subtechniques) such as "Credential Dumping: LSASS Memory." Techniques definitely provide more concrete information that could be used for building detections. However, as we've already seen, a technique can be implemented in a multitude of ways. As a result, building a detection at this level has the potential to leave out some of these variations and be less resilient to changes.

The final level in the TTP Pyramid is that of procedures. Procedures provide information about not only the (sub-)technique that is being used but also about how exactly it is implemented—in other words, performing Credential

Dumping: LSASS Memory through the use of a tool such as Mimikatz or Sharp-Dump, each of which has this capability. Because procedures provide this fairly unique granularity of information, they appear to offer a greater value for detection. Therefore, creating detections at this level might allow us to ensure that the threat actors' choice of method does not break them. So, how can we be sure this conclusion is accurate? The best way is through testing. It is to this topic we now turn.

Testing

Focusing exclusively on detections for tools can be problematic, as we've seen. However, Atkinson notes that tools still play an important role in determining whether a detection rule is effective. He contends that the way attack techniques are instantiated is in the form of tools. Therefore, tools are what we typically use to help test and validate detections. If we can understand how tools are constructed, we can start to understand the differences between them, why those differences matter, and how to best validate any detections in place. The majority of the following discussion relies on content from the talk "Mapping Detection Coverage" in which Atkinson and his coworker Jonathan Johnson cover the core concepts of accurate testing in order to perform proper validation.[x]

Literal Level

Tools are often examined and compared initially at what Atkinson calls the literal level, which is the specific instance of a tool. Traditionally, comparing tools at this level to look for differences means inspecting elements like raw code, hash values, or file creation times. Unfortunately, from this perspective there are effectively an infinite number of tools that could be instantiated for a single technique like dumping LSASS. Testing any percentage of tools at this level is not helpful because we never will get close enough to the total to matter. Therefore, he asserts that we need to find a more useful way to compare and contrast tools. Instead, he suggests using the concept of abstraction, which is essentially taking a step back in order to understand or view something in a different way. Abstraction can be used to group things that are similar in the ways that matter to us in order to reduce the infinite to the finite. In this case, it is the key to being able to observe some important similarities between tools.

Functional Level

Atkinson and Johnson begin their search for similarities by first examining two tools at their functional level, the first level of abstraction. They compare

SharpDump and Out-Minidump, both of which instantiate the technique Credential Dumping: LSASS Memory. Because these are both open-source tools, they explain that we can examine the code to view the functions that each uses. The result of this examination is that although these tools are different at the literal level, as in the first is a C# binary and the second is a PowerShell script, they share the same three functions: NtQuerySystemInformation from `ntdll .dll` to enumerate processes to find the process ID of LSASS, OpenProcess from `kernel32.dll` to open a read handle to LSASS, and then MiniDumpWriteDump from `dbghelp.dll` to generate a crash dump.

Because these tools use the exact same functions to achieve the goal of dumping credentials from LSASS memory, Atkinson calls them functional synonyms. The differences between tools that are functionally synonymous are, generally speaking, relatively superficial because they are only a single layer of abstraction away from each other. There is still some benefit to testing at least two functional synonyms, though, because it helps determine if what you have is a tool-based detection. For example, if you have a detection rule that can only detect either SharpDump or Out-Minidump, it is likely a tool-based detection or a signature. Both of these detection types are so focused on the specifics of the tool in question that they won't detect even minute changes. However, testing more than two functional synonyms can result in diminishing returns because they become redundant.

Operational Level

Next, they bring in a third tool called Dumpert and compare it against Out-Minidump. Dumpert also instantiates Credential Dumping: LSASS Memory. They note that this tool contains the following functions: NtQuerySystemInformation from syscall, NtOpenProcess from syscall, and MiniDumpWriteDump from `dbghelp.dll`. Atkinson explains that while both tools achieve the goal of dumping credentials via LSASS, they differ in terms of which functions are used to arrive at this goal.

From here, Atkinson introduces the next abstraction layer in order to find ways in which these tools might be similar. In this case, abstraction allows us to focus on the desired outcome from the use of the tool rather than the specific way in which it accomplishes that goal. He calls this level of abstraction "operations" and contrasts it with the functional level. With that idea in mind, he then explores which operations each function maps to. It turns out that in both cases, the first function maps to Process Enumerate, the second to Process Access, and the third to Process Read in this same order.

The problem with focusing on just operations is that they can be used in multiple types of attacks. For example, not only is Process Access an operation in Credential Dumping: LSASS Memory, but it is also used in the technique

Process Injection. Therefore, if you focus on the operation itself, you wouldn't know for sure what you were testing, and you may wind up with unproductive detections. Instead, we need to focus on procedures. Procedures, Atkinson explains, are a "sequence of operations that, when combined, implement a technique or sub-technique."[xi]

Atkinson and Johnson note that these are not the only functions that can be used to achieve Credential Dumping: LSASS Memory. There can be a multitude of ways to create a procedure that will achieve the same outcome, and threat actors only care about outcomes. For each of the operations that make up a procedure, a variety of functions could be called. Testing at the operational level would require considering every possible functional variation that makes up each operation and then multiplying each of those totals together. For example, if Process Enumerate has 21 functional options, Process Access has 7 functional options, and Process Read has 8 functional options, the total number of functional variations for this procedure would be 1,176. This is certainly a far cry from the infinite possibilities that we saw with the literal level, but it's still not realistically manageable from a testing standpoint.

Atkinson refers to tools that can produce the same outcome but are functionally different as procedural synonyms. It is important to note that it's not just that these tools use the same set of operations, but that they are used in the same order. How these operations are sequenced is what makes a procedure unique, not just what operations exist. What that means, then, is that an adversary can use either tool to reach the same objective, dumping credentials with LSASS. Because adversaries focus on the outcome of an engagement rather than a particular tool, they're going to want whatever tool will help them reach that objective. Therefore, they are likely to want a procedurally synonymous tool that will avoid detection over one that might be caught.

Technical Level

The last level of abstraction that we will discuss here is the technical level. Tools that contain different operations and thus different procedures but achieve the same outcome are called technical synonyms. For example, if Credential Dumping: LSASS Memory is being done via process injection rather than using something like Out-Minidump, the outcome would be the same but the procedures would be different.

The benefit of moving to this additional abstraction layer is that we can simply ignore the differences between the functions that are being used to achieve a particular operation. Once we do, it becomes clear that the number of potential operational variations for a given procedure is significantly smaller than the number of functional variations for a given operation. For example, from their research Atkinson and Johnson assert that for Credential Dumping: LSASS

Memory they have uncovered only four operational variations that could be used for a single procedure, such as through the use of Dumpert. Four is certainly an easier number to conceive of for the purposes of testing. As a result, they assert that this level of abstraction must be the right space for building detections.

Because we now know this level of abstraction is the right place to build detections, it is also the correct place to test those detections. Procedure-based testing involves testing all of the operational variations of a technique or subtechnique to determine how many are included in or covered by the detection. In other words, we must be able to answer questions about whether a detection fired when a particular technique was executed for each procedural variation for which we have a test.

Of course, the goal here isn't to teach you how to become a detection engineer, but with a better understanding of these challenges in mind, hopefully you'll understand why testing the detections you do have in place is so important. Now, let's move to a discussion about how best to validate the detections you already have, since as an Active Defender that subject is likely a valuable, practical consideration.

Proper Validation: Both Telemetry and Detection

When beginning to implement testing initially, just having the ability to test any detections in place is a significant improvement in your organization's security posture. However, as your institution continues to mature in this space, you will realize that it is better to focus on the quality of the tests than the quantity of tests available. We know that security vendors often focus their visibility, detection rules, or preventative controls around function calls and particular tools rather than procedures. Therefore, as an Active Defender, it is our responsibility to consider these limitations when validating the detections they provide.

As Johnson asserts, proper testing requires validating two different things: telemetry coverage and detection coverage. Determining telemetry coverage is important because we need to know whether telemetry was created for a particular operation. If telemetry is somehow bypassed, then evasion can happen. Ultimately, detection cannot happen unless telemetry generation is possible. Therefore, testing must be done for each of these elements and not just for one or the other. Figuring out an organization's detection coverage provides insight into the percentage of possible detections for all techniques/subtechniques that an organization has, which plays into their overall security posture.

Telemetry Coverage

Telemetry coverage is operational in nature. Johnson notes that because an operation can be implemented by more than one function, we need to be able to determine whether telemetry is created by each functional variation, not just one. For example, the operation Process Read alone contains eight different functional variations. We'd want to make sure that telemetry is generated regardless of which of these variations are used. It is important to note that until you answer questions about telemetry coverage, you cannot hope to determine gaps in detection coverage. Furthermore, if you cannot trust your telemetry, you cannot trust your detections.

Detection Coverage

Detection coverage, on the other hand, is procedural in nature. In other words, we need to examine a whole procedure rather than the individual operations in order to determine if a detection will work properly. The problem with focusing on just operations, as we've seen, is that they can be used in multiple types of attacks. Instead, we need to make sure that all procedural variations are covered by an organization's detections.

Ultimately the ability to determine what the detection coverage is for an organization is difficult at best because it requires knowing what the absolutely possible testing coverage looks like. While we will not be able to fully answer that question here, Atkinson and Johnson suggest that their work on abstraction may provide the key to ultimately finding the answer. They note that although it may be impossible to know what the absolute detection coverage is, we can instead use abstraction to create a representative sample set of procedural variations. Using this set we can approximate our coverage across the entire set. Just as pharmaceutical companies test new medications across a representative population of the world, we can use a similar representative set to estimate our detection coverage. With this sample set, we can then use some form of atomic tests to validate detection coverage.

Testing Solutions

Fortunately, there are a couple of publicly available, free platforms with which one can do some telemetry testing. These platforms will at least provide some initial insights into detection testing. The first is Atomic Red Team, which was mentioned earlier. The second is AtomicTestHarness, which we'll dive into in a bit.

Atomic Red Team

Atomic Red Team, as previously discussed, is a great platform to start with if you have never tested any detections in your environment. However, because it was created specifically to test security products and detection coverage, the tests it has tend to focus on tools rather than operations. As a result, Johnson explains that although Atomic Red Team has 12 different tests for Credential Dumping: LSASS Memory, it turns out that only 10 different tools were being used, which means there is repetition within the tests. Furthermore, at the time of the presentation, these tests only covered two of the eight possible ProcessRead functional variations, meaning that there is likely some significant redundancy there as well. Having that much redundancy suggests that we may not be obtaining the right telemetry. Therefore, having more tests does not mean that we have better coverage, and we can see why focusing on quality is so more important.

AtomicTestHarness

With a more robust understanding of the challenges of detection, hopefully you can now see why another platform for testing has evolved. AtomicTestHarness, also available through Red Canary, is a newer testing suite that provides much greater flexibility and more granular control over what exactly is being tested and how the operation is performed. [xii] As a result, we can eliminate the literal level and the functional level and focus on the procedural level.

It has a PowerShell module for running tests against Windows and a Python package for running these tests from MacOS and Linux. Specifically, AtomicTestHarness allows the user to select different functional variations when testing in order to determine whether the expected telemetry is created for each operation, regardless of how it is instantiated. Furthermore, it validates the telemetry generated during execution such that you know whether or not the tests fired successfully.

For example, consider the operation Process Access, which as we know is the second operational step for Credential Dumping: LSASS Memory. Johnson illustrates that there are six different functional variations that perform that particular operation. One function it could use is OpenProcess from `kernel32 .dll`, whereas another could be OpenProcess from `kernelbase.dll`. Therefore, in order to determine whether telemetry is generated for each one of these variations, you must run a test for each one. Furthermore, telemetry differences can occur in some security products depending on the specific function that is called during an operation. For example, Sysmon will always log Event ID 10 for Process Access, so long as there are no conflicts with the configuration files, such as entries that might disable logging of these events. However, at the time of this writing, Microsoft Defender for Endpoint will alarm on credential dumping from LSASS memory only if OpenProcess is called specifically for the LSASS process. Knowing what telemetry differences exist is extremely important because, as previously discussed, assumptions about them can render detections worthless.

By using AtomicTestHarness for the process of validation, they were able to account for six of the functional differences across the eight possible options for

Process Read instead of just two. The only reason they were unable to validate all eight is that while AtomicTestHarness has significant flexibility in terms of selecting which functions are being used in a test, it does not have the ability to use system calls directly. Therefore, any variations that rely on system calls, such as what we saw with Dumpert, cannot be tested.

Summary

The purpose of this chapter, as stated at the beginning, was not about having enough information to become a detection engineer but rather to provide insight into the challenges they face when building detections. Understanding what we want to detect requires both recognizing why we want to do detection and appreciating the bigger picture in which it is situated. Jared Atkins's Funnel of Fidelity provides a formal model with which to think about this larger detection and response process. Once we know where in this model detection is situated, we can then begin to examine what is needed to build an effective detection.

Effective detections require not only properly addressing both the identification and classification phases of detection but tackling some broader challenges as well. For example, we saw how complications with the topics of focus placement, telemetry perception, abstraction level, and rule validation can add to difficulties in building useful detections. With those challenges in mind, we then returned to the Pyramid of Pain and the TTP Pyramid to explore why defenders have difficulty detecting an adversary at specific levels. In particular, we saw how the emphasis on building detection rules specifically for tools, a common practice by many vendors, involves flawed thinking.

Ultimately, we concluded that the best level for building detection rules was likely that of procedures, because of the unique granularity it offers. However, in order to confirm that decision was accurate, we considered what testing might look like at each of the levels at which detection could be accomplished. After determining that the procedural level was the correct choice for building detections, we then explored what was necessary for proper testing: validating both telemetry and detection coverage. While detection coverage is not easily determined, because it requires having knowledge of every possible procedural variation, we saw how using abstraction might provide a direction to pursue. Finally, we explored two available platforms for telemetry testing and discussed why Atomic Test Harness, in particular, has the capability to provide more accurate results.

Notes

i. https://posts.specterops.io/introducing-the-funnel-of-fidelity-b1bb59b04036

ii. https://posts.specterops.io/thoughts-on-detection-3c5cab66f511

iii. https://twitter.com/jaredcatkinson/status/1461028108199358467

iv. https://learn.microsoft.com/en-us/windows/security/threat-protection/auditing/event-4697

v. David J. Bianco, Enterprise Detection and Response, "The Pyramid of Pain," December 17, 2022. http://detect-respond.blogspot.com/2013/03/the-pyramid-of-pain.html

vi. https://twitter.com/_wald0/status/1501692940254466048?s=20&t=j2l8IxFEEOK3PLd0VO2DPQ

vii. https://twitter.com/_wald0/status/1501692946625679360

viii. Christopher Peacock, The TTP Pyramid, December 30, 2022. https://scythe.io/library/summiting-the-pyramid-of-pain-the-ttp-pyramid

ix. www.scythe.io/library/summiting-the-pyramid-of-pain-the-ttp-pyramid

x. www.youtube.com/watch?v=tNfWSE4M4qg&t=2s

xi. https://medium.com/specter-ops-posts/on-detection-tactical-to-function-810c14798f63

xii. https://redcanary.com/blog/introducing-atomictestharnesses

Actively Defending Cloud Computing Environments

Cloud computing environments involve delivering technology services such as servers, storage, databases, networking, software, analytics, and intelligence over the Internet instead of buying, owning, and maintaining physical data centers and servers. These services can be provided on an as-needed basis via pay-as-you-go pricing, which eliminates the need for up-front IT infrastructure costs. The benefits of cloud computing include not only the potential for these services to be less expensive but also for an organization to be more agile because it can deploy resources in a matter of minutes. Furthermore, it allows an organization to have greater elasticity because it provides the ability to scale up or down resources as there are shifts in business needs.

Choosing to deploy cloud computing services may seem like a foregone conclusion given the benefits just discussed. However, it is not as simple as just replacing local infrastructure with what is in the cloud. There are a significant number of details that need to be considered before moving forward. For example, there is not a one-to-one mapping from a data center environment to cloud services. The potential to be locked into the use of a single platform is another important consideration. Furthermore, contrary to common assumptions made by those deploying these services as well as vendor claims, the use of cloud computing does not provide a guarantee of greater security. In addition, costs for cloud computing can become prohibitively expensive, sending some organizations to bring services back on-prem.

The goal of this chapter will be to provide an overview of cloud computing environments, how they differ from physical ones, and the general security implications of these differences. I will provide examples from at least one of the main three cloud environments when feasible: Amazon Web Services (AWS), Microsoft Azure, and Google Cloud Platform (GCP). In addition, I'll examine these security ramifications from the offensive security professional's point of view to provide insights for the Active Defender. With these insights in mind, I'll discuss how to best defend a cloud computing environment.

Cloud Service Models

There are three main types of cloud service models: Infrastructure as a Service (IaaS), Platform as a Service (PaaS), and Software as a Service (SaaS).

IaaS

IaaS provides fundamental networking features, computers, and data storage space. Computers can be either virtual or created on dedicated hardware hosted and managed by the cloud provider. The consumer can then deploy and run any software they choose, which can include operating systems and applications. While the consumer does not manage or control the underlying cloud infrastructure, they do have control over operating systems, storage, and deployed applications. They may also have access to a limited set of networking components.[i] Some examples of IaaS include Amazon EC2, Azure Virtual Machines, and Google Compute Engine.

PaaS

PaaS provides the ability for the consumer to deploy applications of their own or acquired elsewhere onto the cloud infrastructure without having to manage or worry about the underlying infrastructure (e.g., hardware and operating systems). However, these applications must use programming languages, libraries, services, and tools that are supported by the provider. The consumer controls the deployed applications and may have the ability to control configuration settings for the application-hosting environment but does not control the underlying infrastructure.[ii] Some examples of PaaS include AWS Elastic Beanstalk, Azure Web Apps, and Google App Engine.

SaaS

SaaS provides the ability for the consumer to use existing applications offered by the cloud provider and running on their cloud infrastructure, often through a subscription. These are usually end-user applications, such as web-based email. The provider controls the underlying infrastructure as well as the operating system, software maintenance, and storage. The consumer only has to concern themselves with the use of the application and perhaps some limited user-specific application configuration settings. Some examples of SaaS include Microsoft Office 365, Google Workspace, and Salesforce CRM.

Cloud Deployment Environments

While it is important to have a general understanding of these original service models, there is now significant comingling of all three because virtually all cloud providers offer a range of products along this spectrum. It can still be a useful but somewhat subjective descriptor for individual products. For example, Amazon's Elastic Kubernetes Service (EKS) is more IaaS whereas its Elastic Container Service (ECS) straddles the line between IaaS and PaaS. Its Elastic Beanstalk is most certainly a PaaS. Therefore, the taxonomy is no longer as useful as it was initially. Instead, the focus tends to be more on the distinction between private and public cloud deployment environments.

Private Cloud

A private cloud involves an infrastructure implemented and maintained by a single organization for its own private use. Typically, these organizations want some of the benefits of cloud computing but may have reasons, such as regulatory requirements, that necessitate keeping control over the data. They are usually deployed by extraordinarily well-funded entities such as a large bank or insurance company.

Public Cloud

A public cloud involves an infrastructure implemented and maintained by a service provider. Public cloud environments serve multiple customers and organizations, typically with access over the Internet. The best known examples of public cloud environments are those offered by Amazon, known as AWS, Microsoft, known as Azure, and Google, known as GCP.

Fundamental Differences

Traditional IT and cloud computing share some basic similarities. They both provide computing resources that can be used for many different kinds of organizations. They both need to be managed at least to a certain degree, and someone needs to take responsibility for the data each houses. However, there are some essential differences that are important to understand even before we can discuss the security implications.

On-Demand Infrastructure

One of the biggest differences between traditional infrastructure and cloud computing is the fact that cloud computing is considered to be available on demand. In other words, requests for cloud services by consumers are not required to be provided manually through an administrator or IT support staff. Traditional IT requests can take days, weeks, or months, depending on the size of the organization and the resources it has available. Instead, cloud resources such as server time and network storage can be provisioned whenever they are needed. Rather than having to purchase each piece of hardware and software, consider power and cooling capabilities of existing space, or provide networking access to deploy a new service, you can instead rely on someone else's existing infrastructure.

The options available to request are extremely broad. For example, you can request a server as a single system provided in a bare bones capacity or a fully configured cluster of machines and either can be provisioned within minutes. Furthermore, in traditional IT, storage and the servers doing computing functions are tightly coupled. Typically, all of a server's components such as processing power, storage, and networking, were tightly coupled such that when one piece needed upgrading, it made sense to upgrade all of these pieces. If, for example, an organization wanted to increase the amount of storage available to a server, the process to add this storage could be a disruption. However, on most cloud environments, storage is a separate application programming interface (API) and can scale completely independent of these computing resources. Therefore, even thinking of the "server" as the most discrete, basic computing component of a network is becoming outdated. Instead of requesting a full "server" for storage, you can simply deploy a bucket of storage, such as an S3, which is the AWS storage solution.

While the flexibility of cloud computing can make it very attractive to entities within an organization who wish to avoid the hassles of traditional IT, appropriately securing this space comes with a number of great challenges. Therefore, adding these services should not be undertaken lightly. Furthermore, because cloud computing has the potential to become shadow IT, organizations should be monitoring for its use and take appropriate steps to prevent unauthorized use of these resources.

Shared Responsibility Model

One substantial difference in moving to a cloud computing model from a traditional data center one involves determining who is responsible for security at each layer. The shared responsibility model attempts to draw a line between what the cloud provider is responsible to secure and what the customer is responsible to secure. In a public cloud, the provider is always responsible for the bottom layers, which include the physical security of the data center, network, storage, host servers, and the layer of virtualization. In other words, they are essentially responsible for the security of the cloud itself. The customer, in contrast, is responsible for security of what is in the cloud.

However, specifically what the customer is responsible for securing depends on the service being provided, and each cloud provider handles it a bit differently. For example, with an EC2 instance, AWS is responsible for just the lower layers, while the customer is responsible for all the other layers, including client-side data encryption; server encryption; network traffic protection; proper configuration of the OS, network, and firewall; platform and application management; and customer data.[iii] However, with something like Microsoft Office 365, Microsoft is responsible for not only the lower layers but also the operating system, network controls, and applications. By comparison, the customer is responsible for the identity and directory infrastructure, accounts and identities and devices as well as any information and data.[iv] Figure 8.1 illustrates these distinctions.

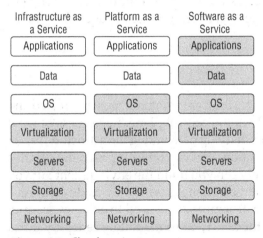

Figure 8.1: Cloud service types

One way to think about shared responsibility is in terms of trust. With the traditional data center model, in theory you can trust your bare metal infrastructure but not your people. With cloud environments, there is an implicit trust in at least the bare metal infrastructure. However, because that's out of the client's control, the reality, as we'll see later, is that it cannot always be trusted either.

Control Plane and Data Plane

Another significant difference between traditional infrastructure and cloud computing is that there are two layers of operations instead of just one. These two layers are called the *data plane* and the *control plane*. While this abstraction is not specific to the cloud, it is more clearly defined as we just saw in the cloud service models. Furthermore, in cloud environments, unlike virtualization in traditional environments, all services are required first to be accessible via the network API.

The control plane is used to manage resources within your public cloud instance. For example, it is what you use to create a virtual machine, storage account, or database. The data plane, on the other hand, is used to interact and use the capabilities provided by your instance of a particular resource. For example, you'd use the data plane to remotely connect to a virtual machine, read and write data in the storage account, or query data in the database.

Traditional IT is most familiar with the data plane because it is the space where they currently work with networks and servers. However, in the cloud you cannot initially access anything without the control plane because the control plane is what manages the entire data plane. Furthermore, not only can the control plane communicate with resources in the data plane but these resources can also access the control plane through API requests. Unfortunately, observing each of these planes is done independently, which can be problematic. The inability to have a holistic view of the entire cloud computing environment can hamper the identification and detection of unintentional misconfigurations or nefarious activities.

Infrastructure as an API

Unlike traditional data centers, an entire cloud environment must be created and managed through the use of an API via the control plane. Regardless of what options you want created, including underlying networking infrastructure, server architecture, storage space, or application, you can build it programmatically. The power of these APIs is that not only can you build the environment but you can also use the APIs to make any and all changes on-the-fly as desired. As a result, immutable or ephemeral infrastructure can be used to enhance security opportunities. In addition, having the ability to immediately redeploy infrastructure when needed is a significant advantage. Furthermore, infrastructure code can be treated like application code and inspected before runtime.

Data Center Mapping

Fundamentally, the traditional data center model with which most IT professionals are familiar is quite different and cannot map directly to the cloud. These networks generally rely on perimeter security, which depends on some assumptions about trust. Typically, they presume that systems and services outside the network cannot be trusted, but what is inside the network from a hardware and data perspective can be trusted. Access to company resources is generally tied to physical hardware via an IP address or VLAN and permissions. Often this approach is represented as a castle surrounded by a moat. Cloud environments, in contrast, are hyperconnected. In other words, deployed infrastructure often has no single ingress or egress point and can easily reach the Internet directly, even when using network isolation techniques like virtual private clouds (VPCs). Likewise, these resources can be located in any part of the world. Therefore, no clear-cut perimeter exists by default. While tools such as VPCs and ACLs can provide the same effect, the existence of the cloud control plane and the hyperconnected nature of cloud resources means that network-based boundaries are far less effective here.

While technically possible, attempting to blindly replicate traditional networking in the cloud, referred to as "lift and shift," removes many of the advantages that the cloud provides. That said, it is common for enterprises to implement some form of perimeter control by routing all traffic through cloud-based appliances, DMZ VPCs, or something similar to allow for an approximation of data center patterns, often in order to facilitate a migration. Ideally, organizations on or moving to the cloud should ultimately be looking for ways to embrace hyperconnectivity and flexibility rather than remaining stuck in the older data center model of tiered networks.

Another important distinction is that in a traditional network, segmentation often functions as a security boundary. However, with cloud computing, identity generally replaces network segmentation for this purpose. "Identity is the new VLAN," according to Bren Briggs, a security and DevOps engineer known as 0xfraq in the hacking community.[v] What he means is that in the way that traditional networks use ACLs and VLANs to segregate traffic by risk level of function, cloud providers use digital identities. This concept will make more sense after the subsequent discussion of identity and access management (IAM).

IAM Focus

Because cloud computing cannot rely entirely on network boundaries for security purposes in the way that a traditional data center model typically does, the concept of IAM becomes undeniably critical. As I've already mentioned, the access model for resources includes both a data plane and a control plane, which have the capability for bidirectional communication. In other words, resources can mutate themselves, not just other objects. Therefore, the security boundaries for cloud computing are far more porous and require significantly more careful consideration.

IAM systems allow the right entities, whether individuals or systems, to access the proper resources, whether applications or data. There are two parts to IAM: authentication and authorization. Authentication is the process of verifying who you are (i.e., your identity), whereas ensuring that entities can only access the data they should and perform the tasks necessary for their IAM roles is called authorization. The power of IAM systems is the flexibility to grant a more selective level of access than with just a traditional username and password combination. One way to accomplish this flexibility involves using attribute-based access control (ABAC) to define permissions. ABAC can use a fantastic array of possible attributes, such as requesting principal, region, tags, method used to initially authenticate, the presence of a multi-factor authentication (MFA) token, and more. See Figure 8.2 for an example of ABAC.

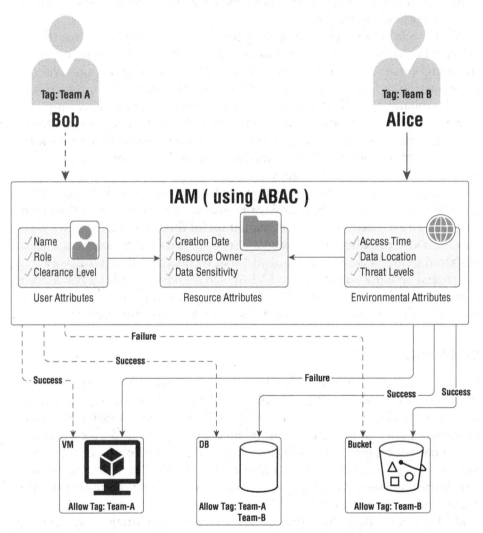

Figure 8.2: ABAC

Another way is to use the more traditional role-based access control (RBAC), which typically defines access based on a person's job functions. See Figure 8.3 for a comparison of these two methods.

RBAC

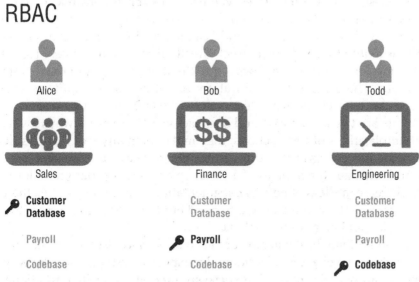

Figure 8.3: RBAC

A unique digital identity is assigned to each entity that is authorized to access resources. When the entity attempts to gain access to a resource, the IAM system first authenticates them to verify they are who they claim to be and then authorizes this identity to access specific resources via a set of permission policies. These two steps, however, are intimately tied together. Proper authorization relies on the accuracy of the authentication step. In other words, if there are mistakes or errors in the verification process, then there is a substantial risk to the resources to which the identity has access.

IAM also allows for the management and monitoring of this identity over time. As the need for access changes, authorization to resources can change as well. Instead of an entity being granted full access for a system, they may only need access to a particular application or API endpoint.

Cloud Security Implications

The fundamental differences between cloud and traditional data center models give rise to some significant security implications. We'll explore a few of them in the following sections.

Larger Attack Surface

One of the major security implications of implementing cloud services is a significant increase in the overall attack surface of the network. An attack surface of a network describes all of the places where it is possible for an attacker to try to enter. As we've seen, one of the essential differences between the traditional data center model and that of the cloud is a lack of single ingress or egress point and the ability to reach the Internet directly from any resource. In some cases, allowing this direct access does require making changes to the default configurations. These default configurations are often initially quite secure. However, because the changes needed to allow direct Internet access to cloud environments are trivial to make, and because people are not always aware of the full implications of their actions, they make them anyway. As a result, this environment becomes less secure. In addition, because an API can be used to create and manage all resources of a cloud environment programmatically from anywhere, regardless of network segmentation or customer status, there are many more points where an unauthorized entity could gain access into a cloud network than into a traditional one.

More important than the expansion of the attack surface itself is the fact that not only are there novel ways to accidentally expose a system in a risky way, but it's significantly easier to do. To expose an internal server in a traditional data center environment, for example, typically requires a networking change such as moving it to a DMZ in front of the firewall. However, in the cloud it's easy to just make a configuration mistake with a simple check box, thereby exposing it to the Internet.

Furthermore, the network will be exposed to more threats, such as traffic analysis and sniffing attacks as well as address spoofing and adversary-in-the-middle attacks, because the vast majority of the cloud traffic will pass through the public Internet.

New Types of Exposed Services

Implementing a cloud environment introduces some new services a company can deploy. For example, one new commonly introduced service is serverless computing, which allows for developers to build and execute application code without having to manage or provision servers. Serverless computing is often referred to as Function as a Service (FaaS). In AWS, serverless computing resources are called Lambdas, whereas in Azure they are referred to as Azure Functions. Google has its own version called Google Cloud Functions.

Object storage is another new service available within cloud computing in which you can store objects such as files and metadata. They are referred to as buckets in Google and AWS and Azure Blobs storage in Microsoft's environment. The benefit to these containers is that as with serverless computing, no provisioning or management of servers is required.

While not an entirely new service offering per se, the way that IAM is implemented in the cloud is new. IAM used with traditional infrastructure is an add-on layer, whereas cloud environments are built on top of IAM. Without IAM, the data center environment will still function, but cloud environments will not. Furthermore, it involves API endpoints that are always public such that they can be accessible from anywhere. In contrast, best practices with an on-prem IAM solution such as Microsoft's Active Directory (AD) recommend that domain controllers, the heart of AD, be protected at all costs from exposure to the public Internet. To protect domain controllers typically entails placing them behind multiple layers of security such as host-based and network firewalls.

While each of these new services brings a wealth of flexibility and functionality to an organization, they also introduce new risks. Unfortunately, because all cloud resources have the ability to connect directly to the Internet, the potential exists for additional services to be exposed. As a result, it becomes unnecessary to compromise one system and then pivot to other key systems or services to compromise cloud resources as needed. Instead, just by obtaining the right credentials you could have enough information to log directly into the cloud consoles. Credentials with any kind of create or write permissions to the control plane allow you to just create your own system and move forward from there.

Application Security Emphasis

As we have discussed, essentially everything within a cloud environment is created and managed through the APIs of the control plane. However, the same Infrastructure as Code (IaC) that uses these APIs to build the system can be subverted to attack it. The idea behind Infrastructure as Code is that either the desired state of what is being designed or the steps taken to reach this state are defined in code. These servers, applications, or other resources require code for creation rather than, as an example, the result of a script's execution or manually performed steps on an already provisioned resource. Once these desired states are defined, IaC tools are used to provision the infrastructure elements such that the desired state is achieved. In addition, any software that utilizes those APIs is a potential path to the control plane. Therefore, it should be obvious that cloud environments require a greater emphasis on security throughout the application development process.

Challenges with API Use

Unlike with traditional models in which security concerns begin at the configuration of a server, security concerns in cloud environments begin at the point of provisioning the resource, which is performed through the use of the control plane APIs. Use of these APIs comes with some significant challenges. Let us examine a few.

Ghost Resources

One problem that an organization can run into is the potential to wind up with what are called "ghost resources." When a resource is provisioned, it is a best practice to also apply a tag. A tag is a string that makes the resource easy to search for later. Ghost resources are created when these tags are not applied. Without a tag, it becomes difficult to detect and remove these resources, and as a result, they can become potential attack vectors.

The best way to avoid this challenge is to make tagging part of the official provisioning process. In addition, organizations should be sure to monitor for untagged resources and then tag them whenever possible.

Base Images and Templates

Another challenge with the use of APIs involves the provisioning of resources using base images in templates. A base image contains the operating system and software dependencies and is used in conjunction with IaC templates to provision resources. If the base image utilized does not come from trusted locations, they are more likely to introduce security flaws. Additional vulnerabilities can occur if the templates in which these images are specified contain misconfigurations or sensitive data. Templates are meant to be regularly reused and thus could regularly introduce security flaws into the network.

To mitigate the issue of problematic base images, ideally obtain them from trusted locations. In addition, run vulnerability assessments against them. To avoid issues with templates, run IaC scans to examine all configuration files, including templates, for known vulnerabilities whenever possible. Furthermore, be sure to avoid hard-coding sensitive information in these templates or version control software.

Configuration Drift

Configuration drift is another way for vulnerabilities or other security risks to be introduced into cloud environments. It occurs when post-deployment changes are made directly in a production environment rather than performed via code.

Directly editing the infrastructure can introduce human errors, configuration mistakes, or other issues.

To prevent issues with configuration drift, an organization must enforce proper configuration update procedures. These procedures should avoid any manual editing of infrastructure after deployment, such as while performing updates or remediations.

Improper Access Management

As with any other platform, using an API includes challenges such as improper access management. Excessive permissions are often granted to those programming APIs rather than only the subset of what is necessary to complete needed tasks. As a result, if their accounts or the service accounts they're using are compromised, attackers could easily pivot to other potentially mission-critical resources.

In order to mitigate this particular risk, organizations must utilize the built-in monitoring and auditing tools that their cloud provider offers. For example, Amazon offers CloudWatch and CloudTrail, Microsoft offers Azure Monitor and Azure Log Analytics, and Google offers Cloud Monitoring and Cloud Audit Logs for this purpose. In addition, because IaC service accounts are almost always highly privileged, it's critical that tools to confirm/enforce least privilege access should be employed whenever possible. For example, Amazon offers IAM Access Analyzer, Google provides the Google Policy Analyzer, and Microsoft has Privileged Identity Management (PIM), which while not quite the same, provides similar information.

Custom Applications

Custom applications can also bring with them considerable unanticipated risk if not secured properly throughout development. Any flaws in an application written to run on the data plane not only have the potential to compromise the system but could also lead to a compromise in the control plane because of the bidirectional communication nature of these operational layers. If the application talks directly to the control plane, there is an even more direct route for potential exploitation.

Cloud Offensive Security

The goals of an offensive security professional with a cloud engagement are essentially the same as their on-premises counterparts. They still view the environment through the lens of an attacker, looking for ways to gain access and move throughout the space, including potential avenues from the cloud to on-premises. The possible attack surfaces they can explore include external, which is completely unauthenticated, requiring a hunt for keys, credentials, or public resources; internal, which involves first authenticating, such as from one virtual machine to another; or internal after authenticating at the API level, examining vulnerabilities, and doing configuration analysis. Regardless of the specific approach chosen, getting initial access ultimately becomes key.

It is important to note that in order to test a public cloud environment, the offensive security practitioner not only must obtain permission from the customer but may also need to obtain it from the cloud provider. For example, AWS specifically requires prior permission for the use of C2 as part of the testing process.[vi]

Enumeration of Cloud Environments

Just as with an on-premises offensive security engagement, the first stage performed is targeting, which requires some reconnaissance. The first challenge for the offensive security professional is to find the organization's cloud footprint. Unlike with the on-premises engagement, however, there is no such thing as a public IP "range" that can be used as a starting point. Instead, the focus must be on DNS names and single IPs. Fortunately, there are helpful tools such as *Cloud_enum* that can be used to enumerate resources in GCP, Azure, and AWS.[vii] There are also ways to potentially brute force buckets/blobs based on predictable URLs.

One of the challenges with cloud environments is that even if you do not have access into the specific cloud space being used by a particular company, there can be ways to access it from another organization's cloud environment. For example, an account in one AWS environment can enumerate valid AWS account IDs and IAM accounts from another.[viii]

Another way in which cloud-based assets can be discovered is through OSINT. Hunting through the same types of organizational intel as we discussed earlier can provide some useful information. For example, public source code and documentation can sometimes contain a wealth of useful references to locate infrastructure. Let's examine a few of these spaces in more detail.

Code Repositories

Just as with testing performed against traditional networks, access keys and credentials are often found by offensive security professionals in code repositories such as GitHub, Bitbucket, or GitLab. These repositories are either public or inappropriately configured to leak secrets to unauthorized users. One well-known example of this mistake is the storing of hard-coded credentials within an application located in a code repository, providing easy access to the offensive security practitioner. Furthermore, if hard-coded credentials did exist at one time but commit histories have not been properly scrubbed, prior versions can still provide this information.

API key exposure can occur not only by directly saving keys in a public repository but also accidentally through plug-ins that require authentication to GitHub.[ix] Malicious packages can also leak keys through typo-squatting and dependency confusion. Typo-squatting is a technique where an attacker intentionally but subtly misspells the name of a popular software repository in order to trick developers into installing it instead of the legitimate one.

Dependency confusion occurs as the result of the default behavior of a package manager when resolving a dependency conflict. Dependencies are additional packages that are downloaded during a program's installation. If the package manager finds more than one repository with the same name, it defaults to selecting the library with the highest version. An attacker can take advantage of this behavior by creating a repository with the same name and uploading a newer version of a malicious library to it. As a result, the malicious version will be installed by default when the package is updated. Unfortunately, these techniques are becoming more and more popular.[x]

Publicly Accessible Resources

One of the easiest ways to obtain credentials involves publicly accessible resources such as a bucket or blob, or the configuration file for one of these, with no authentication necessary. Because it is exceptionally easy to accidentally misconfigure cloud resources to be public, this avenue is particularly common.

Another example of resources that are publicly accessible are misconfigured web applications or functions that are exposed externally. For example, it is trivial to accidentally make a web application or function public. Consider a situation where an organization creates a web app and deploys it privately but leaves open some ports or eliminates certain restrictions for testing and debugging purposes. However, someone forgot to remove these changes prior to the application being made public. As a result, sensitive data could become exposed. The same situation is true for serverless computing such as AWS Lambdas, Azure Functions, or Cloud Functions in GCP. Similarly, databases with weak credentials may be misconfigured to be publicly available.

Some of the sensitive data commonly found on these resources includes not only credentials but also access keys, including those for protected resources. With these credentials or keys, the offensive security professional can then potentially gain programmatic or console access elsewhere, including access to the underlying server infrastructure.

Initial Access

Initial access to cloud resources can be gained in a number of ways. The easiest, of course, is to use the information obtained through OSINT to gain a direct entry into the cloud environment. Other methods are more involved and require some technical expertise to perform correctly.

Phishing/Password Spraying

Just as with traditional networks, another way to gain initial access in a cloud environment is to either run a phishing campaign or perform password spraying to obtain a set (or more) of credentials. Sometimes, phishing campaigns use targeted emails specific to the cloud environment of choice. Overall, though, they use standard phishing techniques to encourage a user to give up their credentials.

Password spraying involves trying a single common password with multiple accounts. Usernames can sometimes be obtained through OSINT or dumped using command-line tools. Because cloud environments are by their nature open to the Internet, password spraying against them can be particularly straightforward.

Stealing Access Tokens

Not only can acquiring user credentials or keys be used to obtain initial access, but so can stealing authentication tokens. Authentication tokens, also known as access or security tokens, are issued to a user once they essentially prove who they say they are, typically based on a username and password combination along with MFA, depending on an organization's policies. These tokens are then used to potentially grant access to every single request for any resource online within the organization's cloud environment that needs authorization. As a result, users do not have to enter their credentials or MFA each time. Therefore, these tokens are particularly useful for circumventing MFA.

As the popularity of cloud computing environments increases, the value of authentication tokens continues to rise. Beyond phishing for traditional credentials, offensive security professionals often use adversary-in-the-middle techniques in order to obtain tokens as well as credentials. They can then replay the session token with the MFA check completed and gain access to the website without needing user intervention.

Another way to steal access tokens is through the use of a rogue application or website. Any mobile app, social media site, personal email, or professional account that uses OAuth is at risk. OAuth is a protocol/framework that allows for secure authenticated access to applications, servers, and other unrelated services without directly sharing credentials. Let's consider a situation in which someone is convinced to authorize a malicious service or application to use their credentials, perhaps through a variety of social engineering methods. As a result, the legitimate token that was granted via this authorization is then passed to the rogue application, giving the threat actor the same level of access as the initial user. This method is known as an application consent attack.

Resource Exploitation

Resource exploitation is another way to obtain initial access in a cloud environment. All deployed resources such as virtual machines, databases, buckets/blobs, functions, and web applications are at risk for vulnerabilities, whether through misconfiguration, missing patches, or problematic code. Standard vulnerabilities such as weak authentication, SQL or command injection, cross-site scripting (XSS), and especially server-side request forgery (SSRF) are often present in cloud environments as much as in traditional environments. SSRF allows you to cause a web server to send a request on your behalf. We'll explore why this vulnerability is particularly problematic in cloud environments later. Any one of these vulnerabilities can lead to remote code execution, providing an easy entry. Furthermore, they can also potentially lead to additional role-based access, depending on the cloud platform.

Post-Compromise Recon

Once the offensive security professional has gained initial access, much like in a traditional engagement, they need to get a feel for the environment into which they've landed. It is important to develop situational awareness in order to figure out what steps are possible to take next. To that end, they typically consider a number of questions, including the following:

- Who do we have access as?
- What role(s) do we have?
- What group(s) exist?
- What policy(s) impact us?
- What security protections are in place (e.g., MFA, logging tools, etc.)?
- What resources can we access (web apps, storage, etc.)?
- Who are the administrators?
- What options do we have to escalate privileges?[xi]

Answering these questions often takes very little effort, such as running some basic command-line tools. Their responses can provide some insights as to how to best proceed.

Post-Exploitation Enumeration

Although as we have seen it is common to obtain a list of some of the accounts or resources as part of the process of obtaining initial access, once the offensive security professional lands inside the cloud environment, a far more complete listing can usually be acquired. Once they are authenticated in some fashion, enumerating other accounts and resources in cloud environments becomes trivial and is a great next step. For example, certain queries made at the command line can result in the enumeration of all public resources in this environment. These resources might include those that the offensive security practitioner was potentially unaware of previously, perhaps because of an unusual naming convention used when generating the resource. Running tools such as ROADtools, AzureHound, or the aforementioned *Cloud_enum* can be used to tease out more of this information as well.[1]

Roles, Policies, and Permissions

Given the importance of IAM in cloud environments, it should not be surprising that IAM roles, policies, and permissions that are improperly configured provide a gold mine of opportunity for the offensive security practitioner. While nuances exist for each cloud provider, generally speaking IAM roles are a way to delegate users, applications, or services access to a set of resources. Policies determine the permissions that these IAM roles provide. For example, if a user moves from one job to another within an organization, they often need access to a different set of resources. Instead of granting each one of these individually, it can be much easier to provide this access through a change in role. Furthermore, when doing RBAC for cloud environments, groups and IAM roles can both be used for role-based assignment of permissions, but groups are considered permanent, whereas IAM roles are a hat you put on for a short, time-delimited session.

Dangerous Implied Trusts

Each cloud provider offers a way for users or services to assume a temporary set of credentials for accessing other resources that they do not directly have permissions to access. While this functionality is extremely useful because it allows for access without managing credentials for each service account, it also comes with some implicit trusts that, if not properly understood, carries with them inherent substantial security risks.

---

[1] https://github.com/dirkjanm/ROADtools; https://bloodhound .readthedocs.io/en/latest/data-collection/azurehound.html

Traditionally, when someone thinks about account management, they recognize that there are user or service accounts that via direct permissions, groups, or IAM roles have access to certain resources. By reviewing these accounts and their associated groups or IAM roles, it is fairly straightforward to produce a resultant list of permissions for what they can access. However, this additional mechanism for access can bring with it permissions that are not so easily observed. Let us examine how these functions work in each of the major cloud providers.

AWS

AWS provides this functionality through what it calls an AssumeRole policy. With AssumeRole policies, a user or service account temporarily assumes a new role. As a result, the user is granted a new set of permissions that are specifically provided through this role. However, these permission sets are not cumulative. Any permissions granted to the user by their previous role are lost until they are no longer using the temporary role.

For example, a programmer might regularly call AssumeRole to obtain the database read role for day-to-day development. This role only grants the ability to read from tables in the database. If, instead, they need to perform actual modifications to the database, they would then call AssumeRole to obtain the database maintenance role. This role would only grant the ability to perform database maintenance such as modifying table structure or adding/removing indexes. As you can see in Figure 8.4, while the developer is acting under the database maintenance role, they cannot read information from tables in the database; they can only do so when they return to the database read role. It is important to note that while a user or service account may have the ability to assume more than one role, they can only assume one role at a time.

The challenging aspect of this feature is that a user or service account can have different privileges based on the context, which is not obvious. They can be acting as themselves or under another role. Therefore, determining a resultant permission set for a user or service is not straightforward. As a result, when the offensive security professional (or likewise an attacker) gains access to an account, they have access to not only resources via their original role but also the resources that they're granted through the new role(s). Adding this new role creates some implicit trusts that, we'll see later, can become a security challenge if not fully understood.

Azure

Azure managed identities are a way for a service to temporarily gain access to additional resources. Like AWS, managed identities are a way to authenticate to a resource without having to manage a set of credentials. However, unlike with AWS, the focus here is on services such as a VM needing to connect to another resource such as Azure Blob in order to write log files.

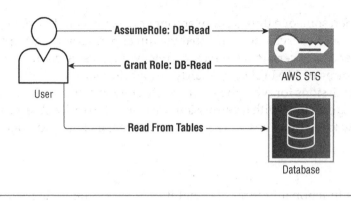

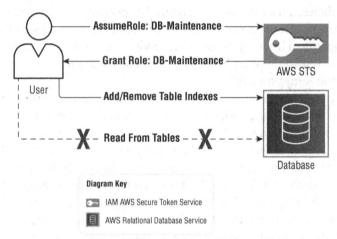

Figure 8.4: AWS AssumeRole

There are two types of managed identities. One is a system-assigned managed identity. For example, you can enable a managed identity directly on a VM, which will create a special service account called a service principle that is tied to this VM's life cycle. It is this account that facilities authenticating between the VM and Azure services that support managed identities. The other is a user-assigned managed identity, which can be used by one or more resources and is not tied to the life cycle of a VM. For example, if we needed to automate shutting down VMs after hours, a user-assigned identity may be given access to an Azure Automation account.

The challenge with managed identities is that by giving a resource access to another resource to perform a function, an implicit level of trust is created. By extension, if a resource that has access to a managed identity is compromised, the possibility exists for the resources it is linked to also to become compromised. For example, imagine a situation in which an offensive security professional gains access to a particular VM through credential theft. The VM itself is running a managed identity that has "contributor access" to another Azure subscription that the offensive security professional could not originally access. However, as Figure 8.5 illustrates, it would be trivial for them to use those implicit rights to ultimately gain access and establish a further foothold in an Azure environment.

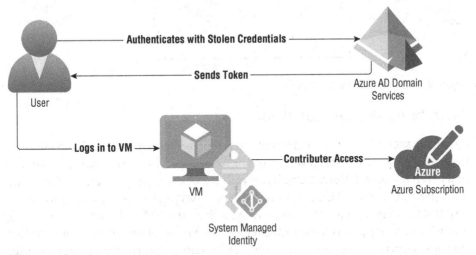

Figure 8.5: Azure managed identity

GCP

GCP uses service accounts as a way for a resource to temporarily gain access to other resources without managing credentials. The service account can be granted IAM roles that allow it access to these resources. For example, applications can authenticate via service accounts in order to make API calls to other resources such as a VM or a Cloud Storage bucket.

The service accounts of GCP, like Azure's managed identities or AssumeRole policies in AWS, also provide an implied trust between whatever authenticates as the service account, such as an application, and the service account itself. Where that becomes a problem is when whatever is authenticating as the service account becomes compromised. Let's look at an example.

Imagine a situation in which a VM runs an application, such as a web server, that is vulnerable to remote code execution (RCE). An RCE allows someone to run arbitrary commands on a remote machine. While performing tests against this application, an offensive security professional triggers the RCE. As Figure 8.6 illustrates, by triggering the RCE, the commands run will execute as the local account the web server runs under, effectively allowing the operator full control over the VM. However, in addition, it is possible for them to authenticate as the service account and access anything it has rights to as well. Therefore, even if the web server itself does not have any data of significant value, but the service account happens to have rights to a Cloud Storage bucket that does, they can access this data.

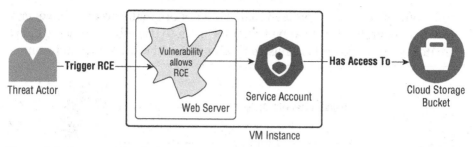

Figure 8.6: Dangerous implied trust

Overly Permissive Configurations

Offensive security professionals will often look for overly permissive configurations such as policies applied to users or resources where they have ownership or a privilege on a different object/resource. For example, in Azure, an account with the role of subscription owner, despite having no direct rights to access any VMs, can run commands on any system as the SYSTEM account. In AWS, offensive security practitioners might look for the use of one of the many built-in policies, which change regularly and could lead to overly permissive permissions. One way this can occur is using wildcards to designate what accounts have access or what can be accessed. Using a wild card in a policy in this way is similar to using the "any" setting on a firewall, which allows any traffic to or from the network in question. In other words, there are no restrictions at all. By using a wildcard, it means any account can assume the role in question.

Multi-Level Access

Another situation involving an overly permissive configuration is not recognizing that there are two levels at which access can be set for most resources. For example, a resource may be restricted to prevent public traffic (e.g., external entities) from accessing it but not further restricted to prevent internal entities from accessing it.

Consider the case where a virtual machine in Azure contains both a public and private IP address. If certain ports on the virtual machine are only accessible on an internal Azure virtual network, an attacker would not be able to gain access to it from an external network. However, anyone operating within the right Azure account's context could still access this virtual machine. For example, as Figure 8.7 illustrates, if an account has contributor access at the subscription level, by default they have access to virtual machines within a subscription. Therefore, if an offensive security professional authenticates to the tenant with an Azure account that has those rights, they would automatically have access to this virtual machine, even though they weren't explicitly granted.

Think of this example like an open share on an internal network. An authenticated user can access it as long as they are on the network and have the rights to do so, but it wouldn't be unavailable to anyone outside of the network.

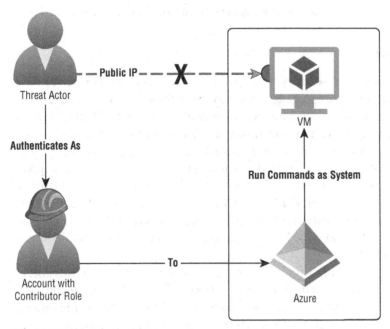

Figure 8.7: Contributor Access

Persistence/Expansion

One of the distinct differences between the traditional data center model and cloud environments is that in order to maintain persistence, it is unnecessary to compromise a machine. Instead, having the right identity with the right IAM roles and privileges is often enough. As you've seen in the section "Dangerous Implied Trusts" earlier in this chapter, with the right identity it is possible to obtain additional information that will allow access to unexpected information.

In addition, AssumeRole policies in AWS or guest access in Azure could provide not only inappropriate access internally but cross-tenant access as well, meaning another organization's systems. Furthermore, because the IAM roles attached to a particular account can be hidden or obscure, there are a variety of unique and interesting places for the offensive security professional to hide. Backup user accounts are not always obvious. Policies specific to vulnerable machines or a Lambda are other convenient ways to set up persistence without compromising the system directly.

Another way to retain access, though not specific to cloud environments, is to create backup user accounts. What is unique to the cloud is how that is managed.

For example, in AWS there is an option to create more than one authentication key for a single user. Therefore, the offensive security professional could take over an administrative account and create a second key for another user. If defenders recognize that the admin account was compromised and reset it, the offensive security practitioner still has a way to maintain persistence.

Lateral Movement

The goals of the offensive security professional for a cloud engagement remain the same as an on-premises engagement and, once they have obtained a set of credentials in the cloud, are conducted in much the same way. Using the keys or credentials obtained from either initial access or post-compromise reconnaissance, they may be able to impersonate an identity and, assuming it has the correct permissions, move laterally to access other cloud resources via API commands. We explored some of that earlier in the section "Roles, Policies, and Permissions." With the right identity or the ability to escalate privileges, an existing identity can result in the complete takeover of a cloud environment. In addition, they may also be able to access systems that allow remote connections such as SSH or RDP.

Another somewhat more involved means to performing lateral movement is abusing cloud-hosted continuous integration (CI), which is an automated process developers use to integrate new code changes to a shared repository, and continuous delivery (CD), which is how those code changes are deployed. CI/CD, as this overall process is generally referred to, is viewed as a pipeline for automation and continuous monitoring for application development.

There are several ways an offensive security professional could use a cloud CI/CD pipeline in order to facilitate lateral movement. We'll examine two in particular. The first involves an organization that provides a CI/CD SaaS solution to their customers. In this scenario, the offensive security professional obtains a set of credentials that has access to the production infrastructure of the organization. If these credentials also provide the offensive security practitioner the ability to generate production access tokens, they can then create new tokens to move laterally across a variety of systems. As a result, they are able to access and exfiltrate data from databases and other storage locations, including customer environment variables, tokens, and keys. This form of lateral movement is what we saw with the breach suffered by CircleCI.[xii]

The second involves an organization responsible for developing a library we'll call libA. LibA is a widely used dependency for many other software packages. In this scenario, the offensive security professional gains access to the organization's CI management service through methods such as exploiting a vulnerability or misconfiguration within it or using existing credentials discovered previously. Once this access is obtained, they modify the code for libA in such a way that allows them additional access to any environment in which it is deployed. These modifications are then pushed out to the organization. Their clients then subsequently incorporate this new version of libA into their software. As a result, the offensive security practitioner can not only move laterally within the organization but also potentially access downstream cloud infrastructures owned by other organizations. It is this form of lateral movement that was essentially used in the SolarWinds supply chain attack.[xiii]

Privilege Escalation

One common situation for the offensive security professional is gaining initial access through an account that has limited permissions or access to resources but needing a greater level of access to achieve whatever goals they have. When this limitation is recognized, next steps typically involve finding ways to obtain elevated access to resources that are ordinarily protected from an application or user, which is called privilege escalation. Privilege escalation can be accomplished by exploiting a bug, design flaw, or misconfiguration in an operating system or application as well as obtaining credentials or keys directly through OSINT techniques.

Unencrypted Credentials in Serverless Environments

Another way that the offensive security practitioner may be able to escalate their privileges is through information left behind in serverless environments, such as Lambdas, Azure Functions, or Google Cloud Functions. Rather than the recommended practice of leaving secrets in a key vault, it is not uncommon for plaintext values to get added to the source code as connection strings or as environment variables. These values could include a variety of secrets including access keys, slack tokens, API credentials, or SSH keys. Having access to read information from any one of these environments is enough to make a call out to view the code or any configuration files that could contain this sensitive data. As a result, this information can be used to easily escalate privileges.

Instance Metadata Service

One service that can be found on every virtual machine in all three of the main cloud providers that we have been discussing is the instance metadata service (IMDS). This service is used to help orient the server within the cloud environment because of its dynamic nature. Specifically, it allows any processes running on the instance to query the server for information about the instance it runs on and the application it resides in, such as hostname, region, subnet, MAC address, and security groups that control the system. However, more critically, certain pieces of sensitive data can be retrieved from this service as well.

Anytime a virtual machine is created, it spins up an IMDS web application endpoint on the non-routable IP address 169.254.169.254. Because this is a non-routable IP address, this site should only be accessible locally and not externally. If an offensive security professional is able to get shell access on a resource in Azure, they can query the IMDS to obtain managed identity credentials if any exist on the VM. However, a simple get request is not sufficient. Instead, a specially crafted request with additional specific headers based on the cloud provider is required. The ability to craft this special request is what requires shell access. As a result, they may be able to access anything that the resource has rights to access, such as the bucket illustrated in Figure 8.8. Likewise, under GCP, they obtain service account tokens that could allow access to anything this service account can access.

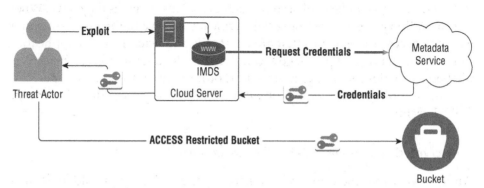

Figure 8.8: IDMS exploit

AWS, however, is a little different because it offers two different versions of IMDS. Version 2 behaves similarly to Azure and GCP in that a query against IMDS could reveal IAM role credentials, which could allow access to anything that role permits. However, version 1, which is still the default deployment of IMDS on AWS, has some other inherent problems. For starters, the offensive security professional does not even need to have shell access to exploit this feature. By using any HTTP client, including a simple curl, they can make an unauthenticated request and retrieve information about that instance from its instance metadata endpoint. Furthermore, not only does version 1 come enabled by default in AWS, but in order to use version 2, you have to both enable it and explicitly disable version 1.

Even more concerning, though, is that under version 1, requests to IMDS can be proxied through a misconfigured proxy server or via an external-facing web application that is vulnerable to server-side request forgeries (SSRFs). Therefore, despite the fact that the site is technically non-routable, these vulnerabilities mean that external access is possible. It is the SSRF vulnerability that was responsible for the Capitol One breach in 2019.[xiv]

Defense Strategies

The best way to actively defend cloud computing environments is, as the core of this book attests, understanding how offensive security professionals might approach an engagement there. Beware of assumptions about standard controls and how they are supposed to work, realizing the various ways there are to get around these controls. In particular, be sure to fully grasp the implications of the connection between the data plane and the control plane. Given that everything is effectively an API and can be programmed, it is crucial to understand how this relationship can offer new vectors for access not previously considered.

Furthermore, be aware of how IAM works within the specific environment(s) you are responsible for defending. Spend time reviewing configurations of all IAM roles, policies, and permissions. Look for ways that having access to one account could allow this account to access unanticipated resources. Proactively search for plaintext data that might be used to gain unexpected access from serverless environments or public resources. Keep an eye open for situations where the initial use case for a set of permissions may have changed. Where possible and approved, consider running some of the third-party tools that the offensive security professional uses for these engagements, such as *cloud_enum* or AzureHound, as well as some of the built-in scripts to get a feel for what information they provide.

Ultimately, the Active Defender must consider each of the steps that the offensive security practitioner is likely to take against their environment and examine possibilities where additional controls and proactive changes in configurations and policies might be beneficial. Specifically, it is crucial for the Active Defender to understand how the components of any PaaS offerings in their environments are intended to work together. Without this knowledge, they cannot know if a deployment is truly secure.

Summary

Actively defending cloud computing environments requires both an understanding of these environments and how they differ from the ones housed in a traditional data center. For example, although infrastructure can be provisioned or deprovisioned on demand, which can be handy, it is impossible to directly map a data center onto a cloud environment. Furthermore, having resources in the cloud introduces a shared responsibility for security between the provider and the customer.

One of the most important distinctions between these types of networks is the addition of a large, complex control plane, which provides ample surface area for attack. As with all other resources in the cloud, the control plane can be managed through an API. The bidirectional communication that exists between the control plane and the data plane opens up new and alarming ways for compromise to occur. Effectively, not only can landing on a resource allow you to make changes to it but you can also alter how its underlying network is set up, alter other instances, or create brand-new ones.

Some additional security implications created by these differences include a much larger attack surface, new types of exposed services (such as serverless computing), object storage, and heavy reliance on IAM for authentication and authorization. Furthermore, application security becomes pivotal because effectively everything in the cloud can be managed with an API.

Generally speaking, offensive security engagements against cloud environments are very similar to those conducted on-premises. However, given the larger attack surface, there can be many more opportunities for the offensive security professional to gain access, move laterally, or escalate privileges. Understanding how the IAM roles, policies, and permissions work in a particular cloud environment can be key to finding some unique paths to persistence and expansion. Ultimately, knowing how the offensive security practitioner approaches a cloud computing engagement is the key to illuminating the areas that the Active Defender must engage with to best defend their networks.

Throughout this book, I've tried to provide a glimpse into the current challenges that the Active Defender faces as well as some insights as to how immersion into the world of the offensive security professional can help. In the next chapter, I will explore some future challenges that defenders are just starting to face and why they could push the defender even further toward a passive stance. It is to this final chapter that we turn now.

Notes

i. https://csrc.nist.gov/glossary/term/infrastructure_as_a_service

ii. https://csrc.nist.gov/glossary/term/platform_as_a_service

iii. https://aws.amazon.com/compliance/shared-responsibility-model

iv. https://learn.microsoft.com/en-us/azure/security/fundamentals/shared-responsibility

v. Per personal communication 1/16/2023 and used with permission.

vi. https://aws.amazon.com/security/penetration-testing

vii. https://github.com/initstring/cloud_enum

viii. https://medium.com/@cloud_haxor/enumerate-aws-account-ids-and-iam-resources-c374843cfdf4

ix. www.securitymagazine.com/articles/96422-how-a-layered-defense-strategy-protects-organizations-from-security-incidents-occurring-at-the-seams

x.   www.cpomagazine.com/cyber-security/hackers-use-malicious-npm-packages-to-steal-data-in-the-iconburst-supply-chain-attack and www.csoonline.com/article/3684468/pytorch-suffers-supply-chain-attack-via-dependency-confusion.html

xi. Beau Bullock. "Securing AWS Discover Cloud Vulnerabilities via Pentesting Techniques" (www.youtube.com/watch?v=fg_hey18tio) and "Getting Started in Pentesting The Cloud–Azure" (www.youtube.com/watch?v=u_3cV0pzptY).

xii. https://circleci.com/blog/jan-4-2023-incident-report

xiii. https://unit42.paloaltonetworks.com/solarstorm-supply-chain-attack-timeline

xiv. www.fugue.co/blog/a-technical-analysis-of-the-capital-one-cloud-misconfiguration-breach

Future Challenges

We've spent time discussing what led to the passive stance defenders often find themselves in as well as the current challenges they are facing. The goal of this chapter will be to look ahead to some of the latest threats starting to become more common that would continue to perpetuate passivity. For example, we'll consider the increasing use of software supply chain attacks, attacks against the Unified Extensible Firmware Interface (UEFI), exploitation of vulnerable drivers, and counterfeit hardware (e.g., hardware supply chain attacks). In addition, we'll discuss the increasing pace and scale of attacks by organized cybercriminal groups and the ease with which they can attack entities thanks to many of the existing frameworks in place.

Software Supply Chain Attacks

Software supply chain attacks occur when a threat actor gains access to a software vendor's network and deploys malicious code to compromise the software before it is distributed to the vendor's customers. As a result, any of the customers' data or systems downstream can also be compromised. Unfortunately, any company that produces software for other organizations can become a target of this kind of attack, including but not limited to those that produce security software, drivers, libraries, or operating systems, regardless of whether they are commercial or open source. As a result, the attack surface of the typical enterprise has been significantly altered, causing it to grow substantially larger than ever before.

A Growing Problem

While this form of attack has been less common in the past, its prevalence has been steadily increasing. For example, consider the 2015 XcodeGhost attack where a compromised version of Apple's Xcode, which is used to build iOS and macOS applications, was used to build hundreds of compromised apps.[i] Because these apps included not only banking and stock trading apps but games, mobile carrier apps, and maps, hundreds of millions of users were impacted. In 2017, attackers were able to modify the performance optimization software CCleaner by software company Piriform by adding a backdoor called ShadowPad.[ii] Over 2.27 million users were affected by this incident.[iii] In that same year, the update servers of a small Ukrainian company, Linkos Group, were hijacked, and a backdoor was built into their accounting software package called M.E. Doc. Unfortunately, this software was used by nearly all companies doing business in Ukraine. As a result, the attackers gained backdoor access to every system running this software. To make matters worse, thanks to that backdoor the attacker was able to release the NotPetya wiper malware to over 12,000 systems in Ukraine as well as 80 victim organizations in 64 countries.[iv]

Perhaps the most notable software supply chain attack to date was the one that occurred on December 13, 2020, against SolarWinds, which I mentioned briefly in Chapter 8, "Actively Defending Cloud Computing Environments," during the discussion of lateral movement. What made this attack particularly noteworthy was the attacker's goal to gain persistent access throughout a number of crucial networks. This nation-state attack was ultimately attributed to Russia and compromised at least 250 organizations. To accomplish this goal, they added malicious code to the legitimate software package Orion, which was developed by the company SolarWinds to track IT performance and statistics monitoring.

Between 2020 and 2021, software supply chain attacks continued to increase, growing 300 percent.[v] By the year 2022, there were at least 10 different significant software supply chain attacks, including against the popular JavaScript Node.js packager npm and the official repository for the Python language, the Python Package Index (PyPi).[vi]

Actively Defending

With software supply chain attacks on the rise, it's no surprise that defenders may feel powerless to prevent them, leading to additional passivity. Building an inventory of all software being used, both commercially and open source, can seem particularly daunting. However, this is yet another area where the

Active Defender's hacker mindset can be useful. For example, given their hacker mindset, they are more likely to recognize the risks associated with software supply chains. Furthermore, they also are more likely to recognize the relationships between software packages deployed in their environments. That information, together with an understanding of what the organization views as its critical data, can help the Active Defender determine where high-risk supply chains are likely to be and thus where to appropriately implement additional segmentation.

Counterfeit Hardware

Another form of supply chain attack involves counterfeit hardware. Rather than an attack involving the software supply chain, this version involves threat actors seeking to compromise the hardware in routers, switches, servers, or workstations through some portion of their supply chain. These attacks typically entail the installation of electronic hardware components that are often a cheap imitation of the expected hardware with the intent to defraud the customer as well as potentially infiltrate systems. For example, the manufacturer of these components may install back doors to allow unauthorized access, leaving the system, and by extension the network it is on, completely vulnerable.

Unfortunately, there are very few security measures in place to prevent against hardware supply chain attacks and these modifications can be nearly impossible to detect during the testing process. Because electronics have become so tiny and complex, determining whether someone tampered with, compromised, or changed part of a chip can be exceedingly daunting. Faulty components could not only lead to security risks but also threats to life safety and to national security if they involve military systems.

Fake CISCO Hardware

A recent example of this form of supply chain attack was uncovered in 2022 when CEO Onur Aksoy was indicted for the sale of over $1 billion of counterfeit Cisco hardware to customers that included hospitals, schools, the military, and government organizations.[vii] His enormous operation dated back to as early as 2013 and involved at least 19 different firms in New Jersey and Florida. The hardware was created by Hong Kong and Chinese counterfeiters but offered as new, genuine Cisco products to unsuspecting customers through Amazon and eBay storefronts for a significant discount. Not only did these products include Chinese pirated software and unauthorized low-quality or unreliable components but they significantly damaged customer networks as the results of failures and malfunctions.

Actively Defending

The Active Defender is in a unique position to help educate stakeholders who are responsible for either the procurement of hardware and/or signing off on these purchases. All too often, these stakeholders are on the lookout for the best deals they can get when placing an order. When faced with a higher price for a well-known dealer rather than a lower cost from an unknown entity, they often cannot fully justify why purchasing from a reputable dealer truly matters. However, the Active Defender knows that, as the old saying goes, you get what you pay for and, in this case, sometimes more than you wanted in the form of malware. Therefore, the best way to actively defend against hardware supply chain attacks is to take time to explain to these stakeholders what the real ramifications might be for deciding to proceed with the lowest bidder, who could easily be an illegitimate dealer.

UEFI

UEFI was developed as a new way for operating systems and firmware to communicate. While designed to replace the traditional BIOS, most implementations are backward-compatible with older operating systems. One of the benefits of moving to UEFI is that it includes some enhanced computer security features. In particular, it supports something called Secure Boot, which acts as the foundation of a chain of trust to prevent malware, such as a bootkit, from replacing the original bootloader. Secure Boot is designed to validate the authenticity, source, and integrity of each piece of code being called during the startup process by a digital signature to determine if anything has tampered with the boot loader. If one piece of this chain isn't recognized, Secure Boot is supposed to prevent the device from booting.

The security of the entire system is essentially tied to the reliability and trust of the UEFI because it is the first thing that runs when someone turns on a computer. Therefore, anything that impacts the UEFI also will impact the operating system, security applications, and all other software, making it a very attractive target for attackers. If a threat actor is successful, a UEFI bootkit can disable the security mechanisms on a system such that even if a hard drive is replaced or the operating is reinstalled it will remain infected.

Increasing Vulnerabilities

Unfortunately, there are an increasing number of vulnerabilities in UEFI implementations and bootloaders, which is problematic. Often the malware works either by targeting the UEFI firmware stored in the flash storage chip or by targeting the software stored in the EFI system partition (ESP). For example, bootlicker is a UEFI rootkit that targets VMware hypervisor virtual machines by targeting the firmware.[viii] Once it has been inserted into the firmware, bootlicker ultimately has the capability of achieving arbitrary code execution without triggering any existing security mechanisms such as PatchGuard. Because these vulnerabilities live in such low-level hardware, they are very difficult to find and no traditional vulnerability scanner will detect them.

In many instances, systems with these vulnerabilities remain at risk because they have not been patched, are not patched correctly, or cannot be patched because they are no longer supported by the manufacturer. In addition, when these vulnerabilities are discovered, the vulnerable files are not always revoked in a timely manner. The process for withdrawing previously approved signed firmware and software used in UEFI Secure Boot involves using revocation list files to update the Secure Boot Forbidden Signature Database. This database contains the signatures of revoked binaries and certificates that can no longer be trusted. However, operating system manufacturers do not always add their signed binaries to this list. As a result, a large number of vulnerable bootloaders continue to remain in use.

However, until recently, a couple of pretty significant obstacles prevented an attacker from installing malware at this level. First, the attacker would need administrative rights to the system either by tricking a user into installing a piece of malware or by exploiting a vulnerability in the operating system. Second, they would have to get past Secure Boot. While there have been known vulnerabilities to Secure Boot in the past, none of them ever allowed attackers to completely bypass the protection it offered.

Enter BlackLotus

Everything changed with the discovery of BlackLotus, a UEFI bootkit that was determined to be offered for sale through underground criminal forums for $5,000 since at least October 2022.[ix] This bootkit is the first of its kind in-the-wild that has been able to compromise the boot process while running on a fully patched version of Windows, even with Secure Boot and other protections enabled. Furthermore, it has the capability of disabling other OS security mechanisms such as BitLocker, hypervisor-protected code integrity (HVCI), and Windows Defender.

BlackLotus takes advantage of an older vulnerability in Windows, CVE-2022-21894, that was fully patched in Jan 2022. This flaw, known as "baton drop," allows attackers to bypass Secure Boot. Despite providing the patch, Microsoft did not originally add the vulnerable signed binaries to the UEFI revocation list. Therefore, even if a machine is fully patched, the attacker can simply replace the patched files with the previous, vulnerable versions as part of their attack process.

To address the issue of vulnerable signed drivers being used, Microsoft released another patch in May 2023.[x] This initial version of the patch does not automatically enable the full set of protections provided, which includes the revocation of boot managers, because they could render some systems inoperable. Instead, a number of steps must be performed manually. First, the May patch must be applied to each vulnerable system as well as to all bootable media and full backups of these systems. Then, an onerous five-step process to revoke the vulnerable signed binaries must be performed on each system to complete the protections against this vulnerability. It is important to note that both the patch and this revocation process come with some significant warnings.

A second version of this patch, scheduled to be released in July 2023, still will not enable the protections by default but is supposed to make the process easier. Finally, a third version will be made available in the first quarter of 2024 that will enable these protections by default. As a result, older, vulnerable versions of the bootloader will no longer be trusted and render older boot media unbootable on all patched Windows PCs.[xi]

Clearly, threat actors are paying attention to the fact that not only are there UEFI vulnerabilities on many devices that have gone unpatched but that the UEFI revocation lists are also not being updated regularly. While BlackLotus is the first publicly available UEFI bootkit that can bypass Secure Boot, it's not likely to be the last. There is every reason to believe that attackers will continue to look for new and unique ways to use UEFI vulnerabilities to their advantage.

Furthermore, nothing about these kinds of issues can be addressed simply by "just patching" a vulnerable system. The unfortunate reality is that the options available for dealing with threats of this nature are imperfect at best. Each one discovered will likely require a significant amount of time and effort to research, uncover any ramifications of proposed mitigations, and apply whatever fixes are available.

MSI Key Leak

Concerns about a supply chain attack that occurred against Micro-Star International (MSI) in April 2023 are already swirling. Although at this time no indications of misuse are known, this well-known hardware manufacturer had its Boot Guard signing keys leaked in a ransomware attack. This leak impacts products from many different device vendors industry-wide, including Intel and Lenovo. Unfortunately, MSI does not have an automated patching process nor any key revocation capability. Furthermore, there is no easy way for MSI to prevent its products from trusting firmware updates signed with the compromised key. Although technically complex, it is possible these keys could be abused in targeted attacks.[xii]

Actively Defending

Because UEFI vulnerabilities are particularly difficult to address, attacks against them are another area that can seem overwhelming to defenders encouraging a continuing passive stance. The best way to actively defend against UEFI attacks is to stay on top of the latest research and the novel ways that these vulnerabilities can be used against a system, much like an offensive security professional. Having timely knowledge of these new attack vectors is partially what sets the Active Defender apart from their counterparts. Knowing what UEFIs are in use within your environment can help you target this research, but be ever mindful of the bigger picture so that you do not miss information about newer attacks. Furthermore, make sure to add patching UEFI vulnerabilities part of your business processes wherever possible.

BYOVD Attacks

Another type of attack that is becoming more popular with threat actors is the Bring Your Own Vulnerable Driver (BYOVD) attack. Because kernel-mode drivers have such low-level access by default, they have the potential to do significant damage if they are malicious. What makes this type of attack particularly problematic is that because the attacker is facilitating their actions via a driver, they are acting with kernel-level privileges. As a result, they are able to bypass any of the kernel protections that are ordinarily in place.

To prevent this problem, Windows can require that these drivers be digitally signed and checked each time they are loaded into memory. This policy is called Driver Signature Enforcement (DSE). If DSE is enabled and a driver is not signed Windows will not load it. By default, DSE is now enabled on all 64-bit versions of Windows. Therefore, to use a malicious driver, an attacker must find a way around this protection. Enter the BYOVD attack that uses the vulnerabilities in a legitimately signed driver to perform malicious activities on a system.

Microsoft claims to prevent these attacks through a combination of two of its features: hypervisor-protected code integrity (HVCI), which is meant to provide memory integrity, and attack surface reduction (ASR), which supposedly prevents malicious drivers from being written to disk. However, testing performed by security researchers such as Will Dorman, a senior vulnerability analyst at security firm ANALYGENCE, indicates that these tools do not work as expected.[xiii] Not only did he discover that ASR failed to block vulnerable drivers, but at the time, the driver block list only contained two drivers for Server 2019. Microsoft has since released a tool that can be used to perform an update of the server block list. However, there appears to be no mechanism to push automatic updates to this list going forward yet.

Lazarus Group

One of the more recent instances of this type of attack was CVE-2021-21551 in May 2021, where the Lazarus Group used vulnerable legitimate BDUtil drivers provided by Dell.[xiv] BDUtil drivers are Dell BIOS drivers that allow interaction between a system's BIOS/hardware and the OS/system applications. Through this 12-year-old vulnerability, the attackers were able to disable security monitoring in many areas on compromised machines—like the Registry, file system, process creation, event tracing, and more—normally performed by the operating system.[xv] As a result, defenders were completely unaware of many actions being taken against these systems.

Cuba Ransomware Group

Using kernel drivers to disable antivirus and EDR solutions has also become a more common method used by attackers. However, at the end of 2021, research by Stroz Friedberg's Incident Response services discovered a new and effective technique used by the Cuba Ransomware group to bypass antivirus by weaponizing a legitimate antivirus driver.[xvi] By using a signed legitimate vulnerable anti-rootkit kernel driver from Avast, they were able to disable processes with kernel-level permissions. Consequently, the attacker was able to escalate their privileges and disable protected processes such as security software without any special consent.

Actively Defending

Just as we saw with the UEFI vulnerabilities, the best option is to stay on top of the latest research and the novel ways that these vulnerabilities can be used. For example, reviewing recent tradecraft intel locations used by offensive security professionals can often provide some insights as to which drivers are being used in the wild and how these exploits are conducted. Actively watch for announcements from security researchers or software manufacturers about driver updates and any new ways to block vulnerable signed drivers. Conveniently, there is an open-source project called Living Off The Land Drivers that contains a list of Windows drivers used by adversaries to bypass security controls and execute code, which is one place the Active Defender can monitor.[xvii] As with UEFI vulnerabilities, know what hardware is used in your environment and be sure to update all kernel-mode drivers as soon as possible.

Ransomware

Ransomware, while not a new challenge, is expected to continue evolving. The first waves of ransomware were as early as the late 1980s. The PC Cyborg virus, also known as the AIDS Trojan, was one of the first documented ransomware attacks. Released in 1989, it was spread via floppy disk. Victims were asked to send $189 to a post office box in Panama in order to decrypt their files and restore access to their computers.[xviii]

However, this form of attack did not become widespread until around 2012 after cryptocurrencies, such as Bitcoin, became available. Cryptocurrency provided a much easier, untraceable way for attackers to receive payment from their victims. By 2013, attackers started using more advanced forms of encryption such as 2048-bit RSA key pairs, creating a situation in which the only way for victims to retrieve the data was to pay for the key. Attackers then realized that they could get a better return on investment by combining ransomware with other targeted attacks and focusing on larger organizations. This approach is called "big game hunting" and was one of the most prominent forms of attack by 2020.[xix]

The next evolution of ransomware was also observed in 2020 when attackers began to include data exfiltration along with their original encryption with extortion techniques. As a result, not only are files and systems in the victim organization encrypted, but the attackers threaten to leak this data if the extortion is not paid. Some variations on this same theme continue, with credentials of individual employees of an organization being used to target other employees or instances of harassment against employees via a phone call after a ransomware attack.[xx]

Continuing Evolution

According to the *2022 Verizon Data Breach Investigations Report*, 2021 saw an explosion of ransomware attacks with an increase larger than the number of attacks in the last five years combined. Furthermore, that year ransomware was involved in 25 percent of all breaches.[xxi] This upward trajectory is expected to continue in coming years. However, we will undoubtedly see ransomware evolve in some additional ways. Ransomware of cloud resources is likely to become more prevalent.

Because enforcement and response to data theft has been historically weak, we will also likely see attackers more often motivated to perform extortion on directly exfiltrated data for ransom instead of encrypting data and decrypting it on the backend. Data theft is a business for these threat actors, and this change in methodology is ideal in that it allows them to conduct their operations more efficiently. Furthermore, as the value of cryptocurrency flattens, they will have a more difficult time getting paid.[xxii] Yet the data that belongs to an organization will still have significant value, requiring attackers to obtain even more of it to ensure they will get the payout they desire.

Actively Defending

Actively defending against ransomware mostly means staying on top of the methods threat actors are currently using as things change. As a result, the information in the following sections is highly fluid and is likely to change in response to the specific TTPs being used by threat actors at the time. That said, there are some basic recommendations the Active Defender can pursue that are unlikely to change significantly, including having your incident response vendor run tabletop exercises, the creation of playbooks, and advanced conversations about ransom situations with appropriate stakeholders.

Tabletop Exercises

Tabletop exercises are verbally described scenarios meant to mimic a cybersecurity incident. They are a fantastic way to test an organization's ability to respond to a particular type of attack, such as ransomware. In particular, tabletop exercises provide a way to evaluate how effective a company's incident response plans are before an incident occurs. Furthermore, they lend some insight into how aware an organization's stakeholders are of their roles and responsibilities during an incident, including both internal employees and third-party providers.

Ideally, an organization should regularly engage its IR vendor to schedule tabletop exercises focused on ransomware for both practitioners and stakeholders. Because the Active Defender understands the methodology behind many common attacks as well as the functions and goals of the business, they are in a unique position to both facilitate convincing management of the value in running a tabletop exercise and help guide how it is planned.

Tabletop exercises usually involve a moderator who describes a situation to the participants and participants who then describe the actions that they would take given that scenario. It is extremely important to make sure that all of the right people attend the exercise from both the business and the technical side. The business side should include folks from legal, communications, senior leadership, and HR. The technical side should be sure to include the relevant subject matter experts as well as those responsible for hands-on analysis and recovery.

While having the right people at the table during the test is critical, an organization should avoid combining testing both the technical and business responses in the same exercise unless they are exceptionally tiny. In other words, unless the company has literally only two or three people who make all of the decisions, it is best to have separate tests for the technical and business sides of the house. Technical exercises can take significantly longer than the business exercises and might bore the business constituents. Furthermore, trying to combine them can be confusing to participants, and facilitators might lose the ability to highlight specific problems in each area.

Technical Exercises

During a technical exercise, the participants typically jump headfirst into the ransomware scenario they are given. The moderator describes a ransomware situation and then observes how the participants respond and what actions they would take, providing feedback based on these actions. The focus with this kind of exercise is generally how the teams involved facilitate the entire incident response process, which includes the investigation, containment, and recovery steps of the situation provided. The scenario evolves based on what the participants choose to do throughout these steps. If the investigation they perform is not appropriate to the scenario, they may not be given the necessary information to take the appropriate next steps. Ultimately, these exercises should help to illustrate any gaps in the current technology, any plans or processes that an organization has to get systems recovered and back online if possible, as well as deal with potential data loss.

Business Exercises

During a business exercise, the participants are led through a scenario focusing more on the specific business decisions that they will need to make during the incident. In other words, the emphasis here would be on how the ransomware attack impacts the business rather than the actions that must be taken by technical staff to get things up and running again. The moderator would spend time to explain to the team what to expect during the particular scenario and what risks the organization is likely to face, such as downtime or potential data theft.

One way to proceed during a business exercise is to break the scenario down into a series of stages that are likely to occur and then address what specific decision points they might need to make for each stage. For example, at the first stage they might be told that the organization was just hit with ransomware but not provided anything about scope of the incident. At that point, attendees would have to consider questions involving initial communications, legal protections, and first steps to take. Once the scope is well understood, including the ransom information, they would begin the next stage. Here, participants would need to consider questions surrounding communications with the attacker and potential payment of the ransom.

At each stage, the participants are given additional twists to the scenario and must determine what actions they must take, what communications should be made and to whom. For example, they might be told that the attack group publishes that they stole data, but before it is confirmed, and later that the data is confirmed not only to be stolen but to be of a sensitive nature. Still later, they might be told that the attack group released the data to the public. In the end, having these discussions prior to an actual ransomware incident can be really enlightening and allow the organization to actively better prepare for an incident of this nature.

Ransomware Playbooks

Another way to actively defend against ransomware is to build out a cybersecurity playbook for a ransomware scenario. Generally speaking, a playbook is a predefined plan that outlines the steps an organization should take in the event of a security incident. In this case, the playbook would be focused on the organization's response to ransomware. It should also provide the members of the organization a clear understanding of their roles and responsibilities during each of the basic stages of the incident as well as what tools and processes they should be using.

A ransomware playbook needs to cover all of the standard incident response steps but with the key questions and strategies for ransomware specifically. These steps include investigation, remediation (which involves containment and eradication), communication, and recovery. Containment is particularly crucial during ransomware incidents and should be given significant priority.

Note that despite what appears to be the linear nature of a playbook, ideally, some of these phases should occur in parallel. For example, while the individuals or group responsible for investigating systems begins their examinations, another can be determining the scope of the event. Yet another group should be communicating the relevant details to those who need to know. Let's examine some of the actions typically included as part of this playbook at each stage. The steps discussed in the following sections essentially follow those recognized by SANS as part of its Incident Response process.[xxiii]

Investigation

During the investigation phase, those assigned to this task will usually attempt to determine what type of ransomware (e.g., what family or variant) is involved by looking for any related messages, analyzing affected or added files, and determining what kinds of software was impacted on an infected system. They will also work on determining the scope of the incident in terms of both systems and data, assess the impact to the organization in order to prioritize resources, and attempt to determine the initial infection vector.

Containment

The containment stage involves quarantining infected devices, affected users and groups, file shares, databases, and backups at a logical and/or physical level where needed to prevent spread from infected systems to critical systems and data. It also includes making sure that command and control domains and addresses are blocked, any related emails are purged from inboxes, and systems are fully patched as well as verifying that endpoint protection is running and current on all systems. Where possible, custom rules to endpoint protection and network security tools based on any IOCs discovered should be added.

Eradication

As one might expect, the purpose of the eradication stage is to remove the attacker from the network. The individuals or team responsible for this step will need to rebuild infected systems from known-good media and restore data from clean backups. Detailed procedures for this process, including a list of tools, should be part of the playbook. In addition, they will need to confirm that the systems are fully patched, that endpoint protection is running and up-to-date on these systems, and that any additional custom signatures or network tools have been added. It is critical to note that reinfection may still be possible and monitoring for this possibility should be a priority.

Communication

The communication stage begins by escalating and communicating the incident to leadership per an established, documented procedure. It then involves establishing necessary communications with internal and external legal counsel, internal users, customers, insurance providers, and regulators. Furthermore, any security partners such as managed providers or incident response consultants should be contacted. Communication to one or more levels of law enforcement (e.g., local, state/regional, federal) may also be included at this stage.

Recovery

The recovery stage involves launching the organization's business continuity and/or disaster recovery plans. Once systems have been rebuilt to a known-clean, patched, monitored state, data can be recovered. Backups must be examined to ensure they too do not contain indicators of compromise. If known resources are available to decrypt systems, they should be tested. If the organization decides that the ransom should be paid after considering all of the implications, the details of how this process will work should be fully documented as part of this stage. It is important to note that the deciding factors for when a ransom should be paid should *not* be documented because it is likely the threat actor will find them and intentionally rise to them.

Frameworks

Another future challenge that defenders face is the ever-increasing pace and scale of attacks by organized cybercriminal groups, which have been made possible in part by some of the frameworks that have been released. These frameworks effectively lowered the bar to entry for a threat actor to be able to attack an organization by providing a way to facilitate exploits without writing additional code in some cases or potentially without the need for the threat actor to remember console commands. The capability of these frameworks is now equally accessible to everyone. Furthermore, the flexible configurations of these frameworks allow threat actors to find ways to continue to bypass EDR/AV without necessarily writing new code. In other words, an attacker doesn't need to know all the little tricks for bypassing detections or hiding in the noise because configured the right way, the framework does that for them.

It is important to note that I will not be engaging in what is known as the offensive security tool (OST) debate. In this debate, people argue for or against restricting the release of these tools to the public. Instead, I am taking the position that because these tools are often available to anyone, an Active Defender must both be aware of them and understand how they work.[xxiv]

Cobalt Strike

As we've already discussed in Chapter 4, "Understanding the Offensive Toolset," Cobalt Strike is a favorite of offensive security professionals because of its flexible ability to simulate adversary activities. However, as with any tools, not only can it be used for legitimate purposes but it can also be used for nefarious ones. Attackers find it exceptionally versatile and particularly easy to use because it has an intuitive, well-documented, solid GUI-driven interface. An operator is able to simply right-click on a beacon and run a process list or file browser against a victim host, which means not needing to figure out or learn specific syntax to type at a command line.

Silver

Because defenders are becoming more aware of and gaining knowledge about Cobalt Strike, they are having more success in being able to detect and mitigate when it is being used. Therefore, at least some attackers are beginning to look for something else to use in its place. Enter Silver, an open-source C2 framework that was developed by Bishop Fox.[xxv] One of the major advantages to Silver is that it was written in the Go language (Golang) and freely available on GitHub. In addition, it can be used across multiple operating systems including Windows, macOS, and Linux. With more built-in modules than Cobalt Strike and smaller payloads, an attacker has an even greater variety of options to exploit systems right at their fingertips. Furthermore, because of its relative obscurity compared to other products, it is possible that some security tools will be less likely to be able to detect its use.

Metasploit

Like Cobalt Strike, the Metasploit Framework was discussed in Chapter 4. Originally conceived of and developed by H. D. Moore in 2003, it has become the world's leading open-source framework used by both offensive security professionals and attackers alike to test for vulnerabilities in systems as well as create tools and exploits to abuse these flaws.[xxvi] It's popularity with attackers is due in part to an extensive database that contains hundreds of exploits and a number of payload options, making it easy to customize. In addition, because it's been around for so long and is used by so many people, there are a ton of custom modules that can be added as well as well-documented workflows.

Brute Ratel

Brute Ratel Command and Control Center (BRc4) is a commercial post-exploitation framework designed by Chetan Nayak, formerly of Mandiant, for use by offensive security professionals.[xxvii] Released in 2020, BRc4 is similar to Cobalt Strike in that it allows "Badgers," which are similar to beacons, to be deployed to victim hosts and facilitate C2 connectivity. As of 2023, a one-year, single-user license for BRc4 is $3,000. The main benefit of BRc4 over Cobalt Strike is that it was designed specifically to evade EDR and AV detection. The official web page for BRc4 indicates that they do have a verification process before selling to a company or an individual that is supposed to check for an official business email address/domain and an individual's work history.[xxviii] However, attackers have been able to bypass this requirement by creating fake US companies, including those formerly involved with Conti ransomware. Furthermore, cracked versions of the product are also known to be circulated among threat actors.

Havoc

Havoc is an open-source, post-exploitation C2 framework created in September 2022 by a malware developer named C5pider.[xxix] Not only is this tool cross-platform, it specifically can bypass Microsoft Defender on fully patched Windows 11 machines using sleep obfuscation, return address stack spoofing, and indirect system calls. Havoc can generate a variety of malicious agents in different formats, including Windows Preinstallation Environment (PE) executable, PE DLL, and shell code, making it particularly flexible. As a result, threat actors can more easily adapt their attacks to specific targets and avoid detection. Furthermore, all of its activities can be monitored and managed through a web-based console, which provides visibility into all of the compromised devices, events, and tasks output.

Mythic

Formerly known as Apfell, Mythic is a multi-user post-exploit, C2 framework designed for offensive security professionals. Created by Cody Thomas in July 2018, it was built with Python3, Docker, and Docker-Compose and includes a web browser UI to be user friendly. ˣˣˣ Instead of only using Docker containers, it can leverage either remote VMs or physical computers to use as equivalent "containers" for agents and C2 profiles. Mythic contains four different agent types, including Poseidon, which works for both Linux and macOS; Leviathan, which acts as an extension of the Chrome browser; Atlas, which is a .NET agent written in C#; and Apfell, which is a JavaScript for Automation agent for macOS. There are several benefits of using this particular framework, including collaboration capabilities, a file browser, support for SOCKS5, and full cross-platform support with additional options for macOS.

Actively Defending

The best way to actively defend against these frameworks is first to know that they exist and then to take the time to understand their capabilities. Some of these frameworks have a great deal of documentation, which can be particularly useful. In addition, reading some of the case studies where attackers have used these tools can be instructive in understanding what kinds of evidence they leave behind. For example, Team CYMRU has detailed write-ups on Mythic and Silver.ˣˣˣⁱ Engage with offensive security team members to understand how they find these tools beneficial and the kinds of use cases they find for various features. In addition, stay on top of any new frameworks as they are released. Threat hunting for the kinds of capabilities these frameworks offer can also be extremely useful, regardless of which framework is being used.

Living Off the Land

One of the consistent pieces of tradecraft practiced by offensive security professionals and attackers alike is to use what is readily available to them on a system whenever possible rather than writing new code to reinvent the wheel. Using existing software packages that are considered known good and trusted makes the job of the adversary much easier because they can automatically bypass EDR or other security software and blend in with normal administrative tasks. This general methodology is called living off the land. We've already seen how it can be particularly beneficial with LOLBins in Chapter 5, "Implementing Defense While Thinking Like a Hacker."

However, this practice goes beyond the operating system and extends to all of the software on a device, including legitimate tools. For example, earlier in this chapter, you saw how attackers were able to use a valid but vulnerable driver to disable security monitoring tools and another to bypass antivirus. Another set of tools commonly abused by offensive security professionals and attackers alike are remote access tools such as VNC, LogMeIn, GoToMyPC, TeamViewer, or AnyDesk.

The use of living off the land techniques by attackers and offensive security professionals is not new. Some of the earliest well-known attacks using this approach include malware such as Code Red and SQL Slammer, which date back to the beginning of the current century. This methodology will no doubt continue to be a growing trend as attackers find new and creative ways to use existing software packages to disguise their activities. Newly developed tools, such as the open-source Iscariot Suite released in 2022 by Bad Sector Labs, can even leverage some of these applications such as Velociraptor, which is a DFIR tool; Splunk, which is a log aggregation tool; osquery, which is a monitoring framework; and various EDR products to create a C2 environment.[xxxii]

Actively Defending

Actively defending against living off the land techniques requires understanding both the extended capabilities of these applications and how they might be used by an adversary. Spend time reviewing sites with offensive security tradecraft intelligence for unique usage of existing software packages. If your organization has not implemented a particular package that could be used in this way, do not merely skip over it. Instead, establish detections for if or when they are used, since that behavior would be unexpected. For the packages that are implemented, establish baseline patterns of usage to determine what is normal in your environment. Monitor them for unusual behavior both in terms of how they're being used and who is using them. Be aware that additional unauthorized instances of existing applications are sometimes used by adversaries to hide their activities and actively monitor for these imposters. For example, while you might use Splunk in your environment and therefore expect specific certain activities associated with Splunk, be sure that any activity you are seeing is the instance of Splunk that is authorized and not a random installation somewhere else, whether on-prem or in the cloud.

API Security

We have already discussed how integral APIs are to cloud services and why, in that environment, they are so important to protect. However, let's more generally explore what an API is, how it's used, and why API security is so critical.

Defining APIs

An API is a piece of software that provides a layer of abstraction between some type of functionality a company wants to provide to others, be that a user or another application. As a result, how that functionality is implemented can change so long as the API stays the same. For example, APIs are what allow you to use third-party software to connect to multiple social media applications at one time rather than switching back and forth between them. Tools such as Sprout Social offers a single place to check messages or run search terms rather than having to go to Facebook and Twitter individually.[xxxiii] Another example is Buffer, which provides the ability to create and schedule posts to multiple social media accounts such as Facebook, LinkedIn, and Twitter at one time.[xxxiv]

API Impact

Regardless of whether the infrastructure is cloud or on-prem, the development of APIs by businesses is expected to grow exponentially in the coming years to continue to facilitate consumer interaction. From a business perspective, APIs can be used to provide new features or services to a company's existing portfolio, which they can charge a fee for others to use. They can also be used to increase the efficiency and/or reliability of a company's existing services, which can provide a form of soft savings. Additionally, revenue can be generated directly by people paying for access to the API or indirectly by selling usage data collected through the use of an API.

Security Significance

While the eyes might be the windows to the soul, APIs are effectively the windows to an organization's applications and underlying systems. Thus, if the security of an API is compromised, there is a significant risk of exposing the data and systems it can access. APIs, just like any web software, can suffer from HTTP header misconfigurations, insecure default configurations, or even error messages that reveal too much information. They can also suffer from DDoS attacks or malware attacks such as SQL injection, AiTM, or credential stuffing.

Actively Defending

Actively defending against API security issues is similar to considerations for any web application, which means looking at them from the offensive security perspective. In particular, for each API that an organization is implementing, it is critical to determine what information and systems it can access. For example, an offensive security practitioner will look for ways that too much information can be made unintentionally available by the API such as password hashes or locations of users, known as inappropriate information disclosure. In addition, they will look for situations where data the API accesses can be overwritten, which could potentially allow privilege escalation. This vulnerability is known as API mass assignment. Furthermore, they will examine the behavior of the

API for inappropriate or no input validation, such as a name field accepting JavaScript, which is known as XSS.

Each of the vulnerabilities mentioned previously is listed in the OWASP API Security Top 10.[xxxv] Much like the traditional OWASP Top 10, which was mentioned briefly in Chapter 4, this list includes the top 10 critical security risks, but specifically to APIs rather than traditional web applications. While traditional vulnerability scanners are sometimes able to uncover weaknesses in APIs, tools like Burp/ZAP can be used to validate whether specific exploits are possible against these flaws.

Additional proactive steps that can be taken include enabling logging at both the application and system level of any system that interacts with APIs. In addition, auditing of interactions between internal or third-party APIs and other organizational resources should be enabled and regularly reviewed. In particular, be on the lookout for SQL keywords (e.g., SELECT, FROM, or INSERT), keywords from operating scripting languages such as shell code or PowerShell, or programing language keywords. Moreover, looking for authentication anomalies or obfuscated code in the logs might be indications of a potential security issue as well.

Everything Old Is New Again

I am frequently asked how I am able to stay on top of all the changes in security over time. While I admit it can be daunting, after a while you begin to see repeat patterns appear that make it much easier to manage. The reality is that so many "novel" attacks are really just a rehash of old ones with the threat actors creating new procedures with existing code, techniques, or sub-techniques. Let's look at just a few upcoming challenges that defenders are likely to face that, underneath, are not so original.

OWASP Top 10

Coding vulnerabilities never seem to significantly change and continue to remain problematic. First released in 2003, the OWASP Top 10 is a list that "represents a broad consensus about the most critical security risks to web applications (`https://owasp.org/www-project-top-ten`)," as we've already discussed in Chapter 4. It has been updated fairly regularly, every three or four years. Although the list does see some changes for each update, many of the same vulnerabilities persist, sometimes just in a different order. For example, Injection Flaws, XSS, and Broken Authentication have consistently made the list since its inception. Because web applications continue to be developed with vulnerable code, attackers are able to reuse the same old attacks against new applications.

Old Malware Never (Really) Dies

One of the common misconceptions about malware is that there is no longer a need to worry about any of the older varieties either because they are not currently in use or because existing tools will easily catch them. However, it is not uncommon for detections for older malware to simply be removed from current detection/prevention tools, perhaps to make room for something newer. Furthermore, attackers are well aware of older forms of malware and are actively reviving the code for these outdated and long-forgotten techniques to their advantage.

Not only is there evidence that botnets are able to be resurrected by attackers, but in 2022, researchers Aamir Lakhani and Joseph Muniz gave a presentation at RSA, a large information security conference held in San Francisco, illustrating the process.[xxxvi] They described how even when a botnet is taken down, usually what is taken down is the controller, leaving many of the infected hosts behind. As a result, these hosts often retain many resources that could be used in the future. For example, once a system has been made part of a botnet, they often still contain the C2 remote shell software, modified routing tables, infected Registry, bootup modifications, a hijacked execution path, modified AutoStart settings, and new services installed.

In the following sections I will explore just a couple of well-known malware botnets that were taken down at one point only to later return with a vengeance. Emotet, which was first detected in 2014, was taken down in January 2021 only to return by November of that same year. REvil, which was first detected in 2019, was taken down in January 2022 but appears to be active again as of May 2022.

Emotet

Originally a Trojan virus that targeted small banks in Germany and Austria, Emotet was first discovered in 2014 through its unusual patterns of network traffic. It was delivered through a variety of emails containing infected attachments and embedded malicious URLs. The goal of this malware was to steal personal information as well as bank account and credit card numbers. The second version of Emotet even included a new script that could instantly transfer money out of an account.

Over the coming years, additional features were added and the threat actors using it expanded their focus to include banks in other countries such as Switzerland, Canada, China, the United Kingdom, Mexico, and eventually the United States. Finally, in January 2021, the Emotet botnet infrastructure was taken down through a joint effort of law enforcement agencies and authorities from a number of countries.[xxxvii] All infected systems were pointed at infrastructure managed by law enforcement where an uninstaller module was added, removing the malware as of April 25, 2021.

The uninstall event was considered the end of an era. However, by November 2021, the threat actors using TrickBot had begun adding an Emotet loader into the systems that it infected. As of 2023, not only is Emotet still active and being distributed in Microsoft OneNote files to avoid detection but other malware groups can rent access to computers infected with it as part of a Malware as a Service in order to infect the computers with other malware such as TrickBot, Qbot, and Ryuk ransomware.

REvil

REvil is the name of a prolific Ransomware as a Service operation operating out of Russia. Their malware was first detected at the end of April in 2019 and they became known for targeting high-profile and extremely lucrative entities, demanding enormous payments from them. They were also one of the early adopters of the extortion tactic involving both exfiltration and encryption of the victim's data. The original REvil group officially folded up operations in 2021, as the result of sanctions against them. Furthermore, in January 2022, raids were conducted by Russian authorities at the request of the United States, resulting in a number of arrests and the supposed complete demise of the group.

Fast-forward only a few months later. In late April 2022, the REvil's ransomware servers in the Tor network were discovered to be back online, as was their blog. However, this infrastructure redirected visitors to new URLs with a completely different look. The new sites contained novel information as well as information previously stolen by REvil. The new entity assumed the name Sodinokibi. Despite this rebranding, security researchers began to suspect that code originally used by the REvil group might have been making a comeback. It turns out that Sodinokibi was another popular name used by REvil in the past. [xxxviii] Furthermore, when the Secureworks Counter Threat Unit analyzed a new REvil malware sample in May 2022, they concluded that those writing it must have had access to the original REvil source code. [xxxix] While it is unclear whether these resources are being managed by the original developers, new victims were once again added to the group's leak site, including a US university.

Actively Defending

The best way to actively defend against older malware and well-known vulnerabilities is to be mindful of security lessons from the past. As Spanish philosopher George Santayana wrote, "Those that fail to learn from history are doomed to repeat it." [xl] Never assume that because an attack method or malware is old it cannot still be relevant and reused. Expect to see these "oldies" return and be prepared to address them if they do.

Summary

It important for the Active Defender to understand not only how to deal with the challenges of today but also to look ahead to what they may face next. Software and hardware supply chain compromises are already on the rise and expected to continue to increase in the coming years. Likewise, attacks relying on vulnerable drivers are growing and anticipated to become more common. It is crucial that the Active Defender stay on top of the research in these areas, knowing what hardware and software their organization utilizes and where those risks are likely to be the greatest.

Ransomware will continue to evolve, requiring the Active Defender to encourage their organizations to regularly find ways to run effective tabletop exercises and set up appropriate playbooks. Frameworks have lowered the bar to entry for some threat actors, allowing them to build attacks more easily while also bypassing certain defenses with fewer difficulties. While only a handful have been discussed, many more exist, and still others will be developed over time. Relying entirely on detections for these tools, as we saw in Chapter 7, "Building Effective Detections," is not always effective. You must also understand the capabilities of these frameworks and then ideally spend time threat hunting for their activities in your environment rather than the tools themselves.

Because the easiest way to hide nefarious activity is by using what is readily available to an adversary on a system, no doubt we will see new and creative uses for existing software, whether it be binaries, drivers, or any other package. Furthermore, remember that relationships are the key to how an adversary knows how to move through your network and that APIs are a way of extending those relationships beyond an internal network. Therefore, with the explosion of new APIs in use, API security is paramount to keeping your resources secure as well. Finally, do not think that just because an attack methodology or form of malware is old that it is not still relevant.

All of these future challenges are either emerging or re-emerging threats that are difficult to prevent and/or particularly hard to detect in part because they are often not the kind of things that lend themselves to passive alert monitoring or traditional vulnerability reporting. Therefore, only an active defense makes sense, which requires constantly staying aware of current attacker trends. As you've seen, that involves keeping abreast of the latest news through social interaction with offensive security professionals who can provide input on what attack paths they're exploring and find promising as well as what they might be hearing in their own circles. Furthermore, it requires maintaining a constant situational awareness of potential risks within the organization that cannot be directly prevented or detected, such as in the case of supply chain compromise, in order to consider mindful and intentional business decisions to manage that risk.

Notes

i.   https://unit42.paloaltonetworks.com/malware-xcodeghost-infects-39-ios-apps-including-wechat-affecting-hundreds-of-millions-of-users

ii. https://blog.avast.com/update-to-the-ccleaner-5.33.6162-security-incident

iii. Ibid.

iv. www.reversinglabs.com/blog/a-partial-history-of-software-supply-chain-attacks

v.   https://venturebeat.com/security/protecting-your-organization-from-rising-software-supply-chain-attacks

vi. www.reversinglabs.com/blog/10-supply-chain-attacks-your-software-team-can-learn-from

vii. www.bleepingcomputer.com/news/technology/ceo-charged-with-sale-of-counterfeit-cisco-devices-to-govt-health-orgs

viii. https://github.com/realoriginal/bootlicker

ix. www.welivesecurity.com/2023/03/01/blacklotus-uefi-bootkit-myth-confirmed

x.   https://support.microsoft.com/en-us/topic/kb5025885-how-to-manage-the-windows-boot-manager-revocations-for-secure-boot-changes-associated-with-cve-2023-24932-41a975df-beb2-40c1-99a3-b3ff139f832d

xi. https://arstechnica.com/information-technology/2023/05/microsoft-patches-secure-boot-flaw-but-wont-enable-fix-by-default-until-early-2024

xii. https://arstechnica.com/information-technology/2023/05/leak-of-msi-uefi-signing-keys-stokes-concerns-of-doomsday-supply-chain-attack

xiii. https://arstechnica.com/information-technology/2022/10/how-a-microsoft-blunder-opened-millions-of-pcs-to-potent-malware-attacks

xiv. https://cybernews.com/security/bring-your-own-vulnerable-driver-attack

xv. www.eset.com/int/about/newsroom/press-releases/research/lazarus-targets-aerospace-company-in-the-netherlands-and-political-journalist-in-belgium-to-steal-da

xvi. www.aon.com/cyber-solutions/aon_cyber_labs/yours-truly-signed-av-driver-weaponizing-an-antivirus-driver/#_ftnref1

xvii. www.loldrivers.io

xviii. www.crowdstrike.com/cybersecurity-101/ransomware/history-of-ransomware

xix. Ibid.

xx. Ibid.

xxi. *2022 Verizon Data Breach Investigations Report,* www.verizon.com/business/resources/reports/dbir.

xxii. 2022 saw exchanges like FTX going completely under and the value of Bitcoin dropping to a quarter of what it was the previous year. See www.npr.org/2022/12/29/1145297807/crypto-crash-ftx-cryptocurrency-bitcoin for more details.

xxiii. www.sans.org/white-papers/1516

xxiv. For some detailed information about this debate, see https://medium.com/@anthomsec/misconceptions-unrestricted-release-of-offensive-security-tools-789299c72afe and https://catscrdl.io/blog/opensourceredteamtooling.

xxv. https://bishopfox.com/blog/sliver

xxvi. www.simplilearn.com/what-is-metaspoilt-article#:~:text=CybersecurityExplore%20Program-,A%20Brief%20History%20of%20Metasploit,was%20entirely%20rewritten%20in%20Ruby

xxvii. www.bleepingcomputer.com/news/security/ransomware-hacking-groups-move-from-cobalt-strike-to-brute-ratel

xxviii. https://bruteratel.com/pricing

xxix. https://github.com/HavocFramework/Havoc

xxx. https://github.com/its-a-feature/Mythic

xxxi. www.team-cymru.com

xxxii. https://gitlab.com/badsectorlabs/iscariot-suite

xxxiii. https://sproutsocial.com

xxxiv. https://buffer.com

xxxv. https://github.com/OWASP/API-Security

xxxvi. www.youtube.com/watch?v=O8DFCoUi3JY

xxxvii. www.bleepingcomputer.com/news/security/emotet-botnet-disrupted-after-global-takedown-operation

xxxviii. https://vpnoverview.com/news/revil-ransomware-resurfaces-with-rebranded-operations

xxxix. https://therecord.media/researchers-warn-of-revil-return-after-january-arrests-in-russia

xl. https://iep.utm.edu/santayan

Index